Dancing has its place in all societies; yet the phenomenon of dance has been oddly neglected by most anthropologists. This volume is intended to further anthropological awarenesss of its critical relevance. It is claimed that in a very important sense, society creates the dance, and it is to society and not just to the dancer's experience that we must turn to understand its significance. Performance has meaning within the social process.

The anthropological analysis of dance can be approached in a variety of ways. These are identified in the introduction to the volume, and then illustrated by seven case examples drawn from Africa, Southeast Asia, Melanesia, and Oceania. In successive chapters, dancing is presented as a controlled emotional outlet whose form reflects cosmology; as a creative experience that draws adolescent girls into the adult world; as an extension of speech and gesture that adds further levels of meaning to formal occasions; as a strategy for orchestrating the climax of a successful exchange; as a challenge to the power of elders that generates an alternative reality; as a communal response to crisis that recreates order out of confusion; and as a sequence of transformations that periodically resolves an inherent social dilemma. The volume concludes with an assessment of the relevance of the work by a dance scholar.

By revealing dance as an aspect – often the most spectacular aspect – of ritual behavior, this work is intended to stimulate more anthropologists and those in related disciplines to realise the full potential of its study. It also offers insights to those who are principally interested in dance itself, as well as appealing to any reader who shares a curiosity about the ways in which the spectacle of dance can be interpreted.

Society and the dance

Society and the dance
The social anthropology
of process and performance

Edited by
PAUL SPENCER
School of Oriental and African Studies
University of London

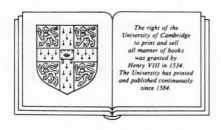

The right of the
University of Cambridge
to print and sell
all manner of books
was granted by
Henry VIII in 1534.
The University has printed
and published continuously
since 1584.

CAMBRIDGE UNIVERSITY PRESS
Cambridge
New York   Port Chester
Melbourne   Sydney

Published by the Press Syndicate of the University of Cambridge
The Pitt Building, Trumpington Street, Cambridge CB2 1RP
40 West 20th Street, New York, NY 10011, USA
10 Stamford Road, Oakleigh, Melbourne 3166, Australia

First published 1985
Reprinted 1988, 1990

Printed in the United States of America

Library of Congress Cataloging in Publication Data
Main entry under title:
Society and the dance.
Includes bibliographies.
1. Dancing – Anthropological aspects – Addresses,
essays, lectures.   2. Rites and ceremonies – Addresses,
essays, lectures.   3. Dancing – Social aspects – Addresses, essays, lectures.   I. Spencer, Paul,
1932–
GV1588.6.S63   1985   306'.484'0967   84–29212

ISBN 0-521-30521-7 hardback
ISBN 0-521-31550-6 paperback

Contents

Contents

Figures and tables

Preface

The popular appeal of dance has barely touched the imagination of most anthropologists. We regularly explore such topics as symbolic interaction, sexual opposition, religious experience and body language, all of which seem to bear on dance, whereas dance itself is oddly neglected. It is generally excluded from our curricula, and so we tend to assume that it lies beyond our immediate concern. And there in general it remains, an obscure rather than a challenging phenomenon, unwanted and dispersed as fragments in the anthropological literature. Most of us have encountered some form of dancing in our field studies, often as a highlight of social gathering; it is too big to miss – and yet we still somehow miss it. Meanwhile, non-anthropologists who are interested in dance itself are increasingly aware of the rich possibilities of non-Western forms, but may find themselves hampered by a culture-bound approach to their subject and by the lack of a clear lead from those who specialise in cross-cultural analysis.

Over the past decade and especially in the United States, volumes and articles on the anthropology of dance have begun to appear, and these are forerunners of the present work. However, a somewhat different approach is intended here, summarised in the title of this volume. The difference is essentially between *cultural anthropology* in America, where the approach seeks to embrace the whole of culture, and the narrower view of *social anthropology*, which stems largely from the sociology of Emile Durkheim. Adrienne Kaeppler (in a personal communication) has expressed this difference by suggesting that American anthropologists generally view dance as culture, whereas in social anthropology it would be seen as social action; but from neither perspective, she adds significantly, do we have a truly satisfactory study of dance for any society. The more restricted view searches for significance and meaning in the interaction between social pheonomena and their wider context. It is the contextual view

Preface

that is adopted here, not as a uniquely British approach (*vide* Kaeppler), but as a necessary one.

It was this opportunity that provided the theme for an intercollegiate seminar held at the School of Oriental and African Studies in 1979, and attended by the various departments of social anthropology in London University. Earlier versions of five of the following chapters were presented originally at the seminar, while the chapters by Andrew Strathern and Alfred Gell are welcome later additions to the collection. These seven case studies constitute the core of this volume. The authors themselves pursue their own lines of enquiry, but each chapter aptly illustrates successive themes identified in the Introduction, which seeks to establish that a scattered repertoire of anthropological insight into dance already *does* exist reflecting the various trends of anthropological interest since Durkheim. Peter Brinson's Epilogue was also initially presented to the seminar as a dancer's challenge to social anthropologists to demonstrate their skills in relation to dance. Taking our contributions here as our response to this challenge, his final comment from the world of dance should reassure nonanthropologists that the work can appeal to a wider audience.

In expressing my warmest thanks to everyone involved in producing this volume, I would single out John Blacking, both for his encouragement and for sharpening our awareness of the need for the study of dance to become an established procedure in anthropological enquiry. I am grateful to John Blacking and Adrienne Kaeppler for their perceptive comments on an earlier draft of the Preface and Introduction. I am also grateful to Sue Jennings for her moral support when this work was still in its infancy, before other commitments claimed her time. The volume has been greatly enhanced by Angela Turnbull's editorial skills on behalf of the publishers, and by Alfred Gell, whose anthropologist's eyeview on the cover beckons us. However, above all it is each of my fellow contributors that I have to thank for their collaboration, patience and intellectual thrust, which has provided the justification for this volume.

PAUL SPENCER

March 1985

x

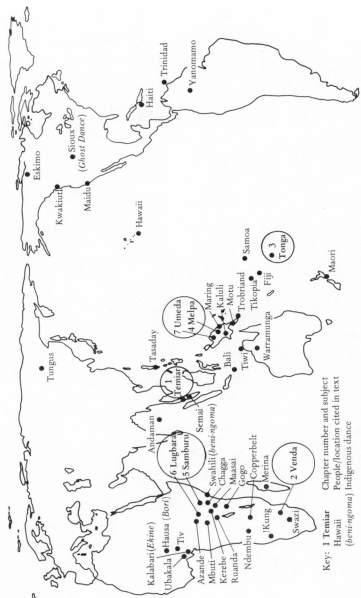

Distribution of peoples cited in the text.

Key: 1 Temiar   Chapter number and subject
      Hawaii   People/location cited in text
      (*beni-ngoma*) Indigenous dance

Introduction: Interpretations of the dance in anthropology

PAUL SPENCER

Dance provides a spectacle in most societies and an obvious topic for anthropological curiosity, yet curiously it remains largely unresearched. It has an elusive quality, which adepts and those who have known it all their lives find easier to demonstrate than to explain in so many words. It has to speak for itself, and although often far from uninviting towards the visiting anthropologist, its hidden code remains hidden, and research remains in an impasse. Because we have no initial ideas about dance, we ignore the opportunity that it provides, and because we ignore it the stock of ideas remains low and it continues to be ignored.

It is against this background that some recent writings have attempted to stimulate interest, and these should be regarded as precursors of the present work, providing useful discussions on particular points and daunting glimpses of the vastness of the field with extensive bibliographies.[1] However, apart from Blacking's work, which focuses primarily on music, these surveys tend to reflect the dancer's viewpoint with a rather eclectic approach to anthropology. There is, for instance, a widespread concern with definitions of 'dance', many of which emphasise its patterned movement as an end in itself that transcends utility.[2] Such definitions assume that dance is self-contained, to be justified essentially on aesthetic grounds; one is lulled into looking no further. Yet there is an arbitrariness in confining the term 'dance' to nonutilitarian patterned movement which becomes clear when, for instance, one considers the description of the Warramunga fire ceremony in Australia that so impressed Durkheim. Here dancing merged into leaping, prancing, singing, yelling, shouting, taunting, practical joking, processing, mock attacks with blazing torches, and ultimately a mêlée among the flying sparks and embers; there was moreover a highly utilitarian purpose – to patch up old quarrels and live in peace.[3] Similarly, in the Ghost Dance in North America, dancing merged into ceremony, trance, prophecy, and ultimately into the surge of a millenarian movement with the very

1

Paul Spencer

specific (even if unrealistic) purpose of restoring lost lands and traditions.[4]

The inner experience of the dancer is another topic that is often emphasised in these works. This raises the hoary question facing any anthropologist in the field: how does one plumb the inarticulate emotional depths of people of other cultures, even over an extended period of fieldwork? Even Rudolf Laban himself in his attempt to establish the universal principles of dance maintained that it was up to the individual dancer to interpret 'the manifestations of human mind and spirit, as perceivable through dance'.[5] Hence merely learning to perform the dances of another culture offers no solution in itself. It may be a useful step in establishing rapport in other respects, but it does not automatically hold the clue to other people's inner feelings.[6]

The solution, which is the keynote of this volume, is to broaden the issue, extending the search outwards to the wider context and taking clues of the inner world of the dancer only as these offer themselves.[7] One may take, for instance, a definition of 'dance' proposed by Franziska Boas that may appeal to some dancers: 'ordinary gestures and actions can become dance if a transformation takes place within the person; a transformation which takes him out of the ordinary world and places him in a world of heightened sensitivity'.[8] This definition would seem to extend 'dance' to all active forms of religious experience and spirit possession, but the relevant point here is that it is precisely these kinds of social phenomena that anthropologists have successfully approached by considering the institutional frameworks that constrain the individuals and even fashion their inner experiences and alternative realities. In the title of this volume, the use of the definite article, *the* dance, is quite deliberate; one is not just concerned with dancers or their dancing, but with an institutionalised arrangement. Merriam makes a similar point: 'Our only reason for separating dance from the rest of culture is conceptual; our modes of thought force us to deal with reified entities. But, in fact, the entity of dance is not separable from the anthropological concept of culture.'[9] Also, one might add, the entity of dance is not separable from the anthropological concept of institution.

Directly relevant to the present approach are those relatively few anthropologists who have been lured as much by their own field experience as by any personal whim to consider the dance seriously. The excitement of the throng and the aura of the occasion alerts some sixth sense that the dance reflects powerful social forces and demands some explanation; or perhaps an intriguing pattern reveals itself and leads to further enquiry. Yet because this is an uncharted area, premature attempts to summarise the relevance of dance have tended to lead to sweeping generalisations and ultimately to confusion. Consider, for instance, the disjointed dialogue that has focused on women's collective dances in Africa when they adopt male traits. These were portrayed as a temporary release from their subservience (Gluckman 1963), followed by a denial that they are subservient (Rigby 1968); as a veiled protest against male domination (Lewis 1966 and 1971), followed by a denial of any protest on the evidence that competition between women is stronger than their resentment (Wilson 1967). There was the suggestion that as transvestites the women were merely fulfilling their traditional role in rites of passage (Norbeck 1963); this may be contrasted with the view that in adopting a warrior stance they were to be regarded as potential revolutionaries (Hanna 1977a:122–3). The moral is clear: Africa is a vast continent, and dance is a complex and varied topic. Only by breaking this topic down and considering it in relation to specific societies can one begin to appreciate this complexity.

In the sections that follow, I try to select from among the various published studies by anthropologists to suggest that the field *is* finite, that there *are* a number of recurrent themes, and that dance *can* be relevant even for those who (like me) regard themselves as left-footed, though curious. Although there may up to a point be a certain correspondence between these themes and different types of dance, this is only a matter of degree. The themes are intended as basic models, presented in a logical sequence, which apply in varying extents to most dances.

The contributions to the body of this volume elaborate certain aspects of dance in the context of particular societies and reflecting the insights of each author. Very broadly, and very largely by luck, each successive theme in the Introduction happens also to be illustrated in depth by one of the contributions. These are therefore presented, chapter by chapter, in the same sequence to give some shape to the work as a whole.

Dance as a safety valve: the cathartic theory (theme 1)

The notion that dancing may have some therapeutic value is at least as ancient as the dancing epidemics of the Middle Ages. Following the harvest in certain years, alarming symptoms would sweep through the poorer communities of Europe: a burning sensation (St. Anthony's fire), a sense of suffocation, cramp, twitching limbs, convulsions,

Paul Spencer

frenzy, mental confusion, hallucinations, necrosis, and death. These were popularly associated with an invasion by demons and a heightened terror of death and eternal torment. In this climate, the notion developed that these conditions could be avoided and even cured by resort to a contorted form of dancing that matched the convulsing limbs, and this dancing (St. John's and later St. Vitus's dance) spread as the terror mounted. Backman (1952) has examined the probability of an association between these symptoms and alkaloid poisoning from a rye fungus (ergot), and concluded that the dancing would indeed provide a symptomatic relief for the victims until the poison had worked its way through their systems. His systematic sifting of the medical and historical evidence provides an outstanding model of analysis on one aspect of dance. But Backman might have pursued further his evidence that the dancing mania was altogether more widespread than the incidence of poisoning. Whole sectors of a local population would be caught up compulsively in an epidemic of ceaseless dancing until they collapsed in sheer exhaustion, and then later, somewhat recovered, they would return to dancing. This raises the possibility that the terror itself provoked the compulsion to dance and was perhaps relieved through the dancing – a relief that might even be extended to other anxieties of the age such as the repressive domination of church and state feudalism. Certainly, there is strong medical evidence that dancing can induce a relief of this kind. Various authorities have noted the effects of rhythms in creating tension, anxiety, and stress under certain conditions, and of releasing them once they have built up; and they have pointed out the implications of this for tribal and other dancing.[10]

The literature on dance frequently emphasises its carthartic value, releasing pent-up emotions. This notion was developed in stages in the writings of Herbert Spencer when he explored the variety of emotions that expressed themselves in muscular action, first in relation to an ingenious theory of the origins of music (1857), then of laughter (1860), and then briefly of dancing (1862:234–5). He viewed emotion as a form of nervous energy that became intensified when denied its natural outlet, and had to be released through some other channel. This concept of dancing as a safety valve for releasing emotional steam foreshadowed Freud's concept of the libido – a psychic force analogous to hunger that requires some direct or indirect physical outlet. More recently, anthropologists too have made the point, as when Evans-Pritchard suggested that the Azande beer dance served among other things 'to canalize the forces of sex into socially harmless channels'. Similarly, Margaret Mead suggested that the informal dances

Introduction

of Samoan children provided a release from their rigorous repression
and subordination by adults in other spheres. At a popular level in
a survey of young people in London, Rust makes the same point. At
a more professional level, it was a guiding principle in the innovations
of Isadora Duncan.[11] One may compare the view of Rudolf Laban as
a choreologist that man feels the urge to dance after the disturbances
and frustrations of everyday life with Lorna Marshall's comments on
the frictions and accusations typical of a gathering of !Kung Bushmen:
'But the next moment, the people become a unit, singing, clapping,
moving together. Words are not dividing them. They are doing something together that gives them pleasure. They are enlivened in spirit
and body by the music. They are lifted out of the arduous unremitting
search for food, and out of the anxieties that fill their days.'[12] Clearly
the notion of a tension release achieved through dance is not just a
flash of insight among some recent writers interested in dance therapy
as a topic with its own jargon, journal, and professional association.
It is either a very general experience, or an established metaphor in
our own pattern of thought, a reflection, perhaps, of the stresses of
our own society.

However, this can never be more than a partial explanation. Curt
Sachs, introducing his *World History of Dance*, made a pertinent point.
If dance, he noted, is a necessary expression of excess energy and
the joy of living in all mankind, 'then it is only of slight importance
for anthropologists and social historians. If it is established, however,
that an inherited predisposition develops in many ways in different
groups of man and its force of direction is related to other phenomena
of civilization, the history of dance will then be of great importance
for the study of mankind.'[13] The intriguing aspect of this assertion is
that it is at the hub of social anthropology, although Sachs himself
belonged to an intellectual tradition far removed from modern comparative social science. Universally shared biological or psychological
considerations do not account for the differences between societies;
hence one has to look both at the variety of dance and at the variety
of its social context in order to arrive at a fuller understanding.

Certainly, with reference to specific examples, the notion of tension
release provides a plausible explanation. Hartwig describes precolo-
nial dancing among the Kerebe as an intervillage competition during
the slack dry season that provided an emotional outlet for men in
striking contrast to their toil at other times under the stagnation and
decay of an oppressive regime. The dance craze during and following
World War I in Britain is sometimes portrayed in these terms.[14] Gluckman's interpretation of the Swazi first-fruits ceremony is a release of

5

Paul Spencer

tension following a period of economic anxiety, and a diversion of potentially rebellious forces against the king; there was an acting out of these tensions in a dance that rose to an emotional climax as the king was at first rejected by his followers and then, appearing isolated as a wild monster executing a crazy elusive dance, was reunited with his nation. Lewis's analysis of religious cults associated with spirit possession portrays dancing as a widespread activity leading to catharsis, as in tarantism in medieval Italy, voodoo in Haiti, *Bori* in West Africa, and Tungus shamanism in Siberia; they appealed to the downtrodden sectors of society, notably women.[15]

Gluckman and Lewis are not without their critics, but these criticisms focus primarily on the nature of the initial tensions and do not seriously question that tensions exist and are released through dancing.[16] This in itself is revealing, for it demonstrates how plausible the safety-valve hypothesis is on the one hand, and how difficult it is to disprove on the other. The problem is that it can sometimes be too glib an explanation that on reflection does not adequately account for the facts. Thus, if the Kerebe dance is viewed as a release from anxiety under a repressive regime, why did it persist and progressively develop to a major preoccupation some time after the demise of this regime? If the dance craze of the 1920s was a response to the tensions of World War I, why did it not continue during the years of economic depression around 1930? Were the new tensions bottled up or released in some other way? The perennial problem is that while this explanation is essentially psychological and seems to account for the element of spontaneity often noted in dancing, it does not account for the formal element in dancing. Even the Swazi king when he executed his 'crazy elusive dance' was required to do so at a particular point in the first-fruits ceremony, and his followers were required to sway and beat their shields vigorously.

In this volume (Chapter 1), Sue Jennings's account of the development of seances among the Temiar of the Malay peninsula shows how dancing may provide an outlet from the emotional straitjacket of their restrained existence. But significantly their dancing and trancing have a distinctive symbolic form that relate to their perception of their own bodies and of space, and even tension release has its place in Temiar cosmology. Their view of catharsis opens up a finer analysis of their dance, rather than precluding it.

The cathartic theory in dance faces the same pitfalls that have bedevilled other topics in anthropology when trying to resolve the chicken-and-egg dilemma of the relation between the build-up and release of tension. As an example, one may consider Judith Hanna's view that among the Ubakala of Nigeria, certain girls' dances anticipate life crises such as marriage and childbirth, and strengthen their ability to face these by allaying their anxieties. This is in fact very close to Malinowski's view of the function of magical rites that serve to strengthen men's resolve by relieving anxiety in situations of stress. As against this view, Radcliffe-Brown's rejoinder to Malinowski, that magical rites might actually generate the very anxiety they are calculated to relieve, may be applied to dance: the Ubakala girls' dances could generate rather than simply resolve anxiety as part of a process in which they learn to accept their subordinate role in their forthcoming marriages, and the importance of bearing children.[17] The relevance of both aspects of this argument has been noted by several writers in relation to competitive dancing, where the act of resolving tension in one context may create it elsewhere.[18] In a situation of competition, the cathartic theory tends to emphasise one side of a more complex argument.

Suzanne Langer has raised a further point concerning the relation between emotion and dance that at first sight poses a serious challenge to the theory of catharsis in dance. She has pointed out that such writers as Duncan, Laban, and Sachs generally assumed that there is a direct expression of emotion in dance, whereas in other forms of art it has been widely accepted that it is the image of emotion that is expressed by the artist in a mood of detachment, raising our awareness of this emotion to a higher plane. Why, she asks, should dance be an exception? 'No one, to my knowledge, has ever maintained that Pavlova's rendering of slowly ebbing life in the "Dying Swan" was most successful when she actually felt faint and sick'. In other words, the dance creates an illusion of emotions that are not really felt, but only imagined as in a novel or a play or a painting, and revealed through symbols. Rather than symptoms of real emotion expressed through spontaneous gesture, one has symbols of perceived emotion, of will, conveyed by the artist through contrived gestures as he creates a virtual world. Langer's lateral insights are relevant to subsequent themes. Here, however, it may be noted that her model is based on dancing as an art form, and hence on essentially theatrical dancing. She subsequently contrasts this with a debased form of popular dancing – pleasure dance – in which emotion is experienced more directly, 'in a spirit of romance, escape, relief from the burden of actuality, without any spiritually strenuous achievement'; and thereby in a throwaway aside, she accepts the principle of catharsis, while rejecting the more pleasurable form as true dance.[19] Once again this becomes largely a problem of definition, but it does pose another question here: in such instances as the Swazi first-fruits ceremony or the Temiar seance or the Ubakala girls' dances where the form of dancing is overladen with symbolic significance, is emotion truly expressed or released, or do such rituals merely create a virtual world of emotion? Langer herself has a view of primitive dance derived from Sachs and ultimately Rousseau that does not help us here. It is a question that touches on the anthropological debate concerning the relation between ritual and sentiment.

Dance as an organ of social control: functionalist theories

(a) *The educational role of dance and transmission of sentiments (theme 2)*
The alternative view, which switches the focus from the release of anxiety through dancing to the generation of anxiety as an educational technique, entails a second theme. The Ubakala girls' dance may be compared with the eighteenth-century practice in Britain whereby a debutante was rigorously trained to take the floor at her first ball in an exhibition minuet before the critical gaze of the assembled company. This has the distinct flavour of an initiation ordeal, as if the minuet epitomised the etiquette and set of values that maintained the distinctiveness of the élite.[20] The notion that a minuet might be primarily an educational device is well supported. Reginald St. Johnston suggested that during the seventeenth and eighteenth centuries it was hardly a dance, but rather one of the finest schools of courtesy and deportment ever invented.[21] Earlier writers had made similar comments about fashionable dances in general. Thus in 1531, 'Dauncing may be an introduction into the first morall vertue, called Prudence' (Sir Thomas Elyot); in 1693, 'the effects of dancing . . . gives to children . . . not mere outward gracefulness of motion, but manly thoughts and a becoming confidence' (John Locke); in 1767, 'is there anything more useful for young people than to be able to enter a drawing room with self confidence, to address a person of rank with decorum, every day? What are children until they have had instruction in the dance?' (Chavanne).[22]
Margaret Mead proposed a similar interpretation of the informal children's dance in Samoa, but with a shift in emphasis. In the European example the dance was regarded as a mould that produced standardised products, whereas in Samoa Mead regarded it as a device that separated adept from inept children, preparing them respectively for success or failure in later life. Through their dancing,

keen children were held to develop an adult grace, proficiency, and confidence, whereas clumsy and stupid children were rebuked by their peers and lost confidence; in this way the more precocious children cultivated adult values that discriminated against clumsiness, while the less skilled came to accept their inferiority. This is an ambitious claim for what was, after all, only informal dancing among children. The unfolding of adolescence is notoriously unpredictable, and Mead was in Samoa for too short a period to assess the progressive development of clumsy or precocious children into later adulthood. Moreover, in trying to combine this theory of selective education with a cathartic explanation of the same dance, she presents a confusing picture. On the one hand, these dances are seen to be educating children towards an adulthood in which they are expected to be 'wise, peaceable, serene, generous, anxious for the good prestige of their village', on the other hand, the dancing children are held to wallow in a 'genuine orgy of aggressive individualistic exhibition'. It is rather as if she is trying to claim that the classroom and the playground are one and the same. It was a pioneering attempt to draw attention to the rich potential of dance for anthropologists; but it overloaded the topic with analytical significance.[23]

The contrast between the European and the Samoan examples is similar to the contrast that Basil Bernstein has drawn between *restricted* and *elaborated* language codes, which he developed with reference to the transmission of two types of culture in the socialisation of children, suggesting also that the distinction might be extended to nonverbal symbolic forms such as music.[24] Extending this possibility to dance, the minuet has a restricted code and the expressive opportunities of Samoan dance an elaborated code.

It is the aptness of such linguistic models for the study of communication within the dance that Maurice Bloch has questioned, also in the context of its educational role. The setting for his discussion is a male initiation ceremony among the Merina of Madagascar. Initiation is an occasion when young men take a significant step towards adulthood, threatening the power of the elders, and the Merina elders responded with a heavy-handed display of ritual, repeatedly emphasising the symbolic trappings of their power, leading towards rigidly prescribed songs and dances that shrouded the naked truth of their regime in a pall of tradition and mystery. In this way, Bloch suggests, the dances served to inculcate the youths with fear and respect.[25] This leads him to conclude that dances in general are totally rigid with no semantic structure or inner meaning and he then rejects dance itself as a topic for further consideration, except as an instrument for ritual

9

domination. Yet in his analysis dancing is only given a cursory mention and he does not even consider the possibility of less rigid forms of dancing that give fuller freedom for expression, such as those discussed by Mead. As a result, the analysis is reduced to a simple dualism that overlooks the complexity of the data. In fairness to Bloch, he makes explicit an issue that tends too often to be taken for granted, and a certain concession is made to his point of view in the final section of this Introduction. Even so, his sweeping generalisation from just one fleeting ethnocentric instance overloads the topic with insignificance.

The solution clearly is to turn to writers who have looked more closely at dance itself and at its role in upbringing. Closer to the roots of education through music, Gehard Kubik has examined African music as a pattern of sound and as a pattern of body movement, both in creating this sound and in responding to it in dance. These patterns are closely associated in African cultures from the time when an infant is rocked as his mother sings to him, and when he is carried on her back and absorbs the rhythm and sound as she joins in a women's dance. After this, the child learns how to perform these patterns as a musician or a dancer. Together sound and movement build up as a single pattern linked as though through a conditioned reflex moulded by his culture, so that in later life when he hears the music, there is an inner response within his body that makes it difficult for him to sit still. He may spontaneously want to dance, or without difficulty he may turn his attention to some novel way of reproducing the rhythm.[26] Similarly, in studies of Balinese music, emphasis has been placed on experience in childhood, and ultimately 'when movement and gesture reach the point where they coincide with [rhythms, melody, and metric construction, then] like well-conditioned reflexes, the dance has "entered" the dancer'.[27]

John Blacking has extended the point, drawing on a Chomskyan rather than a Pavlovian analogy. Man's musical ability, as with language, implies some biologically innate mechanism within every person to organise, create, and respond to sound. At the surface level at which it is perceived, it is a metaphorical expression of indefinable feelings; below the level of conscious awareness, musicological analysis reveals a coherent pattern that must correspond to some deeper structure within the music and to some inherent potential within the performer. There is a rhythmical stirring within his body, a response that music alone can awaken. A performer in any culture has to learn to feel his way into the music through his whole body, and his expression is a part of the total body movement. In the rapport between performers and infecting their audience, it is difficult to separate the unity of their movement from the unity of the music that this movement produces; and they become involved in an experience that is enhanced because it is physically shared. It is an argument that moves almost effortlessly between music, musicmaking, and dancing. Beyond these it extends to the social context in which they are learned and performed.[28] Thus, while Kubik draws attention to the relevance of music and dancing in the process of enculturation and creative expression within the individual, Blacking in effect extends this logically to socialisation and the creative potential of the group. The danger of reducing the analysis of dance to a stimulus–response theory with no outward meaning is averted by extending it to the interaction through dance between the dancer and his social milieu.[29]

In this volume (Chapter 2), John Blacking stresses the narrowness of Bloch's argument and shifts the focus from the power of the older generation to the creative potential of the dance itself with special reference to girls' initiation schools among the Venda of southern Africa. Over a period of one to four years, the girls learn a sequence of dances with contrasting styles that symbolically prepare them for motherhood and culminate in the unforgettable collective experience of the *domba* dance. This is portrayed by the Venda as 'a huge drawing of breath of the whole countryside', a congregating movement of bodies, and the girls are drawn from the dispersed existence of their childhood into the united body of society. They are not in the grip of the elders and alienated from power, but through the power of music and dance they become aware of the transformation within themselves as they pass from girlhood to the adult world.

(b) Interaction within the dance and the maintenance of sentiments (theme 3)

A functionalist approach to the role of dance in society is summarised in Radcliffe-Brown's view that the basic conditions for an orderly social existence depend on the transmission and maintenance of culturally desirable sentiments; and this leads us to turn from impregnating the young with such sentiments, to revitalising the sentiments of adults through dance.[30] In this context, it is useful to consider a verbal–nonverbal scale of human interaction in relation to dancelike behaviour.

A scale of this sort was suggested as early as 1857 by Herbert Spencer in his theory of 'The origin and function of music'. Elaborating on the significance of intonation in ordinary speech, he emphasised the importance of communicating emotion and evoking sympathy. Beyond purely verbal understanding, he perceived the nonverbal expressions of the highest ideals of society that bind people together; and these, he suggested, form the basis of the nonverbal arts. It is a point of view that Langer has reiterated. More recently, Birdwhistell has examined the extent to which gestures and intonation comprise an essential element in normal speech, serving to amplify, emphasise, and occasionally substitute for words, opening out the nuances of meaning. Such gestures are significant in the rapport established during conversation in which attentive people may echo one another's gestures and achieve a rhythm in their interaction; or they may fail to do so where rapport is absent.[31] Given this general observation, dance is an obvious metaphor that has been used to describe this nonverbal signalling. Condon and Ogston, for instance, noted in a film analysis of ordinary conversation that the body of the 'speaker dances in time with his speech [and the body of the listener] in rhythm with that of the speaker'. Alan Lomax has elaborated this metaphor yet further with the suggestion that mutual understanding of conversation depends on a synchrony of movement that is 'more fine-grained than that of any *corps de ballet*'; an extravagant claim perhaps, but at least it conveys the distinct impression that something is communicated at a nonverbal level that has an affinity with dance.[32]

With oratory, the emphasis shifts from informal interaction to a performance before an audience when the nonverbal component is a vital aspect of eloquence. Anne Salmond describes how any great Maori orator captured his audience by striding towards the opposite party, chanting his greeting, gesticulating with a walking stick, and then abruptly spun on his heel to walk back in thoughtful silence. Then he would return with the next few sentences, stressing each point with a stylised gesture, making terrific faces, tongue out and eyes rolling. As the tempo of his speech increased, he moved faster, and stamped his feet so that dust rose. One orator actually took off his shoes to move with greater effect, stamping his feet in a staccato dance at moments of greatest excitement.[33] Whether one describes this as dance to emphasise the nonverbal component or as dialogue to emphasise the verbal is a matter of choice. Both aspects are relevant in the final analysis. Durkheim touched on the topic, noting the development of rapport whereby the orator responds to the sentiments of the crowd and finds his own enlarged and amplified, so that he is able to dominate them with gestures and grandiloquent language, generating a moral force that binds them all.[34]

This natural blend of speech and gesture in performance is elaborated into an aesthetic idiom in Tonga, described by Adrienne Kaeppler in the present volume (Chapter 3). It is not just the metaphoric allusions of poetry that have to be understood at various levels, but also the accompanying gestures in dance that add further innuendo. Public performances proclaim formal allegiance to rank, while at the same time dance gesture may be used to shift and even invert the stress. It is this subtle eloquence that enhances the occasion, legitimising a more complex reality within the formal hierarchy of the system.

A widespread form of interaction that might be compared with oratory occurs where singing is used as a pointed weapon to air grievances or to discredit adversaries, making the issues more explicit and public than mere gossip. Those that have offended public morality are chastised through a popular idiom that carries with it a wide appeal and an element of licence, leaving the victims isolated – unless they can respond with conviction in similar vein. This idiom varies from the song contest among the Eskimos and the drumming duel among the Tiv to miming in the dance among the Mbuti Pygmies when they may reenact any unusual event of the day's hunt. A husband may lead the dance and ridicule his wife who through her laziness as a beater spoiled his chances; on other occasions women may ridicule their menfolk.[35] It is the skill with which the essential message is blended with the nonverbal element that draws popular acclaim and enhances its moral force.

Further still from normal language, many wordless songs are effectively nonverbal. Whether or not they were once more explicit as some authors claim, is irrelevant here.[36] They still retain a certain fascination that merges into the music and accompanies the dancing. It was this power of music and dance, beyond words and beyond mime, to act as a moral force on the individual that was central to Radcliffe-Brown's analysis in *The Andaman Islanders*. In effect he took Herbert Spencer's theory of the relevance of subliminal communication in the arts and in society, and switched the focus, rather as Durkheim might have done, from a shared emotional experience through the arts as an ideal that binds people together, to the intense involvement in society as an emotional experience and an end in itself. It was a switch from a shared happiness to a morally binding force. Through the rhythm of their music, Radcliffe-Brown perceived the Andaman dancers and singers as performing together as one body. The rhythm generated a force that acted on the dancer from without and yet also found a response from within. He was regulated, made to conform in the common acitivity, losing himself in the dance and becoming absorbed in the unified community, reaching a state of elation in which he felt himself filled with energy or force beyond his ordinary state. The precise sentiments varied with context, as when two groups danced together after a long period of separation and generated a feeling of harmony; when warriors danced to induce a collective anger before setting out to fight; or at a ceremony of peace making and reconciliation. On each occasion, the sentiments of unity and concord were intensely felt by every dancer, and this was the primary function of the dance as a central example of his analysis of custom and belief. The Andaman Islander was regulated in his responses, his thoughts and emotions, deriving all these from within himself and at the same time from his society.[37]

Radcliffe-Brown's was essentially a homeostatic model, treating society as a living organism, with the dance, through its rhythm, acting like public opinion to bring back into the fold any individual who was, so to speak, out of time. Through control over his body, his thoughts and sentiments too were brought under control. It is a point of view that blurs the distinction between aesthetics and ethics. Good taste and sensitive judgement in either bears on the other with the community in a mediating role. The rhythm, music, dancing, and social life itself merge into the highest expression of collective emotion.

It is precisely this approach that John Blacking followed when he contended that music among the Venda is an individual experience nurtured within the collective consciousness of the community and hence extremely potent. *Tshikona*, for instance, is the most universal Venda dance, connected with ancestor worship and state occasions. *Tshikona*, they say, is ' "the time when people rush to the scene of the dance and leave their pots to boil over." *Tshikona* "makes sick people feel better, and old men throw away their sticks and dance." *Tshikona* "brings peace to the countryside." Of all shared experiences in Venda society, a performance of *Tshikona* is said to be the most highly valued.' The influence of Radcliffe-Brown and beyond him of Durkheim in Blacking's treatment is clear. Music is seen as a moral force that acts on the individual both from within and without, inducing a sense of elation bordering at times on ecstasy. Venda music creates a special world of time that extends from the living to the dead and the world of the spirit, and makes them more aware of society as a system of active forces. It is as if Blacking is claiming for Venda music (and hence dancing) what Durkheim claimed for the various totemic emblems in Australia when people were collected together; a visible (or in this instance danceable) religious symbol of the invisible force of the collectivity, active within the group as a whole, an expression of

14

sentiments that well up in the individual in response to the established collective symbols of his society.[38]

Susanne Langer too seemed to be intuitively leaning towards a similar interpretation, and indeed Blacking's choice of expression shows that as a musician he has read her works with care. She dwells on the illusion of a consciousness of life and feelings of power conjured up by dance that controls their movement, as though through some conscious will, external to the dancers. Turning then to primitive dance to support her argument, she portrays this as the art form par excellence, a genesis of religious awareness. There is again an illusion of some vital force that animates the dancers, lying beyond their persons, transporting them to a sacred state, creating a realm of virtual power, and inducing ecstasy as they enter this realm. It is this awareness of power that she evokes and elaborates at considerable length, and yet the Durkheimian notion – that it is the dancers' response to the force of society itself that is the true source of the illusion of power in dance – somehow evades her. Instead her enchantment with Sachs's romantic illusion of the world of primitive man diverts a fascinating argument, and she dismisses 'merely magnetic forces that unite a group' as artistically trivial.[39]

If the notion that dance should be viewed as a cathartic release of tension has become a psychological catch-phrase (theme 1), then the corresponding sociological cliché is that it generates social solidarity (themes 2 and 3). The notion of solidarity has been applied to a variety of communal activities including singing, prayer, feasting, drinking, or joint participation in some sacred act. None of these is preeminent in every respect. However, in terms of a whole-hearted communion of joint action, of a sustained coordination of the whole physical being and collection of physical beings, and for sheer spectacle, dance often has a compulsion that these other activities tend to lack.

Dance as a cumulative process: the theory of self-generation (theme 4)

The twin strands of Herbert Spencer's theory of emotions derive perhaps from his earlier training as a railway engineer, and are woven into more recent theories of dance. If the tension release model views dance as a safety valve to let off surplus steam (theme 1), then the functionalist model views it rather as a governor, a constraining mechanism that limits any tendency towards anarchy (themes 2 and 3). What is *homeostasis* in the organic analogy becomes *negative feedback*

15

Paul Spencer

in the mechanical analogy. In theme 4, the analogy can be pursued by reversing the governor to simulate the build-up to an emotional climax. This is a switch from negative to positive feedback, or in Radcliffe-Brown's terms from 'social harmony' at one level of analysis to 'intoxication' at another level as when dancing intensifies excitement and collective anger before a fight. 'As the dancer loses himself in the dance, as he becomes absorbed in the unified community, he reaches a state of elation in which he feels himself filled with energy or force immediately beyond his ordinary state, and so finds himself able to perform prodigies of exertion.'[40]

It is a theme also considered by Durkheim in relation to the mounting collective passion, a sort of electricity, which is formed when Australian tribesmen collect together and 'quickly transports them to an extraordinary degree of exaltation. Every sentiment expressed finds a place without resistance in all the minds, which are very open to outside impressions; each re-echoes the others, and is re-echoed by others. The initial impulse thus proceeds, growing as it goes, as an avalanche grows in its advance.' Apart from several disconnected references, Durkheim was not concerned with dancing as such, but with what he perceived as the genesis of religion among the Warramunga. Nevertheless, in the relevant passages of the authorities he cites, it is clear that dancing (in their fire ceremony) or dancelike movements that accompanied singing (to placate the Wallunqua totem) played a continuous part in the steady build-up to the ceremonial climaxes.[41]

One finds the same description of an evolving social occasion in more recent accounts of dancing, with a cumulative climax, a mounting sense of excitement, and a transformation in the atmosphere, as dancers, musicians and onlookers respond to one another's encouragement; or conversely rapport may simply fail to develop and the dance may limp to a premature end. Very often, the course of a dance one way or the other may hinge on the ability and initiative of some central figure whose effective lead depends considerably on his sensitive response to those around him, as a dancer, drummer, singer or some other key personality, spurring the dance towards its climax.[42]

Edward Schieffelin provides an especially penetrating and dramatic analysis of this process in relation to the satisfactory development of the Gisaro ceremony and ultimately harmony among the Kaluli of New Guinea. This requires a finely balanced increase of tension between visiting dancers and host spectators in which the dancers aggravate the spectators by evoking poignant memories of past bereavements, and the spectators respond by at first joking and taunting the dancers, and then attacking them with burning torches in fits

16

of anger, and finally by weeping in their sorrow. The emotional stimulus is not, however, one-sided; the dancers will only excel in their impassive performance and build up to a climax in response to the open display of emotion and aggression from the spectators. Where a balanced opposition is not achieved, the dance will either peter out or break into a fight.[43] Similarly, one may argue that the atmosphere created in other less exotic forms of dance is essentially the result of balanced oppositions between complementary responses of leaders and followers, of the sexes, of dancers and musicians, and of performers and spectators.

Various authors have emphasised this element of transformation achieved through the dance without paying due regard to the social context. Sachs, for example, refers to dance in its essence as simply life on a higher level, breaking down the distinction between body and soul, giving ecstasy by transporting man from everyday bonds, transforming him into another self; and he cites a Persian dervish poet: 'Whosoever knoweth the power of the dance, dwelleth in God.'[44] Implicit in such treatment is the notion of a release from the humdrum of ordinary life into a rather private and personal experience that unites body and soul; whereas in the various ethnographic accounts, dance is seen to bring a closer involvement between people rather than a release from such involvements. It develops, not just within each dancer, but also in the interaction between all those participating, extending in space, filling the entire hut of the Tungus shaman or the circle of light cast by the fire at a !Kung medicine dance. Ironically, Sachs assumed that the purest form of dance, which induced true ecstasy in a private world, could only be achieved among the least specialised societies furthest removed from modern civilisation; and yet it is precisely among these remoter peoples that we have the best evidence of strong collective bonds and of the close involvement of dancers with one another. The element of religious ecstasy, the shifting boundaries, the transformation of time itself reflect an act of communion rather than of detachment.

It is intriguing to compare this semireligious fascination of dancing with Max Weber's concept of charisma – a *gift of grace* that enhances the moral authority of a leader in the eyes of his followers. A dance performance may be endowed with a similar elusive quality capable of generating an infectious excitement. Weber's elaboration of the *routinisation of charisma* also has its parallel in the development of any particular dance from an innovative experience to its establishment as an institution with widespread expectations. The parallel may have relevance also for other artistic media, but it is especially well illus-

Paul Spencer

trated with reference to dance. In the following example, it was the build-up of a dance that acted as a charismatic symbol, a catalyst in a process with much more at stake.

The cult of the *Bori* spirits among the Hausa of Nigeria has been described in general terms by Michael Onwuejeogwu and with particular reference to the establishment of a market at New Giwa in Mary Smith's rendering of *Baba of Karo*.[45] While the *Bori* dancing itself is largely incidental to their accounts, one is given a clear insight into the relevance of this dancing for the establishment of the market as a thriving commercial centre.

Hausa towns develop around their markets, and their viability as communities in a predominantly rural economy depends on their ability to compete for trade from the surrounding rural areas at each other's expense.[46] Formally, each town was governed within the strictly Islamic hierarchy of the local emirate; but the unpredictable market forces on which the fortunes of the town depended were linked to the pagan belief in *Bori* spirits. These were popularly held to be beneficent and protective beings on the one hand, but with a capricious streak on the other and a passion for dancing. Each spirit was known to have its own characteristic dancing rhythm and guise, such as a prince, a slave, a lame woman, on which its dancing was modelled. Each town had its own *Bori* cult, primarily in the hands of adepts whose status was marginal to Hausa society, notably prostitutes and unattached divorcees between marriages, who fell short of the Islamic ideal, though they had considerable influence with their suitors. A successful market town was thought to have a flourishing community of *Bori* spirits whose presence manifested itself in the vigorous dancing of the adepts, attracting a crowd of onlookers and sustaining the reputation of the market. The higher the reputation of an adept, the larger the number of the spirits who might on different occasions possess her (or him), and the more versatile the range of performance. If several adepts were possessed at a *Bori* dance by different spirits simultaneously, then the scene enacted before the local audience ostensibly revealed the goings-on of the spirit world, but were also a reflection of aspects of the contemporary Hausa scene and the popular feelings and uncertainties in the minds of the onlookers generally. To attract *Bori* spirits to a local market gathering, drummers would beat out their characteristic rhythms, tempting the spirits to possess the adepts. If on some occasion the adepts did not successfully respond, then this was interpreted as reluctance on the part of the spirits to leave their abodes, or they may have been attracted to some other town by a rival dance, reflecting the rivalry between markets. For the

18

Hausa, it was the benign presence of the *Bori* spirits, made manifest in the continuous dancing, that determined the community spirit and the success of the market. Analytically, it is necessary and logical to reverse the causal connection and to regard the community spirit as the source of the belief in a *Bori* presence. Seen from this point of view, the failure of a *Bori* dance was more than the failure of the drummer or the adept to work towards a state of possession: it was essentially a failure of the whole community, onlookers included, to generate the right atmosphere for possessions to take place, and a symptom of a certain apathy and lack of morale.

In the marketplace (and also incidentally within the home), the *Bori* cult may be seen to reflect each of the themes discussed so far: as an emotional outlet for women whose status in Hausa society was generally depressed (theme 1);[47] and as an expression of community spirit and a means of public redress, spreading gossip, exposing deceit and serving as a caution against wrongdoers (theme 3).[48] To appreciate the wider relevance of theme 4, it is useful to turn to the example provided by Baba in which the townspeople of Old Giwa were moved to a new site, New Giwa.

Old Giwa had a serious water shortage during the dry season, and while it was the centre of a thriving farming community and enjoyed considerable autonomy in its remoteness, reflected in the belief in a local community of *Bori* spirits, various attempts to develop the market had only been partially successful. The decision to abandon the old town was taken at a higher administrative level, and the population was moved to the less remote site at New Giwa, which had adequate water. Despite this favourable location, the market at first failed. It lacked a sense of community, it did not attract traders or potential customers, and the *Bori* dancing did not take hold. This impasse was a chicken-and-egg situation often noted in new towns: a viable market would only develop in a place with a reputation as a market centre and a community with its own sense of identity. But these would not develop so long as it remained a commercial backwater. Awareness of the problem was expressed by the people themselves in terms of the *Bori* spirits. The spirits in the vicinity of New Giwa were thought to be strangers, even to Hausa society, with no benign influence, whereas the *Bori* spirits of Old Giwa had remained entrenched in their old abode, refusing to be dislodged. This was popularly thought to portend the eventual return of the human population to their old homes. As they saw it, only the transfer of the *Bori* spirits from Old to New Giwa would generate the dancing, attract the crowds, and transform the situation. Reversing the causal chain analytically, so

19

long as the former residents of Old Giwa remained there in spirit, they lacked a determination to establish a new market, the *Bori* adepts lacked the encouragement to work up trance states through dance, and the *Bori* spirits were felt to remain aloof.

The eventual success of New Giwa hinged on the ultimate acceptance by the local chief of the need to placate the spirits through the cult, and to attract them to the new market. Having first performed Islamic rites without success, he then discreetly approached the local *Bori* cult with promises of gifts, and an impressive dance was organised. Some famous *Bori* dancers were invited from elsewhere and they attracted a large crowd from over a wide area for the occasion. From this point, according to Baba, although the relationship between the *Bori* cult and the chief remained ambivalent and some of the *Bori* spirits remained at Old Giwa, at least one influential spirit was persuaded to adopt the new market as her permanent home – having successfully named her price through the adepts. The market now had a spiritual patroness, the *Bori* cult was firmly entrenched, recognised on its own terms, and the market itself became established and steadily grew.

In terms of Hausa cosmology, their beliefs in the *Bori* spirits may be viewed as a vivid metaphorical expression of their community spirit, their economic viability, and ultimately of the moral condition of their society. The crucial point here is that this metaphor is more than a cultural conception; there is analytically an analogy between a market and a dance such as *Bori* on which this metaphor is based. Both depend at their inception on a communal act of faith, so that in the above example one cannot disentangle the popular enthusiasm and interest generated by the dancing from the growth of economic confidence necessary to establish the market. The development of rapport in a dance depends on intangible forces that are very similar to the development of confidence in an economic venture. At New Giwa they were closer still, because the example was not merely concerned with a single dance, but also with the establishment of a dance as a permanent feature of the community, closely associated in the minds of the people with the establishment of good faith in the market as a permanent venture.

The *self-fulfilling prophecy* is another topic that is quite often cited by anthropologists, but seldom pursued. Merton first coined the phrase in an economic context to describe the onset of the depression in America in 1929 and the progressive loss of confidence that spread like an epidemic across the country. More recently, Gluckman drew on the same concept in his analysis of the interplay between football players and the crowd, in which team morale could build up or be lost against heavy odds in the right circumstances and determine the unlikely outcome of a match. The same argument can be extended to the process of recovery after an economic recession, to the role of morale in the unlikely outcome of battles and ultimately wars, and to the development of rapport among Mbuti Pygmy net hunters, who depend for success on coordination as a team. It is a process of positive feedback that can, I suggest, most usefully be applied to situations in which there is a degree of uncertainty or confusion; and it can be applied to dancing, where success breeds upon success and failure upon failure. Where dancing is an integral feature of millenarian movements, as in the American Ghost Dance of 1870, it may play a central role in generating a climax, however unrealistic this may prove in purely practical terms.[49] So in New Giwa, the build-up of popular expectation in their *Bori* dancing was a vital aspect of the build-up of credibility in their market as an economic venture.

Andrew Strathern provides another illustration of this theme in his analysis of Melpa dancing in this volume (Chapter 4). The Melpa of Papau New Guinea have a system of periodic exchange in which pigs are accumulated over a prolonged period and then given away in a lavish display, depleting the herd of the big-man and his followers, but enhancing his prestige and laying the basis for future exchanges. After the extended preparations, however, the actual giving is a low-key affair, and a climax has to be orchestrated to avoid an anticlimax that would detract from the display of strength. It is the dancing and the decoration of the dancers that provide this display, drawing in crowds of admiring onlookers, and reaching a peak of excitement immediately before the pigs are given away, and then continuing throughout the day. In this way the periodic intensification of the dance plays an essential role in the Melpa exchange cycle, rather as *Bori* dancing is critical to the success of Hausa markets.

There is an element of uncertainty in the dance – as an event or as an institution – that is well expressed by the notion of capricious possessing spirits. This uncertainty makes it all the more spectacular and memorable when it comes off and all the more dismal and regrettable when it fails. In dance as in any performance, nothing succeeds quite like success.

The element of competition in dance: theories of boundary display (theme 5)

Anthropological classics have frequently alluded to the element of mounting competition through display in dancing. The Kwakiutl regarded the exclusive title to a dance as a treasured possession to be jealously fought over if it were captured by a rival through deceit or force; the Maidu held contests in which the victor was the shaman who danced down the others. Rivalries between Trobriand villages built up to an intense emotional display of dancing during the month after harvest marked by envy of successful dancers, fears of black magic, and resort to counter-magic. The Azande beer dance prompted a competitive display among men for leadership and for the attention of girls. In Tikopian night dances there was competition between villages to attract visitors to dance, and then vying for moral supremacy between young men and women, reflecting the conflict of interests in their normal lives.[50]

Such dances may be viewed as confrontations. F. G. Bailey has suggested that in a confrontation, messages are sent across the arena of competition indicating clear intentions and strength in order to intimidate the opponent. If one side or the other does not yield ground, then the next step is a direct trial of strength – an encounter. Each culture, he notes, has its own idiom of confrontation; and, one might add, dance is a highly appropriate idiom because it can display precisely the power, initiative, and coordinated discipline that give strength in the event of an encounter; it can be overbearing. This is well illustrated in Roy Rappaport's description of massed dancing displays among the Maring of New Guinea, where population pressures led to disputed boundary areas and fighting. Dancing was regarded as equivalent to fighting, recruiting potential allies and indicating the military strength of the host should war develop. To the extent that such a display led to the dispersal of a weaker group, direct encounters were avoided. Or again, among the Yanomamo of Venezuela, Chagnon has described the aggressive dancing at their feasts that displayed the fighting strength of different groups in a situation of endemic feuding where alliances were extremely brittle, and any admission of weakness invited intimidation. In such examples, one is reminded of animal displays in boundary situations, parading strength before rivals.[51]

Pursuing the analogy, it has been noted that during the breeding season, a bird will normally flee when threatened outside its territory, whereas inside this territory it is likely to attack a rival swiftly and silently; but on the boundary it may mount a display which seems to signal 'I may attack or I may flee'.[52] The display in other words occurs at the most sensitive point, which can easily give way to a direct encounter if there is further ambiguity.

Where the idiom of confrontation is competitive dancing, this is geared to attract attention, and the scope for display and innovation within the cultural tradition is boundless. With a popular appeal among rival groups of supporters it merges into a type of game on the one hand, while on the other with its eye-catching flamboyance it merges into a form of parade. Both aspects are evident in Terence Ranger's study of *beni-ngoma* in East Africa, which is probably the most penetrating historical investigation of any dance.[53] Ranger found that his Swahili informants had difficulty in discussing recent historical change in general terms, but they would enthusiastically convey their feelings on change when discussing the transformation of this dance over time. *Beni-ngoma*, a 'drum band' or caricature of a military parade, originated with colonialism along the Swahili coast and drew its inspiration from European culture; but it was rooted in the intense jostling for positions in Swahili society with a concern for reputation and success that predated colonialism. Its idiom was one of display and competition between rival dance associations and it adapted to the changing scene as the nub of competition shifted. In the coastal town of Lamu where Ranger undertook his own work, for instance, at first it provided the arena for the rivalry between rich aristocratic families associated with the two factions of the town; then as the traditional order crumbled, it became the vehicle for younger men to use their new wealth to wrest the initiative from the older patriarchs who had previously shouldered the expense; and finally before it died out with colonialism in Kenya, it was the focus of a challenge by low-status immigrants to the town for recognition by the Swahili élite. As *beni-ngoma* spread inland and southwards more or less coincident with the diffusion of Swahili as the lingua franca of the region, it retained this competitive idiom, while adapting to the divisions and aspirations in each locality. In the Copperbelt towns, Clyde Mitchell portrayed it as a relatively docile joking relationship between formerly hostile tribal groups who in the urban context jostled for prestige. Among the Kerebe of Tanzania, Gerald Hartwig described it as a less docile escalation in which local dance associations resorted to magic, sorcery, gimmicks, feats of daring, and in fact any novelty which could be paraded close to a rival dance in a desperate bid to divert attention and lure away curious spectators; it was the dancing team that finally held the largest audience that won the contest. The parallel with intensely competitive team sports is apparent. Significantly, when intergroup competitive dancing in the region was suppressed by the colonial administration, popular interest shifted to football with the same flamboyant rivalry and appeal.[54]

Abner Cohen's study of the West Indian Notting Hill Carnival parallels Ranger's work.[55] A traditional parade with music and dancing that had developed in one area (Trinidad) was exported to another area (London), where it was adapted and extended to the changing dilemma of the West Indian community in a situation of relative poverty, unemployment, and racial discrimination. The principal symbol of the carnival was the transformation of worthless oil drums to produce the finely tuned drums and intensive dance rhythms of the steel band; with these the West Indians themselves were transformed during carnival. Just as *beni-ngoma* was used by Ranger as a key to the study of history and the passing of an era in East Africa, so Cohen has approached the phenomenon of the Notting Hill Carnival as the surface expression of a more fundamental problem, which similarly has absorbed much of the creative talent and limited wealth of its organisers. The differences are also important. *Beni-ngoma* dancing was the idiom for competition between rival dance associations and only in its ramifications outside the arena of dance was it linked in certain areas to protest against the colonial yoke.[56] The Notting Hill Carnival, on the other hand, had been rooted in the spirit of revolution against white domination in Trinidad and was the idiom of protest by all performers as an immigrant minority against the (largely absent) majority of privileged whites. It provided an organisational base for the mobilisation of a political awareness, whereas the heated arguments between rival interests during the preparations were a secondary issue.

At the opposite end of the scale of privilege, one may again consider the dancing of élites. In Georgian England, the element of manneristic display, typified by the exquisite nuances of the minuet, emphasised the exclusiveness of the privileged ranks threatened by an aspiring middle class. The dances and court etiquette of the traditional élites in Ruanda or Hawaii provide further examples.[57] These élite dances were not confrontations that displayed potential strength, but rather displays of finesse that sealed their boundary and kept them above the arena of competition. It was a demonstration of the immutability of their superiority, and in this sense such dances have been considered with theme 3. The contrast between a display of protest at the lower end of the scale of privilege as a step toward implementing change, and a display of unattainability at the upper end as a means of preserving the status quo parallels Ioan Lewis's discussion of spirit possession where he distinguishes between *peripheral cults*, which express the spirit of protest among the downtrodden, and *central cults*, which reinforce the downtreading regime.

These two types of display dance also illustrate once again the contrast between Bernstein's *elaborated* and *restricted* codes. If there is, however, a parallel with language codes, then why should dance and not language be used to articulate these points of view? Cohen considers this problem with reference to a debate between rival factions within the West Indian Carnival organisation: why not convert the festival atmosphere into one that is unambiguously political, emphasising the element of protest more pointedly? Cohen's answer is that carnival, with its distinctive Trinidadian origins, was a more potent symbol of protest with a wider cultural appeal to all sectors of the West Indian population than a more consciously contrived and verbalised demonstration. In relation to dance, David Best similarly notes the power of the skillful use of symbols to arouse hidden passions that might not be touched by an appeal that is more easily comprehended. Cohen's notion of carnival as an irreducible element in West Indian culture corresponds to Best's discussion on the irresolvable problems of any attempt to translate dance into language.[58] It is an argument that could apply equally to *Tshikona* as a potent and irreducible symbol of national unity among the Venda, to *beni-ngoma* and the spirit of rivalry among the Swahili, or to the restricted finesse of the minuet at the privileged end of the social scale.

In societies where dances of display are the idiom of confrontation along a boundary, some association between these dances and the notion of warriorhood is almost inevitable. Competition exists on a sliding scale that extends to violence. From a West Indian point of view the Notting Hill Carnival and indeed the steel band itself were born in violence, and occasionally erupted in riots against the police. *Beni-ngoma* was mounted as a quasi-military parade, which from time to time broke down in street fighting. In similar vein, a Samburu warrior who had served in the King's African Rifles once tried to convey to me his feelings on returning home and joining in a dance of display with other warriors: 'It's like being on parade.' Another worldly warrior stressed the element of escalating competition: 'It's like an auction.' Normally this vying remains within the limits of convention; but it can dissolve into a fight at any time, and no-one can predict with certainty which way it will develop.

In this volume (Chapter 5), these Samburu dances are shown to mobilise along boundaries at various levels. Within the dance, jostling for prestige between warriors of rival clans plays itself out and leads to vying between the sexes and ultimately to uninhibited play. This succession of phases may be seen as a form of reversion that contrasts with the process of reversion noted by Gell in *ida* dancing (Chapter 7). In *ida* the problem is associated with more competitive individu-

Paul Spencer

alism at a later phase of the life cycle and the dancing leads towards the domestication of older men. The idiom of Samburu dancing is one of protest against the regime imposed by the elders; and this is true also of the dances of mature women. As such, dancing in Samburu society provides a gauge of popular feeling against this regime, which the elders cannot ignore. It poses an alternative reality over which they have little control and it confronts them with its own impunity. During the dance, it is the dance that reigns supreme and it leads towards an alternative undomesticated order.

It is the element of confrontation that Judith Hanna has stressed in her interpretation of certain dances in West Africa, where women band together in a united protest against male domination. By their united action, they take the notion of lampooning through song and dance a stage further, defending the boundary of their own domain against abuse. The reversal of roles in which they adopt a masculine and even military stance is interpreted as a veiled threat that they may reject the authority of males altogether.[59] This type of women's dancing also intrigued Gluckman in his analysis of *ritual of rebellion*. However, Hanna has shifted the emphasis from rituals to rebellion, and even the possibility of revolution and anarchy. Surely an overstatement; but certainly in various parts of Africa, men behold women banded together in this fashion with awe.[60] In one incident related to me in East Africa by some Matapaato Maasai, bitterness spread among the women after one of their daughters had been raped, then a groundswell of resentment, then a display of anger against the culprit expressed through a particular dance. Finally, when he foolishly attempted to defend his cattle from their onslaught, they seized him and maimed him for life. No sane man, it was claimed, would ever want to cross the path of Maasai women performing this dance: their boundary had been violated and the response was a dance display that was transformed into an attack. More pertinent still to Hanna's interpretation is the shift in the boundary with men that was achieved by the women's *lelemama* dance associations in Mombasa. Margaret Strobel has shown how the seclusion of married women was a combination of female subservience and the high status of their families; but the desire to acquire prestige within their dance associations led these women to emerge from seclusion, defying convention and male domination, and ultimately expanding their activities and achieving a greater control over their own affairs.[61]

As between Gluckman's *ritual* and Hanna's *rebellion* against male exploitation, the odds are heavily weighted in favour of the status quo. The electric atmosphere generated in such dances seems more

26

likely to lead to a harmless discharge than to provide a quasi-revolutionary spark for a liberation movement. Hanna's own material from West Africa has a clear mythical component.[62] Even Strobel admitted that the Mombasa women's outburst hardly went beyond their immediate frustrations, and their solidarity against male domination was shattered by in-fighting between rival women's dance associations.[63] Nevertheless, it is clear that the licence to dance provides these women with an arena from which to pursue limited grievances with effect.

Social class in its Marxist sense is not a term that one can normally use of traditional African society, and certainly if one sets women in the context of their day-to-day dispersal and regards dance, like religion, as the sigh of the oppressed creature and serving merely to release frustrations – in other words if one follows Gluckman and confines the analysis to theme 1 – then the women are like the proverbial potatoes in a sack, and they do not comprise a class. However, there is an element of uncertainty in the development of these dances that gives the display of protest its cutting edge. In discussing previous themes, we have noted the transformation that takes place: the development of solidarity in certain kinds of dance, the alteration in the level of consciousness, the entry into a domain in which the normal day-to-day order is upset and there is an awareness of a transcendental presence, a spirit generated by the group in their dance. With the present theme, the context is an external threat to the integrity of the group. Translating this process from Durkheimian to Marxist concepts, from a religious experience of the force of society to a political awareness and demonstration of strength in defence of a moral boundary, one may perceive this enhanced consciousness as one of power to assert group interests. It is in their collective dances of protest (theme 5) as in no other traditional context that African women may be said to form a social class. Yet they are still not a class in a fully revolutionary sense, and the role of dancing in the resolution of inherent contradictions within society is central to the next theme.

Dance as ritual drama: the theory of communitas and antistructure (theme 6)

Although Victor Turner (1969) does not consider the dance as such, his concept of *communitas* provides a further insight that builds on earlier themes. Turner points to the paradox present in any society where social inequalities, rivalries, and property interests divide people according to some prevailing structural premiss, yet there is at the same time a generic human bond, a communitas, that unites them

27

Paul Spencer

all regardless of differences in status. In the final analysis, political power is fragile and all humans are mere mortals, ground down to a uniform condition beside the mysteries of life, death, fertility, and the uncertain bounties of nature. These lie beyond the power of individuals and yet are intimately bound up with their destinies. As symbols of the cosmos, they are closely related to the expression of communitas, for they reduce humans to a humble role where they survive only as a species and only by involvement with one another. This leads Turner to suggest two complementary modes of social interaction. It is the structured aspect that dominates day-to-day existence; but when there is some disruption in the normal routine, during periods of anxiety or at ceremonies marking changes in status, boundaries shift, the gaps in the structure are laid bare and the underlying force of communitas rises to the surface. Neither structure nor communitas is complete in itself; together they give shape and meaning to human existence.

The relevance of dance should be at once apparent. It is not just that dancing is a highly social and levelling activity that draws people together in solidarity (theme 3). It is also frequently marginal and anomalous in its own way. It contrasts with normal everyday life, taking the dancers out of their structured routine and into a realm of timeless charm. In their *ecstasy* they literally *stand outside*.[64] Frequently the dance stretches beyond the immediate social milieu to some higher association with spiritual beings, who possess the dancers as in *Bori* or perhaps lurk in the shadows as in the !Kung medicine dance. Analytically, such beliefs provide vital clues as metaphorical expressions of the inexpressible. Thus the *Bori* cult stood outside the formal Islamic structure of Hausa society; pagan, unacknowledged, and socially deviant. Yet through their close association with the spirits, members of this cult were in a unique position to express the popular feelings against the contrived move from Old to New Giwa. Far from being peripheral, they were seen to play a complementary role to the formal hierarchy and to force a concession from the authorities. Only through their dancing, perceived as *Bori* spirit possession, was it thought possible to breathe new life into a spiritually lifeless community. Metaphorically, the patronage of the market by these pagan spirits, interpreted through the dancing of some of the most marginal people in the town, was an expression of communitas and gave a legitimacy to the enterprise beyond the powers of the Islamic lawgivers.

Elaborating on this theme, one may consider Robin Horton's analysis of the ritual cycle of masquerade dances among the Kalabari, also associated with spirit possession in Nigeria. The virtue of the

Kalabari example is that it forms a very clearly defined ideal type, although I suspect that the following treatment would broadly apply to the dance plays performed at Balinese festivals and might well be adapted to other forms of theatrical dancing, including Western ballet with its emotive themes and etherial niche in popular cosmology.[65]

The Kalabari were a coastal people whose traditional economy was based on fishing. Each village had its own *Ekine* men's society organised around the annual performance of a cycle of thirty or more masquerade plays. According to popular belief, the cycle was originally devised by water spirits, who controlled the weather and abundance of fish in distant creeks, but had also been partly tamed by the *Ekine*, bringing creativity and innovation to the Kalabari. Each spirit was represented in the cycle by a particular mask and associated with a drum rhythm. The cycle enacted episodes that reflected the cut and thrust of Kalabari life, where competition for status and influence was keen, but with restricted opportunities for success, and an uncompromising attitude towards failure. Popular interest, especially among the women spectators, centred on the ability of each masked dancer to translate the rhythm faultlessly into the appropriate dance steps as though the drumming had entered his legs and was pushing him around. At this point, the owner of the dance – the water spirit – was held to be walking with the dancer and ideally at some point it would actually take possession and enter the mask itself. In functionalist terms, the whole performance could be regarded as a highly engaging and popular symbolic representation of the competitive ethos of Kalabari society, giving the stamp of approval and serving to reinforce these values. The risk of public ridicule in certain dances and of mystical punishment by the water spirit in the event of a blunder could add further spice to these values. Indeed, there was a certain achievement in advancing through the grades of the *Ekine* society: a youth in the lowest grade needed to impress a senior patron with his dancing ability to advance to the next grade, and then to perform certain routines faultlessly to be accepted into the senior grade – or risk public humiliation, which could even provoke his suicide.

In other respects, however, the activities of the *Ekine* men's society contrasted with the relentless competitiveness of Kalabari life. Within each grade, the *Ekine* strove to be self-consciously egalitarian and uncompetitive. Status and influence were irrelevant. The most prominent members were expected to be relaxed and gregarious. Such men were unlikely to be suspected of sorcery or to achieve prominence outside *Ekine*; they contrasted outwardly with the aggressive and thrusting politicians who succeeded in public office. They also con-

29

Paul Spencer

trasted with ancestral spirits who were thought to sow discord among the living, inciting their descendants to perpetuate the struggle for status between rival lineages. For this reason, members of *Ekine* were expelled from the society at death when they became ancestors, and all reference to ancestry was avoided.

In contrast to the restricted choices of everyday life, each member of *Ekine* was free to select from a wide range of masquerade personalities in order to master one dance pattern to perfection; this could be his consuming pleasure, and provide a sense of secure identity and success. The immediate aim in dancing was to enhance the standing of the *Ekine* as a whole rather than that of the individual dancer, who was expected to remain anonymous and concealed by his mask. When his performance excelled, it was regarded as an achievement of the possessing spirit rather than that of the dancer himself. Indeed the competitive element of the masquerade plays was removed one further step from the performance by the notion that it was not the actual spirits who were betraying relentless opportunism, but the characters in the plays they had devised: the dancers were possessed by spirits who were only acting. Horton emphasises that this separation of competitiveness from *Ekine* activities was an ideal that was only partially achieved in practice: the water spirits by reputation had a vicious streak, which had only partly been tamed by the *Ekine* society; and dancers were not wholly incognito and their successes could bring them into rivalry for the favours of women. Yet the emphasis in *Ekine* was effectively against competition, and the basic ideals of the masquerade served to disentangle the characters and the themes of the plays from the personalities of the dancers, giving a certain detachment essential for true aesthetic performance and for appreciating these performances as ends in themselves.

This reveals an intriguing situation whereby mortals, both the dancing *Ekine* men and the women spectators in convivial mood, were treated to a performance by spirits who parodied the uncomfortable realities of Kalabari existence. It is as if, instead of looking up to the spirits, the mortals were looking down on their own antics with a detached enjoyment, rather like gods on Olympus.

Adapting Turner's model freely to the Kalabari, one has the contrast between their high regard for achievement, which dominated their economic and political reality, and the masquerade cycle associated with recreation and concerted fellowship. It was in the *Ekine* activities that the submerged spirit of communitas became dominant and the notion of struggle and status-seeking became mere play, even if still the focal point of their acting. That dancing and masquerading should be the idiom of expression emphasised that it was indeed a parody. However, beyond the masquerading lay dangerous forces expressed in the grotesqueness of some of the masks, the vicious reputation of the water spirits, the danger of inciting them by inept footwork, and even in the possibility of suicide if a novice was publicly unmasked for some mistake. This was more than mere recreation; it concerned the dialectical relationship between structure and communitas, inequality and equality, opportunistic manoeuvring and conviviality. Each placed the other in perspective and sharpened its meaning. The structure of Kalabari society divided men but in the final analysis they were united in the survival of their way of life. They were all subject to the capricious forces of chance that lay beyond their power to control, and hence these forces, like the water spirits, lay outside social structure. Even within the structure, the trappings of power and success depended on the universal acceptance of their symbolic worth, and on a consensus regarding the rules that governed their competition.[66]

With these points in mind, one can argue that by transforming the competitive ethic into a parody, the dancers demoted it almost to the status of a mere game, a whim of the *Ekine* fellowship; and yet at the same time by lavishing so much loving care in adapting it to a widely acclaimed and demanding aesthetic form, they endowed it with a legitimacy it would otherwise lack. The masquerade can be regarded as both a mandate to the private ambitions of men and an assertion that they were in the final resort accountable to the community. The vicious forces of competition associated with ungovernable water spirits stood opposed by the power of communitas during the masquerade cycle. It may be seen as a dialogue that maintained the vitality of community existence, while preserving it from the Hobbesian chaos into which untrammelled competition would degenerate.

Gluckman's interpretation of the Swazi first-fruits ceremony (noted in theme 1) foreshadowed Turner's opposition between structure and communitas, but it needs to be restated with a shift in emphasis. The ceremony occurred at a time in the agricultural cycle when widespread unrest welled close to the surface, and this was symbolically perceived as a threat to the whole nation of cosmic proportions if the ceremony was not performed meticulously. At such a time of unrest, the ability of the Swazi king to maintain peace by balancing the competing interests of his subjects was severely strained and he was isolated. The problem was not specifically of subjects fomenting rebellion against their king (Gluckman) as of the forces of law and order strained to their limit (Beidelman). The arbitrary powers of the king were closely

Paul Spencer

associated with these forces and with the survival of his nation in a region of powerful, autocratically ruled kingdoms.[67] At the climax of the ceremony, he would show reluctance to continue his rule as his royal kinsmen sang of their hatred for him; then, appearing as a wild monster, he would execute a crazy elusive dance. Once again one is presented with a parody of the dominant political structure, a metaphor that in this instance seems to emphasise the unique isolation of the king, and also the grotesque extremes expected of his autocratic rule in order to maintain the aura of kingship and ultimately the prestige and independence of the Swazi. The king's isolation was countered by his loyal warriors vigorously stamping and beating their shields in an intense dance that was intended to strengthen the king and unite him with his people. The opposition to his rule now modified as renewed loyalty overcame misgivings, and they wooed him back with expressions of national solidarity, reemphasising at the same time that the legitimacy of his rule depended ultimately on the whole-hearted consent of his nation.

One can identify, then, two aspects of social solidarity in dancing, each associated with a form of complementary opposition: the solidarity bred of the complementary opposition between groups of people (theme 5), and the solidarity expressed in complementary opposition to a dominant principle of social organisation, a competition of ideas, so to speak (theme 6).[68] Either may appear in relatively pure form, as with *beni-ngoma* on the one hand or *Ekine* on the other. However, there may be a certain fusion of these principles, especially in dances associated with protest. To the extent that the North American Indian Ghost Dance or the women's dances in Africa are regarded as political movements among subordinate groups against their oppressors, it is the element of competition that is stressed. To the extent that there is felt to be a supernatural presence that extends to all mankind – a redemptive reunion with the lost past in the Ghost Dance or a divine blessing on women's fertility in Africa – it is a more pervasive sense of solidarity based on a religious idea that is stressed. Among the Swazi, the belief that cosmic disaster is avoided by acting out the opposition between king and his people through dance combines both themes. The religious and political aspects of social solidarity, although analytically distinct, are by no means mutually exclusive.

In this volume (Chapter 6), John Middleton considers the significance of dancing among the Lugbara of Uganda in situations where there is uncertainty and disorientation. These include the women's dances following a bumper harvest or a long dry season; and even more dramatically the men's dances after a death. In each of these situations there is a sudden change in everyday existence and a general notion that orderly time and the normal pattern of social relations have been thrown into confusion. The world has gone wrong. After a death, the wilderness associated with the dangerous powers of Divinity and the dead is felt to close in on village as the centre of social life; and it is in the area between the village and the asocial wilderness that the death dances are performed, permitting reversals of normal behaviour and a display of individualism and jostling in a disoriented community that has been caught up in a cosmic hiatus. Out of this display, a sense of order in society and time is re-created, pushing the wilderness back and ultimately incorporating the dead person into the protective world of the ancestors. An intriguing expression of their sense of disorientation is the Lugbara claim that they are then 'like children'. For this seems to parallel the manner in which Samburu dancing transcends structured oppositions, leading to the suggestion that the genesis of communitas lies in the uninhibited play of childhood (Chapter 5).[69]

Dancing may also be viewed as an expression of the paranormal among mythical beings that lie beyond society. With regard to the Dance of Death in medieval art, for instance, Sachs drew attention to the eerie contrast between the youthful vigour of dancing and the awful and eternal stillness of Death. Brought together in one image, the message was intended to serve as a sombre warning for those who abused their position on this earth: that Death claims men in every walk of life at the least expected moment.[70] The figure of Death, dancing convulsively and lording over mortals as his minions may be compared with the dancing of the competitive Kalabari water spirits. In the medieval instance also, the onlookers are presented with a grotesque reflection of the structure of their own society, Death behaving arbitrarily as the supreme feudal lord, and regardless of status differences they are drawn together in awe of this prospect.

More widespread generally are beliefs in the weird dances of mythical witches, as in the witch's sabbath in medieval Europe or at the hut or grave of their victims in parts of Africa. In Africa, the term 'dancer' or 'singer' is often a euphemism for a witch. Where, for instance, an Ndembu chief was ritually humiliated at his installation and told, 'You have danced for your chiefship because your predecessor is dead', the insinuation was that he had killed him through witchcraft.[71] Once again, there is a pronounced anomaly in this belief; on the one hand a notion of unbounded selfishness among witches and a denial of all social virtues, and yet on the other hand an odd impression of communitas among their covens described in widely diverse areas: witches are thought to hold trysts, to share nefarious feasts, to be bonded together by a heavy, perverted, sexual symbolism, and to dance together in a collective orgy. They present a grotesque parody of all that is evil and yet at the same time of something that is prized. The explanation seems to lie in the type of village that believes that witches are abroad. In any balanced traditional community, such a suggestion would normally be denied. However, where there has been a cumulative loss of trust among fellow men, such a rumour becomes credible and suspicion may spread and speculation as to which villagers are the witches, emerging only in their true guise at night. In a generally demoralised village, witches may be blamed for all ills. It is they who are thought to have betrayed every law of human decency, placing themselves beyond the community of mankind. They are no longer people in the normal sense. However, this village is no longer a community in the normal sense; it may have a structure of sorts, but it lacks communitas, and anyone and everyone may be suspected of witchcraft. At such a point, the popular belief in omnipotent witches becomes dominant, and it is they who have in a sense taken away the communitas from the village to display it – as an anticommunitas – in their own perverted way. Figuratively, the village needs to recover the will to dance together, and the power of the coven will fade. This is more or less what witchfinding and also millenarian movements set out to achieve, and what the !Kung medicine dance does achieve at times of vague malaise, as the dancers assert the power of communitas to hold the sinister spirits lurking in the shadows at bay. One has, in fact, a widespread phenomenon that in certain respects is an inversion of the Hausa beliefs in the benign *Bori* spirits: the absence of dancing *Bori* spirits in certain unsuccessful Hausa towns corresponds broadly with the presence of dancing witches in demoralised villages elsewhere; and vice versa.

If the cathartic theme (1) at its crudest portrays dance as a communal sneeze relaxing the tension that has built up, then Turner's model has a closer affinity with a dream world in which the structure and repressions of everyday existence are upturned in a meaningful symbolic pattern. There is in this, as Turner points out, a shift from *structure* as applied to the power relations of everyday life, to communitas at times when normal life is suspended, and here *structure* in Lévi-Strauss's alternative sense becomes more pertinent, referring to the underlying logic of symbolism in ritual and myth, and revealing the basic dilemmas of social existence. The prominence of dancing in both ritual *and* myth emphasises that these paranormal aspects of social life are more than stimulants for thoughtful reflection as Turner has suggested.[72] Through dancing, the individual is caught up in a very dynamic way in the powerful forces underlying community life. It is not just his imagination that is stirred, but his whole body.

It is, once again, a topic on which Durkheim and Langer, representing two diverse traditions and apparently quite independently, show a remarkable convergence. It is the convergence of the twin forces of society and the dance on the senses of the dancer.

Commencing at nightfall, all sorts of processions, dances and songs had taken place by torchlight; the general effervescence was constantly increasing... The smoke, the blazing torches, the showers of sparks falling in all directions and the masses of dancing, yelling men... One can readily conceive how, when arrived at this state of exaltation, a man does not recognize himself any longer. Feeling himself dominated and carried away by some sort of an external power which makes him think and act differently than in normal times, he naturally has the impression of being himself no longer... everything is just as though he really were transported into a special world, entirely different from the one where he ordinarily lives, and into an environment filled with exceptionally intense forces that take hold of him and metamorphose him.... So it is in the midst of these effervescent social environments and out of this effervescence itself that the religious idea seems to be born. *(Durkheim 1915:218)*

The dance creates an image of nameless and even bodiless Powers filling a complete, autonomous realm, a 'world.' It is the first presentation of the world as a realm of mystic forces... the prehistoric evolution of dancing... is the very process of religious thinking, which begets the conception of 'Powers' as it symbolizes them. To the 'mythic consciousness' these creations are realities, not symbols; they are not felt to be created by the dance at all, but to be invoked, adjured, challenged, or placated, as the case may be. The symbol of the world, the balletic realm of forces, is the world, and dancing is the human spirit's participation in it... the dancer's world is a world transfigured, wakened to a special kind of life. *(Langer 1953:190)*

Conclusion: the uncharted deep structures of dance (theme 7)

There remains a final theme that probes the pattern of dance movement for some hidden meaning. A structuralist view of dance has provided a major topic that characterises, almost to the point of dominating, recent writings on the anthropology of dance. Parallels have been sought between dance and language: dance in general with its structured set of possibilities and creative potential, dances in particular with their underlying structural form, and dancing as a shared activity with its nonverbal mode of communication.[73] Much of the literature appears to lead one to the brink of proposing that the patterns of dance, deep down, form a structural whole within any society, but without adequate illustration.[74]

A rare opportunity to tease out this problem is presented by Alfred Gell in this volume (Chapter 7). He examines the pattern of dancing among the Umeda of Papua New Guinea, and shows how the symbolism of their *ida* ceremony exaggerates and distorts culturally significant features of everyday life, and this gives it powerful associations and subtle meaning, rather as poetry draws strength by transforming the nuances of normal language in our own culture. Following this approach, the array of *ida* dance styles can be related to the normal walking gait of different categories of people; and the underlying pattern reveals a structural dilemma, deeply embedded in the social life of the Umeda: the need to contain the bizarre excesses of successful elders. In the course of the ceremony there are successive transformations of the dancing styles evoking the domestication of these men as they are united with the community in an apparent resolution of the problem.

The special value of this example is that it extends Gell's earlier work on the *ida* ceremony, and places the analysis of dance movements fully within the scope of ritual.[75] For this purpose, he devises his own specific notation to examine the gait of either leg; and the notation does not, for instance, indicate the leaping movement to which the Umeda themselves draw attention, nor the sideways movements that distinguish women's style of dance from men's. However, it does reveal a pattern that would have been obscured had he relied on a more conventional method. This partiality poses a problem for choreologists who may insist that dance must be allowed to speak for itself and nothing less than a notation that records the totality of movement will reveal the true language of the body. Yet in this volume at least, Gell has gone further than other contributors, who provide even less comprehensive descriptions of dance movements: their search for underlying truths has led in other directions, ranging from body decoration to perceptions of consciousness, time and space.[76] It is not the search for hidden patterns that is in question, but rather any assumption that these must lie in movement or in any other particular direction.

The nub of the problem is this: is a half revelation (the lower half in Gell's case) a half-truth? It is a topic on which anthropologists who seek to simplify in order to construct models of reality and specialists in dance may always be at cross purposes. In defending the model builders against the choreographers, one can point to the close parallel between the anthropologist's attempts to pinpoint key features in his analysis, which introduces an element of distortion in the process of interpreting an underlying truth, and what the choreographers themselves are attempting to do (like Umeda dancers and Western poets) when they devise the movements of a dance as an interpretation of some aspect of human life. In other words, it is not that the model builders are merely amateur choreographers (although of course they are) but that they have fundamentally different aims, which require a different set of tools. One is concerned with two different levels of interpretation.

In the final analysis any underlying pattern of behaviour or belief that is not consciously perceived by the members of a culture may be described as deep structure; and where, for instance, some inherent pattern of a particular dance form shines through the superficial changes in fashion like a dominant symbol, as in Balinese dances, this persistence invites a structuralist explanation.[77] But this is not to suggest that every nuance of the basic choreographic pattern of all dances must have some inherent meaning or must in some way relate directly to the wider analysis of ritual leaving no possibility of an independent experience. The fact that so often a dance can be exported from one culture to another, albeit with surface adaptations that in themselves may have a deeper meaning, suggests that what has actually been transferred may be regarded in a sense as an artefact: exquisite in its way and with an inherent form, but no longer the natural possession of any one culture with a meaningful deep structure. One has only to glance at the mass of earlier literature on the dances of North American Indians to appreciate how suitable the topic of dance is in any unbounded study of the diffusion of culture.

Even where some underlying dance form persists in a society, its role may modify in what appears to be a wholly arbitrary manner. Adrienne Kaeppler has provided a very neatly argued historical reconstruction of the process of change in Tonga as perceived through the changing roles of certain persistent dance forms. What had been an informal night dance in the past was recognisably similar in form to a contemporary day dance of formal allegiance to the king through the ritual presentation of food, whereas the dance form that fulfilled this precise role toward an earlier line of kings has since been adopted by their fallen dynasty virtually unchanged as a symbolic claim to continuing prestige. At the level of historical analysis, the changing meaning of these dance forms may be seen to reflect the changing fortunes of rival dynasties. At a different level, the persistence of the distinction between percussive informal night dances and more restrained formal day dances is relevant to the symbolic analysis of a

Paul Spencer

persisting social structure. But these two aspects – the persisting choreographic forms and the persisting symbols of hierarchy – appear to
be wholly independent of one another.[78]

This is not to diminish the achievement of the very few authors
who have made good the structuralist claim that within the pattern
of movement in dance there is some hidden code that touches on the
mainspring of social existence. But it is to question any axiomatic
assumption that the basic choreographic pattern of every dance must
be loaded with an inner subliminal meaning. This is to shift the emphasis in analysis from the dance itself as a self-explanatory structural
entity – its choreographic form – to its ritual context. From this certain
corollaries follow, attested by the contributions to this volume:

to the extent that dancing is relevant to boundary situations, evoking an emotional response that may stray beyond the boundaries of
normal consciousness, it is relevant – even vital – to the analysis of ritual
behaviour and to the distinction between normal life and ritual drama;

to the extent that dance can be related to perceptions of the body,
of bodily movements, of time and of space, it is relevant to these in
the broader analysis of the cognitive framework of society;

to the extent that communications occur within a dance – planned
or spontaneous, mimed or implicit, signalling skill or rapport or play
– these should be regarded as symbolic acts with various levels of
meaning, and they should take their place rightly in the analysis of
their ritual context.

It then follows that *dance* may be defined in whatever way seems
most appropriate to the study of any specific situation or society.
Dance is not an entity in itself, but belongs rightfully to the wider
analysis of ritual action, and it is in this context that one can approach
it analytically and grant it the attention it demands. In a very important sense, society creates the dance, and it is to society that we must
turn to understand it.

NOTES

1 Kurath 1960; Rust 1969; Blacking 1973; Comstock 1974; Lange 1975; Royce
  1977; Hanna 1979b; 1979c; Blacking and Kealiinohomoku 1979; Copeland
  and Cohen 1983.
2 Lange 1975:39; Royce 1977:8; Hanna 1979a:19; 1979c:19; Copeland and
  Cohen 1983:1–102; cf. Sachs 1933:6. Best (1978:88–90) discusses the fallacy
  of seeking definitions in relation to (for example) dance. In anthropology
  the intractable problem of seeking cross-cultural definitions has been discussed, for instance in relation to religion (Evans-Pritchard 1965:120) and

38

marriage (Leach 1961:107–8), and very similar arguments could be raised in relation to dance. In the present volume, Kaeppler raises the problem in relation to structured movement among the Tonga, where the Western conception of dance is too narrow in one sense and too broad in another. Yet once the trap of ethnocentrism has been exposed, what better metaphor can one offer?

3 Spencer and Gillen 1904:375–92; Durkheim 1915:218.
4 Mooney 1892–6.
5 Lange 1975:22; cf. Langer 1953:184–5.
6 Cf. Best 1978:31–2, 152.
7 Cf. Best 1978:79; Kaeppler 1978a:34.
8 Snyder 1974:221.
9 Merriam 1974:15–17; cf. Kaeppler 1978a:45–6.
10 Sargant 1957:92, 118–19; Neher 1962; but note also Rouget's reservations (1977:234).
11 Freud 1922:263; Evans-Pritchard 1928:458; cf. Kuper 1947:224; Mead 1928:92–101; cf. Holt and Bateson 1944:328–9; Rust 1969:168; Royce 1977:91.
12 Lange 1975:59; Marshall 1969:380.
13 Sachs 1933:12. Also noted by Blacking p. 68 below and Royce 1977:218–19.
14 Sargant 1957:62; Franks 1963:185; Rust 1969:85–6.
15 Gluckman 1963:124–5, 133–4, 258; Lewis 1971:52–3, 91–2, 102–7, 176, 195.
16 Norbeck 1963; Beidelman 1966; Rigby 1968; Wilson 1967.
17 Hanna 1978:5; Malinowski 1925:59–60; Radcliffe-Brown 1952:148–9.
18 Evans-Pritchard 1928:460; Rust 1969:25; *Encyclopaedia Britannica* 1875–89, cited by Lange 1975:14. This is turn echoes Nadel's critique of the cathartic theory of witch beliefs and accusations (Nadel 1952:29).
19 Langer 1953:177–82, 203.
20 Pemberton 1711, cited by Rust 1969:60; cf. Spencer 1965:245.
21 St. Johnston 1906:142.
22 Cited respectively by Rust 1969:41; Lange 1975:14; Sachs 1933:400.
23 Mead 1928:97–9, 108; cf. Raum 1940:224 for the Chagga.
24 Bernstein 1965:166.
25 Bloch 1974.
26 Kubik 1979:228.
27 McPhee 1938 (1970:213–14); 1948 (1970:311); De Zoete and Spies 1938:262.
28 Blacking 1973:26, 52, 109–11.
29 For a neurobiological interpretation of this process see Lex (1979–:143–4); and also Williams's reservations (1978:212). Cf. Note 10 above with regard to theme 1.
30 Radcliffe-Brown 1922:233–4; 1952:124, 157
31 Herbert Spencer's theory on the relation *speech intonation:music* is also echoed in Gell's *walk:dance* (see pp. 193–4 below). Langer 1953:32; 174–5; 180. Birdwhistell 1970:79–99; 218–19.
32 Condon and Ogston 1966:338; Lomax 1974:199.
33 Salmond 1975:56. See also below pp. 126 (Melpa) and 157 (Samburu).
34 Durkheim 1915:210.
35 Weyer 1932:226–7 (Eskimo); Bohannan 1957:142 (Tiv); Evans-Pritchard 1928:449 (Azande); Mead 1928:93 (Samoa); Raum 1940:222 (Chagga); Smith 1954:222 (Hausa); Turnbull 1965:120 (Mbuti).

Paul Spencer

Paul Spencer

36 Radcliffe-Brown 1922:132, 248; Evans-Pritchard 1928:449; Metraux 1959:187; Marshall 1969:368.
37 Radcliffe-Brown 1922:247, 252, 326; Durkheim 1893:233–4.
38 Blacking 1973:27–8; 48–51, 107; Durkheim 1915:219–22.
39 Langer 1953:175, 183–4; 190–2.
40 Radcliffe–Brown 1922:252–3.
41 Durkheim 1915:215. In so far as Durkheim took note of the relevance of song and dance on this occasion, it was their role in coordinating the movements of the performers to express their collective spirit, but his attention was focused on the mounting tumult of the occasion rather than on the dancing (p. 216).
42 Lewis 1971:53 (citing Shirokogoroff 1935; cf. Jennings p. 54 below); McPhee 1970:297; Sachs 1933:18; Blacking 1973:71; Lange 1975:104; Langer 1953:207.
43 Schieffelin 1976:172–3.
44 Sachs 1933:6, 49, 57; cf. Snyder 1974:220–1; Langer 1953:196; Hanna 1979a:26.
45 Onwuejeogwu 1969:179–305; Mary Smith 1954:188–90, 207–10, 218–30.
46 M.G. Smith 1962:306–7.
47 Onwuejeogwu 1969:290; cf. Lewis 1971:95–6.
48 Mary Smith 1954:222; Onwuejeogwu 1969:283, 289.
49 Merton 1957:419; Gluckman 1959; Brooks 1970; Turnbull 1965:154, 189, 278; Mooney 1892–6.
50 Benedict (citing Boas) 1935:66, 145–50; Malinowski 1929:211–13, 292; Evans-Pritchard 1928:453; Firth 1936:55, 510.
51 Bailey 1969:28–9; Rappaport 1967:26–7; Chagnon 1968: 109–11.
52 Cullen 1972:101; Hinde 1972:177 cf. Huxley 1966:251.
53 Ranger 1975.
54 Mitchell 1956; Hartwig 1969:54; Winter 1956:169; Lienhardt 1968:16–18; Ranger 1975:19, 149, 153–5.
55 Cohen 1980.
56 Notably absent from the idiom of *beni-ngoma* was any element of direct protest against the colonial presence. But the dance associations did attract the talents of ambitious and competent Africans who were denied responsible positions elsewhere, and in the Copperbelt riots in the 1930s it was from these that the organisation and leadership in these disturbances emerged. Similarly, Strobel has noted that women's dance associations, formerly associated with *beni-ngoma*, provided the leadership for mobilising an effective trade boycott against Indian merchants in Mombasa in the 1940s (Ranger 1975:139–140; Strobel 1979:174, 176).
57 Maquet 1961:117–18; Kealiinohomoku 1979:50; Rust 1969:60.
58 Cohen 1980:81–3; Best 1978:150; cf. Langer 1953:32; and p. 13 above.
59 Hanna 1977a:123–4; 1978:7–8.
60 Cf. below p. 159 (Samburu) and p. 177 (Lugbara).
61 Strobel 1979:170–3.
62 In overstating the power of women's dances to initiate social change in Africa, Hanna appears to have repeatedly misinterpreted Gailey's account of the women's disturbances in Eastern Nigeria in 1929. As she presents the incident, the women's *nkwa* dance was a traditional boundary display, mounted on this occasion against a new administrative policy, which went unheeded by the authorities. This led directly to a rampage in which thirty-two women were killed, as a result of which government policies were

modified. Gailey (1970) makes it clear that a single performance of the *nkwa* dance in one province was only one of a long sequence of events that led to the massacre in another province where the organisation among women was quite different (pp. 108, 129). There are only two subsequent references to dancing in his account, both apparently resembling impromptu and unprecedented war dances among women and not *nkwa* (pp. 124, 127, 130–2). Far from being a Women's War in every respect, men appear to have played a significant role in inciting the women at one critical point and in restraining them subsequently (pp. 124, 133). In retrospect, the women had acted more as a catalyst in promoting change than as a direct cause, and it was not these prior warnings (through dance) that the senior administrators had singularly failed to heed so much as those of their own junior civil servants (pp. 133, 155). More limited in its impact, but more directly related to Hanna's theme was the Dancing Women's Movement of 1925; however, again this affected another area and it did not modify government policy (p. 104). This is not to question the extent to which the lead taken by women during this period (nor perhaps their dancing) may in retrospect have built up into a legend within the region. In one sense, this is almost as important as what actually occurred; however, the role of dancing in myth belongs more correctly to theme 6 (p. 33) than to the present section.

63 Strobel 1979: 180.
64 Turner 1969:126; cf. Langer 1953:204–5.
65 Horton 1963; McPhee 1970.
66 Cf. Horton 1962:204 on various Kalabari sayings to this effect.
67 Gluckman 1963; Beidelman 1966:398.
68 Cf. Turner 1969:120.
69 See p. 156 below; and cf. Langer 1953:202. Middleton is careful to note that the Lugbara say they feel 'like children' because of their sense of disorder following a death rather than because of their behaviour. It remains that this sense of disorder does appear to correspond to a lack of adult inhibition at precisely this time (p. 171 below).
70 Sachs 1933:261.
71 Turner 1969:87; cf. Winter 1956:133; Beidelman 1963:64; Buxton 1963:100; Lienhardt 1968:64.
72 Turner 1967:105–6. Cf. also Geertz's reservations (1973:183).
73 Martin and Pesovar 1961; Metheny 1965; Kaeppler 1972; Blacking 1973 (passim); Singer 1974; Bellman 1974; Woodward 1976; Royce 1977:192–211; Williams 1978; Hanna 1979b and 1979c (passim); Gell 1979; Williams 1982.
74 Thus in Williams's example (1978) of counter-clockwise movements on sacred occasions in Ghanaian dancing and clockwise movements in secular dances, this polarity would seem closer to the surface in an analysis of the ritual context than to the 'very fundamental syntactic and semantic features of structure in dances' as she claims.
75 Gell 1975.
76 See below: Temiar p. 58; Venda p. 85; Tonga p. 115; Melpa p. 129; Samburu p. 153; Lugbara p. 179.
77 De Zoete and Spies 1938:263–8.
78 It is this dance of allegiance that Kaeppler describes in this volume. See also Kaeppler 1967 and 1978b.

41

Paul Spencer

REFERENCES

Backman, E. L. 1952. *Religious Dances in the Christian Church and in Popular Medicine* Trans. E. Classen. London: Allen & Unwin.
Bailey, F. G. 1969. *Stratagems and Spoils*. Oxford: Blackwell.
Beidelman, T. O. 1963. 'Witchcraft in Ukagura', in J. Middleton and E. H. Winter (eds.), *Witchcraft and Sorcery in East Africa*. London: Routledge & Kegan Paul.
—— 1966. 'Swazi royal ritual'. *Africa*, 36:373–405.
Bellman, B. L. 1974. 'The sociolinguistics of ritual performance'. In Comstock 1974.
Belo, J. 1970. *Traditional Balinese Culture*. New York: Columbia University Press.
Benedict, R. 1935. *Patterns of Culture*. London: Routledge & Kegan Paul.
Bernstein, B. 1965. 'A socio-linguistic approach to social learning'. In J. Gould (ed.) *Penguin Survey of the Social Sciences*. Harmondsworth: Penguin Books.
Best, D. 1978. *Philosophy and Human Movement*. London: Allen & Unwin.
Birdwhistell, R. L. 1970. *Kinesics and Context: Essays on Body-motion communication*. Philadelphia: Pennsylvania University Press.
Blacking, J. 1973. *How Musical is Man?* Seattle: Washington University Press.
Blacking, J. (ed.). 1977. *The Anthropology of the Body*. ASA. monograph no. 15. London: Academic Press.
Blacking, J. and J. W. Kealiinohomoku (eds.). 1979. *The Performing Arts: Music and Dance*. The Hague: Mouton.
Bloch, M. 1974. 'Symbols, song, dance, and features of articulation: is religion an extreme form of traditional authority?'. *Archives Européenes de Sociologie;* 15:55–81.
Bloch, M. (ed.). 1975. *Political Language and Oratory in Traditional Societies*. London: Academic Press.
Bohannan, P. 1957. *Justice and Judgment among the Tiv*. London: Oxford University Press for International African Institute.
Brooks, J. 1970. *Once in Golcanda*. London: Gollancz.
Buxton, J. 1963. 'Mandari witchcraft'. In J. Middleton and E. H. Winter (eds.), *Witchcraft and Sorcery in East Africa*. London: Routledge & Kegan Paul.
Cohen, A. 1980. 'Drama and politics in the development of a London Carnival'. *Man*, 15:65–87.
Comstock, T. 1974. *New Dimensions in Dance Research: Anthropology and Dance*. New York: Committee on Research in Dance (CORD).
Condon, W. S., and W. D. Ogston. 1966. 'Sound film analysis of normal and pathological behaviour patterns'. *Journal of Nervous and Mental Disease*, 143:338–47.
Copeland, R., and M. Cohen. 1983. *What Is Dance? Readings in Theory and Criticism*. Oxford: Oxford University Press.
Cullen, J. M. 1972. 'Some principles of animal communication', in Hinde 1970.
De Zoete, B., and W. Spies. 1938. 'Dance and drama in Bali'. Reprinted in Belo 1970.
Durkheim, E. 1893. *The Division of Labour in Society*. Trans. G. Simpson 1933. Illinois: Free Press.
—— 1912. *The Elementary Forms of the Religious Life*. Trans. J. W. Swain 1915. London: Allen & Unwin.

Evans-Pritchard, E. E. 1928. 'The dance'. *Africa*, 1:446–62.

Firth, R. 1936. *We the Tikopia*. London: Allen & Unwin.

Freud, S. 1922. *Introductory Lectures in Psycho Analysis*. Trans. J. Riviere, London: Allen & Unwin.

Gailey, H. A. 1970. *The Road to Aba*. New York: New York University Press.

Geertz, C. 1973. *The Interpretation of Cultures*. New York: Basic Books.

Gell, A. 1975. *The Metamorphosis of the Cassowaries*. London: Athlone.

1979. 'On dance structures: a reply to Williams'. *Journal of Human Movement Studies*, 5:18–31.

Gluckman, M. 1959. 'Football players and the crowd'. *The Listener*, 57 (Feb).

1963. *Order and Rebellion in Tribal Africa*. London: Cohen and West.

Hanna, J. L. 1977. 'African dance and the warrior tradition'. *Journal of Asian and African Studies*, 12:111–33.

1978. 'African dance: some implications for dance therapy'. *American Journal of Dance Therapy* 2:3–15.

1979a. 'Towards a cross-cultural conceptualization of dance and some correlate considerations'. In Blacking and Kealiinohomoku 1979.

1979b. 'Movements towards understanding humans through the anthropological study of dance'. *Current Anthropology*, 20:313–39.

1979c. *To Dance is Human: A Theory of Nonverbal Communication*. Austin: Texas University Press.

Hartwig, G. W. 1969. 'The historical and social role of Kerebe music'. *Tanganyika Notes and Records*, 70:41–56.

Hinde, R. A. (ed.).1972. *Non-verbal Communication*. Cambridge: Cambridge University Press.

Holt, C., and G. Bateson. 1944. 'Form and function of the dance in Bali'. Reprinted in Belo 1970.

Horton, R. 1962. 'The Kalabari world-view: an outline and interpretation'. *Africa*, 32:197–220.

1963. 'The Kalabari *Ekine* society: a borderline of religion and art'. *Africa*, 33:94–113.

Huxley, J. (ed.). 1966. *A Discussion on Ritualization of Behaviour in Animals and Man*. Philosophical Transactions of the Royal Society of London, no. 772 vol. 251. London: Royal Society.

Kaeppler, A. 1967. 'Preservation and evolution of form and function in two types of Tongan dance'. In G. Highland (ed.), *Polynesian Culture History*. Honolulu: Bishop Museum Press.

1972. 'Method and theory in analysing dance structure with an analysis of Tongan dance.' *Ethnomusicology*, 16:173–217.

1978a. 'Dance in anthropological perspective'. *Annual Review of Anthropology* 7:31–49.

1978b. 'Melody, drone and decoration: underlying structures and surface manifestations in Tongan art and society.' In M. Greenhalgh and V. Megaw (eds.), *Art in Society*. London: Duckworth.

Kealiinohomoku, J. W. 1979. 'Culture change: functional and dysfunctional expressions in dance, a form of affective culture'. In Blacking and Kealiinohomoku 1979.

Kubik, G. 1979. 'Pattern perception and recognition in African music'. In Blacking and Kealiinohomoku 1979.

Paul Spencer

Kuper, H. 1947. *An African Aristocracy*. London: Oxford University Press for International African Institute.

Kurath, G.P. 1960. 'Panorama of dance ethnology'. *Current Anthropology*. 1:233–54.

Lange, R. 1975. *The Nature of Dance: An Anthropological Perspective*. London: Macdonald & Evans.

Langer, S. 1953. *Feeling and Form: A Theory of Art*. London: Routledge & Kegan Paul.

Lewis, I. M. 1971. *Ecstatic Religion: an Anthropological Study of Spirit Possession and Shamanism*. Harmondsworth: Penguin Books.

Lex, B. 1979. 'The neurobiology of ritual trance.' In E. G., D'Aquili, C. D. Laughlin Jr., and J. McManus (eds.)., *The Spectrum of Ritual: A Biogenetic Structural Analysis*. New York: Columbia University Press.

Lienhardt, P. 1968. *Swifa Ya Nguvumali, the Medicine Man*. Oxford: Clarendon Press.

Lomax, A. 1974. 'Choreometrix'. In Comstock 1974.

Malinowski, B. 1925. 'Magic, science and religion'. In J. A. Needham (ed.), *Science, Religion and Reality*. Reprinted 1948. London: Sheldon Press.
 1929. *The Sexual Life of Savages in North Western Melanesia*. London: Routledge & Kegan Paul.

Maquet, J. J. 1961. *The Premise of Inequality in Ruanda*. London: Oxford University Press for International African Institute.

Marshall, L. 1969. 'The medicine dance of the !Kung Bushmen'. *Africa*, 39:347–81.

Martin, G. and E. Pesovar. 1961. 'A structural analysis of the Hungarian folk dance'. *Acta Ethnographica*, 10:1–40.

Mead, M. 1928. *Coming of Age in Samoa*. New York: Morrow.

McPhee, C. 1938. 'Children and music in Bali'. Reprinted in Belo 1970.
 1948. 'Dance in Bali'. Reprinted in Belo 1970.

Merriam, A. P. 1974. 'The anthropology of dance'. In Comstock 1974.

Merton, R. K. 1957. 'The self-fulfilling prophecy'. In R. K. Merton, *Social Theory and Social Structure*. Glencoe: Free Press.

Metheny, E. 1965. *Communication of Movement in Sport and Dance*. Iowa: Brown.

Metraux, A. 1959. *Voodoo in Haiti*. Trans. H. Charteris, London: André Deutsch.

Mitchell, J. C. 1956. *The Kalela Dance: Aspects of Social Relationships among Urban Africans in Northern Rhodesia*. Rhodes–Livingstone papers no. 27. Manchester: Manchester University Press.

Mooney, J. 1892–6. *The Ghost-Dance Religion and the Sioux Outbreak of 1890*. Abridged A. F. C. Wallace 1965. Chicago: Chicago University Press.

Nadel, S. F. 1952. 'Witchcraft in four African societies: an essay in comparison'. *American Anthropologist* 54:18–29.

Neher, A. 1962. 'A physiological explanation of unusual behavior in ceremonies involving drums'. *Human Biology*, 34:151–60.

Norbeck, E. 1963. 'African rituals of conflict'. *American Anthropologist*, 65:1254–79.

Onwuejeogwu, M. 1969. 'The cult of the *Bori* spirits among the Hausa'. In M. Douglas and P. M. Kaberry (eds.). *Man in Africa*. London: Tavistock, 1969.

Radcliffe-Brown, A. R. 1922. *The Andaman Islanders*. Cambridge: Cambridge University Press.

1952. *Structure and Function in Primitive Society*. London: Cohen & West.

Ranger, T. C. 1975. *Dance and Society in Eastern Africa 1890–1970*. London: Heinemann.

Rappaport, R. 1967. 'Ritual regulation of environmental relations among a New Guinea people'. *Ethnology*, 6:17–30.

Raum, O. F. 1940. *Chagga Childhood*. London: Oxford University Press for International African Institute.

Rigby, P. 1968. 'Some Gogo rituals of "purification" '. In E. R. Leach, (ed.). *Dialectics in Practical Religion*. Cambridge: Cambridge University Press.

Rouget, G. 1977. 'Music and possession trance'. In Blacking 1977.

Royce, A. P. 1977. *The Anthropology of Dance*. Bloomington: Indiana University Press.

Rust, F. 1969. *Dance in Society: An Analysis of the Relationship between the Social Dance and Society in England from the Middle Ages to the Present Day*. London: Routledge & Kegan Paul.

Sachs, C. 1933. *World History of the Dance*. Trans. B. Schönberg 1937, London: Allen & Unwin.

St. Johnston, R. 1906. *History of Dancing*. London: Simkin, Marshal & Kent.

Salmond, A. 1975. 'Mana makes man: a look at Maori oratory and politics'. In Bloch 1975.

Sargant, W. W. 1957. *Battle for the Mind*. London: Heinemann.

Schieffelin, E. L. 1976. *The Sorrow of the Lonely and the Burning of the Dancers*. New York: St. Martins Press.

Shirokogoroff, S. M. 1935. *Psychomental Complex of the Tungus*. London: Kegan Paul, Trench, Tubner.

Singer, A. 1974. 'The metrical structure of Macedonian dance'. *Ethnomusicology*, 18:379–404.

Smith, M. 1954. *Baba of Karo*, London: Faber & Faber.

Smith, M. G. 1962. 'Exchange and marketing among the Hausa' in P. Bohannan and G. Dalton, *Markets in Africa*. Evanston, Ill.: Northwestern University Press.

Snyder, A. F. 1974. 'The dance symbol' in Comstock 1974.

Spencer, B., and F. J. Gillen. 1904. *The Northern Tribes of Central Australia*. London: Macmillan.

Spencer, H. 1857. 'The origin and function of music'. Reprinted in 1868 *Essays: Scientific, Political and Speculative*. London: Williams and Norgate.

1860. 'The physiology of laughter'. Reprinted in Spencer, H. *Essays*.

1862. *First Principles*, London: Watts.

Spencer, P. 1965. *The Samburu*, London: Routledge & Kegan Paul.

Strobel, M. 1979. *Muslim women in Mombasa (1890–1975)*. New Haven, Conn.: Yale University Press.

Turnbull, C. 1965. *Wayward Servants*. London: Eyre & Spottiswoode, London.

Turner, V. W. 1967. *The Forest of Symbols*. Ithaca, N.Y.: Cornell University Press.

1969. *The Ritual Process*. London: Routledge & Kegan Paul.

Weyer, E. M. 1932. *The Eskimos, their Environment and Folkways*. New Haven, Conn.: Yale University Press.

Williams, D. 1978. 'Deep structures of the dance'. *Yearbook of Symbolic Anthropology*, 1:211–30.

1982. 'Semasiology: a semantic anthropological view of human movements

Paul Spencer

and actions'. In Parkin, D. J. (ed.), *Semantic Anthropology*. London: Academic Press.

Wilson, P. J. 1967. 'Status ambiguity and spirit possession'. *Man* (N.S.), 2:366–78.

Winter, E. 1956. *Bwamba*. Cambridge: Heffer.

Woodward, S. 1976. 'Evidence for a grammatical structure in Javanese dance'. *Dance Research Journal*, 8:10–17.

1 Temiar dance and the maintenance of order

SUE JENNINGS

Dancing among the Temiar is a process that can only be fully appreciated in relation to their culture as an integral aspect of their social life. For this reason, this chapter extends beyond dancing as an activity to consider their cosmology, reflecting concepts of body and of space, the socialisation of the young, and the maintenance of values and beliefs among adults.

The Temiar live in villages built on the banks of the main river and its tributaries in the states of Perak and Kelantan in the Malay peninsula. They practise shifting cultivation, the most important crop being cassava; maize and hill rice are also grown. Individual houses sometimes have small vegetable plots for growing tobacco and small quantities of fruit and vegetables. A village can either be a single longhouse, housing several clearly defined families, or a collection of individual houses. A village population can vary between twenty and a hundred people, often organised around a sibling group of adults and their children. Although they also hunt and gather, they cannot be called nomadic. This caused much confusion in the past when the authorities treated all tribal groups as wanderers. The confusion was further increased because the Temiar are a very mobile people, travelling between their villages on ritual and informal visits, visiting their crop fields, and moving village from time to time.

There are over ten thousand Temiar within a total aboriginal population of about seventy-six thousand in Malaysia. Although there is regional variation in belief and practice among the Temiar, they look upon themselves as a defined group, similar to the Semai and with some affinity with other aboriginal groups as opposed to nonaboriginal groups. It is the Semai who are better known through the work of Dentan (1968). Research on the Temiar themselves by Benjamin (1968) remains largely unpublished, and they are less well known.

The Temiar look upon other peoples as strangers or foreigners, to be avoided or even feared. Chinese contract companies, who are making large tracks to enable Land-rovers and machinery to penetrate

47

the jungle areas for timber production, are exposing the Temiar to external influences as a new presence and also as employers who offer a source of income to the Temiar through casual labour. Currently they are surrounded by new influences and redevelopment programmes. The Department of Aborigine Affairs has attempted to bring the aborigines within the Malay system, by providing schools, basic health care, and some economic aid. However, within this dominantly Muslim society, the Temiar have resisted assimilation and have preserved as far as possible their traditional life style and belief systems.

Temiar children are born into a world that is immediately physical, limited spatially, and surrounded by rules concerning diet, behaviour, and the Temiar naming system. Small babies are confined to the house most of the time unless carried for a brief outing by an older sibling. Crawling is discouraged and babies are helped to feel their feet on the mother's lap from a few weeks old. For the early months the baby is limited to an environment that has minimum light through gaps in the bamboo walls, and the gentle springiness of a raised bamboo floor. The first year is dominated by limited space and physical handling. When the child can walk unaided it can leave the house and play with other children in the village. Then it usually becomes the baby in children's family games. Five- and six-year-olds spend a lot of time playing at mothers, fathers, and babies or else mothers and babies. The toddler will be carried in a sarong on the back of a five-year-old, playing at the daily routine of her own mother, fetching cassava, cooking, and so on.

Children's play and play dance

Most of the children's play is imitation of adult life, including the dance and trance sessions. Sometimes these will be imitations of actual sessions that happened on the previous evening. Sometimes the children will spontaneously devise their own. I refer to such behaviour as 'play dance'. These play-dance sessions happen outside or in a corner of the house. Children use small pieces of bamboo to imitate the stompers and they will dance and sing and sometimes imitate the giddiness of the trance behaviour. Occasionally a young adult will join and show them rhythms and tunes. However, if the playing becomes too loud and obtrusive, older people are quick to tell them to calm down. Parents are insistent on obedience to behaviour governed by cosmic rules, even though children do not always take them too seriously. In this way, children are taught to control their spontaneous play.

Yet the Temiar will say that you cannot make anyone do anything, especially children. They say that a good Temiar behaves in certain ways and at the same time that people do what they want. Certainly my experience is that in terms of child rearing there is no pressure brought to bear on children to do everyday tasks, such as fetching water, if they do not feel like it. Parents just shrug their shoulders and do it themselves. Nevertheless, there is one area of daily living in which children never refused to participate – caring for younger siblings.

As well as children's play, spontaneous dancing and singing sessions also occur among adults in the evenings in the house. These can involve anyone who happens to be in the village, even foreigners. There is usually little, if any, preparation and decoration for an adult play dance. It can start with a small group getting together and singing, others gradually joining in. There is an atmosphere of lightheartedness and fun. Usually trancing is not involved, except in a mild spontaneous form among young people, when it is regarded essentially as play. Sometimes older people come and watch, again they sometimes bring the playing to a halt if they think it is getting out of hand. For example, on occasion during my stay among the Temiar there was screaming and shouting to a rhythm beaten on a metal tray. After a short time, an older man or woman would be sure to come and tell those involved curtly to calm down, to do it 'properly', sometimes demonstrating a rhythm.

Temiar dance also provides an opportunity for flirtation among young people, both as an aside during the more serious dances and as a central feature of their play dances. There may be some pairing between the sexes at the play dances, avoiding overt bodily contact. Pubertal girls frequently queue for the attentions of a young shaman who overtly practises his developing skills while covertly responding to their advances. He may place his forehead on theirs, or press the flat of his hand between their breasts, or hold them close from behind swaying with them, and the girls would then start trancing vigorously.

Older people can be critical of this frivolous indulgence in trance. True trance, they feel, can only be achieved by older people; it is a serious matter that requires long practice and considerable self-restraint. Younger people may say 'When I'm trancing, I feel free. It's like flying,' whereas older people disavow the erotic aspect, saying that trance is 'forgetting', and they cannot recall the sensation. Following Benjamin's distinction (1968:261), there is a shift away from

49

the ecstatic experience in youth, towards an ascetic experiece in the more serious trance among older people. My observation is that there is a socially significant contrast between the disorderly movement of the young and the orderly movement of the old.

The trance dance

In complete contrast to the play dances are the more formal sessions of dancing and trancing that take place on a larger scale after detailed planning and organisation. Nevertheless there are some elements of play within the formal sessions just as the play sessions occasionally have some planning. The main difference lies in the seriousness of intention involved. I refer to the more serious sessions as 'trance dances'. Trance is a state of disassociation, often resulting in unconsciousness, and is a central feature of most of the Temiar seances. During trance or sleep, the Temiar believe that a person's head soul, located on the crown, is free to leave the body, and it leaves permanently at death.

It was noticeable on many occasions while I was among the Temiar that the planned event would seem to be in response to a level of tension in the village. For example there would be anxiety after visits from outside: officials from government departments, or the army on patrol for communist guerrillas. Should any of these officials stay in the village, the Temiar would often mount a formal dance, but it would differ from the one they would perform after the officials had left. If the outsiders were staying, there would be an absence of serious trance. There would be serious dancing and singing and some playful trance organised by the shaman. The Temiar seances are famous in the area and beyond, and outsiders will ask for performances and sometimes join in. I attended one formal session that had just started when some passing Chinese loggers dropped by. The shaman discreetly switched gear for that evening and held his serious trance the following night.

On other occasions, when there appeared to be a general sense of irritability in the village and body movements that suggested greater social distance between villagers, one of the older men or women might suggest a trance dance for the same evening. This is an ordered society, where there are rules against conspicuous behaviour and shouting. There is no licence for aggression. The trance dance appeared to be the principal activity that could release any tension that might arise from these constraints.

The location of Temiar dance fits into their major conceptual categories concerning space. The Temiar have two major categories of space, the vertical in terms of 'off the ground'/'on the ground', and the horizontal in terms of 'village' (or 'house')/'jungle'. Earlier I described how Temiar children are not allowed on the ground until they can walk independently; they must stay off the ground, in the house. These spatial categories permeate most of Temiar conceptual organisation. Thus Temiar houses are built in the village and on stilts off the ground. By contrast, temporary shelters built in the jungle, if men stay overnight on a hunting expedition, are on the ground. Most animals that are hunted and killed in the jungle are transformed in some way, such as having the skin burnt off, before being brought into the village, and must then immediately be taken into a house off the ground and stay there. Any waste will be burnt in the house on the fire. It would seem that on the ground and in the jungle belong to the world of nature, and off the ground and in the village or house belong to the world of culture.

Dance and trance belong to the cultural world in terms of their location, and would thus not occur on the ground. The only occasion I witnessed when a group of women danced amid giggles on the ground was when they wanted me to show them an English dance. On another occasion, when some officials tried to encourage a Temiar get-together, they made the mistake of organising it in an open space outside. There was a little desultory singing, which eventually petered out, and even those Temiar attracted by the free food returned to their homes.

Although singing can take place in anyone's house there is usually one house in the village where dancing occurs. If the village is a single longhouse with discreet family units, these are built round a large central area where dancing takes place. Where a village is made up of separate houses, it is usually the house with the largest central area that is used for dancing. They make sure that the supports underneath the house are strong enough for what will be an energetic session. Floors have been known to give way and the proceedings stopped while reinforcements were made. The floor is made of slatted bamboo, which gives a yielding surface for dancing.

It is the women and children who are involved in fetching the leaves and foliage to make the decorations for the session. This usually happens in the morning, the rest of the day being spent in preparing the decorations for the evening. The men will assist in hanging them from the roof inside but the shaman will hang up the central decoration, which he will use ritually. The women weave headdresses from palm and sometimes include flowers or make separate circlets

51

of marigolds. These are only worn by men. Women wear just a single flower in their hair. On the most elaborate occasions, palm and other sorts of leaves are hung at frequent intervals and the centre-piece is either a bunch of leaves or a circlet of rattan from which leaves are hung. Apart from the headdresses, the women split the palm to make fans that the shaman will use and on some occasions large bunches of palm that the men will tuck into the backs of their sarongs. Most villages have a constant supply of bamboo stompers with which rhythms are beaten, but these are checked for cracks and new ones cut if necessary. A banana log is put in place for the musicians to stomp their rhythm. The more formal the occasion, the more dressing up in terms of clean sarongs and elaborate face paint for the women. The final preparation is the rolling of cigarettes from Temiar home-grown tobacco in special leaves. These are placed on a tray and on some occasions there is a dish of charcoal with aromatic plants near the fire.

Dancing takes place at night, commencing after dusk and some-times continuing until dawn but never into daytime. There are few Temiar who do not dance. The exceptions appear to be the older people of both sexes, although older women often join in for a short time. Certain categories of shaman who would not use dance in their special seances still dance in ordinary sessions like everyone else. Pregnancy is not a bar to dance, providing the mother is well. How-ever, the sections of the community who are allowed to trance are far more limited. Parents of young children, midwives and prepub-ertal boys and girls do not normally trance. These are precisely the social categories whose freedom is restricted in other ways, for in-stance with reference to the food taboos and the naming system that differentiates them from others.

An earlier style of dance is occasionally practised by one or two older women in a corner or even in a separate room from the main seance. The shape of the body and positioning of the limbs are rem-iniscent of Indian classical dance. The feet stay apart in one position with the weight being transferred from one foot to the other while the arms undulate and the wrists circle, following the weight of the body from one side to the other.

This contrasts with the contemporary dance movement, which is based on a simple walking pattern, with some variation by men and women. One foot steps forward, transferring the body weight on to it; the second foot is placed alongside the first foot and at the same time the person gives a slight spring forward. This step–spring pattern is repeated with alternate feet leading. Variations can include a small jump emphasising the movement towards the floor rather than away from it, or a forward movement with both feet sliding together.

The dancers initially form a single group, moving in a counter-clockwise direction, though there may be some variation as they turn slightly outwards from the circle and then inwards by the same amount. Women usually dance with their torsos upright, their hands by their sides, whereas the men bend forward ninety degrees from the waist as they spring, each arm alternately extending forward, parallel with the floor. This is the basic movement pattern used by most people in the dance. The grouping may change at the onset of trance and there may be a breakdown in movement and grouping as sometimes occurs with the wilder trancing among younger people.

To the onlooker, the Temiar appears to be divided at the waist into the upper and lower body. This is partially because they wear a sarong that is tied at the waist with the chest left bare unless a T-shirt is worn. It is also reinforced in movement where the lower body is used to support or propel and the main movement activity takes place in the upper body, in the arms and head and bending of the waist (which becomes more vigorous when trancing).

In the old-style dance described previously, the feet stayed in one place and all movement is in the upper half of the body. Once again, this appears to reflect the dichotomy, at a symbolic level, between on and off the ground: dance movements are constrained in the lower body 'on the ground', and tend to allow greater freedom of expression and focus of interest in the upper body 'off the ground'. It belongs to the village and to culture.

Usually, a formal dance session leads into trance, otherwise it is little more than a play dance. Once trancing has taken place, however, then dancing without trancing may well fill the rest of the night. The following is a description of a typical trance dance.

A sense of expectation builds up throughout the day as the preparation and decorations near completion. Once darkness falls there is a feeling of urgency to get started. Most of the village will be present and any visitors from other villages who have heard about it or are passing through. They all assemble in the main dancing area and the women, often with babies slung across their backs, take up a position sitting or squatting behind the banana log. There is a settling down period while they get in sequence, beating out a steady rhythm.

The shaman who is going to lead the proceedings squats in the centre and starts to sing. He is echoed in response by the women playing the bamboo stompers. The fire is dampened down, the children are hushed, the chatter dies away, and as everyone watches,

Sue Jennings

the only illumination is from the kerosene wick. The shaman sings to make contact with his spirit guide, who will assist him in the seance, and to coax the small shy sprites on to the roof of the house, or even to come down to the central leaf decoration. As the singing builds up, the shaman stands and holds on to this centre-piece, through which the power from the spirits can enter him. He is thought to catch it in his palm in the form of a fluid, which he can then use to transmit their good influence. At this point he enters a light trance but is still in complete control of the proceedings.

Men of all ages get up and make a big circle round the shaman, and with the walking step described above, accent the rhythm in their movements. The women play the stompers and increase the intensity of their singing. Those not involved in the music watch and discuss the dancers, sometimes giggling though not loudly. Boys dance with the men, and girls either help with the stompers or sit with their friends. In the shadows, younger people may use the opportunity to flirt as in a play dance until the trancing becomes serious.

The shaman tries to control the development of the session, restraining those who fall into trance too soon so that there can be a slow build-up to a climax by the group as a whole. As he allows the intensity to increase, so the women respond. The rhythm and singing become louder and the dancing starts to get faster; soon some people start to trance spontaneously, those who are not going to trance standing to one side, as do the young boys. The circle breaks up and those already in trance start bouncing round the floor in their own circle. The shaman gives attention to those who are not in trance, and either flicks water with his fan, presses their chest or puts his forehead against theirs, and soon everyone left in the centre is bouncing, twirling and spinning; their arms flay, and they may overbalance and fall over. The onlookers are intrigued, elated, scared and even amused. They step to one side to avoid being hit by a flailing limb while assisting anyone who might overbalance. If the trancing is very chaotic, the musicians break up and move away until the proceedings have calmed down. In contrast the older men are unobtrusively fanning themselves and gently moving backwards and forwards into a trance state, which they achieve with minimum movement compared wih the vigorous efforts required by younger people. Whether trancing, dancing, or just watching, the entire house is involved in this highly charged and energetic experience.

Some of the entranced sink unconscious to the floor, others spontaneously recover. The shaman watches those in trance intently and gives attention to those who are unconscious by massaging their heads, or blowing through a clenched fist into their head soul. As they slowly emerge from the trance, looking dazed and disorientated, cigarettes are placed in their mouths. Often the shaman or one of the elderly women bathes them in smoke from a dish containing burning charcoal and aromatic herbs. During the evening, the shaman may attend to any illnesses; other shamans may take a session and also heal. Sometimes there is a break in the proceedings while everyone smokes cigarettes before getting a second wind.

The observer senses that the entire group has been involved in an experience that is essentially Temiar, whether in trance or not, binding the participants together into a whole, composed of many contrasting elements. They see their trance dance as an event that cannot be shared with non-Temiar. It is felt to be a serious matter that would not be understood by foreigners. I, too, was not allowed into these more serious sessions until I was fluent in the language, and together with my three children had been adopted as Temiar in one particular village.

The trance dance is the most common form of seance. After the men's trance, there may be a women's trance, although far fewer women trance than men because of the taboos. The rest of the evening can be spent in singing, dancing, and light trancing. Sometimes the children get up and caricature the adults, exaggerating their falling movements and so on. Normally Temiar prefer to sleep in their own quarters as a family unit, but after a trance dance many do not bother to return to their own houses. They curl up on the floor in their sarongs, remaining in the company of fellow Temiar and close to the benevolent influence of the spirits. They are at peace. As the excitement gradually diminishes, someone will continue singing until they are all asleep.

In the majority of the seances that I witnessed the focal point of the evening was the scene I have just described, with the men involved in the dancing and trancing and the women in the singing and rhythm. Other writers have reported regional variations and there appears to be less sexual division in the trance in those villages lying further south (Benjamin 1968:244; Dentan 1968:89).

Shamans can practise their healing skills at any time, informally in a person's house, or as an adjunct to the play or more formal dance and trance sessions. However, there is a special form of seance that a shaman will organise if there is severe or chronic illness. It is characterised as the occasion where the shaman himself will perform a stylised dance round the patient while everyone else is inactive but watching intently. People gather in the main dancing room with all the decorations, sometimes travelling from other villages. The shaman opens the seance by singing and then invites the patients to lie in the centre of the room under the cluster of leaves. Through singing and movement the shaman himself goes into trance and starts to dance slowly round the patient, using elongated walks and angular arm gestures, touching the edges of the sick person's body with his whisk. Then he starts work on the offending area and massages it while muttering incantations. He noisily sucks through a loosely clenched fist to bring out whatever is causing the trouble; sometimes he opens his hand and shows actual objects, for example pebbles, or a snail-shell, making sure that the patient and onlookers can see. Sometimes there is in fact no object there, but either way he goes through the same process and disposes of the offending substance outside the door of the hut. Then he milks his own breast on his left side with his right hand and blows through a clenched fist into the same area. The most spectacular device is when the shaman can produce an actual flow of juice from the central decorative leaves with which he bathes the patient. Usually an important healing session of this kind leads on to a dance session, and while people are dancing the shaman sees to any minor ills.

During the healing sessions, the shaman does not always trance. I was told that he needs to go into trance when the patient's own head soul is very weak so that the shaman's head soul can find that of the patient and presumably strengthen it. For minor ailments in the village, the shaman uses the technique of sucking and blowing but does not embroider it with dancing, trancing, or singing.

At the end of a mourning period there is also a special seance before the village returns to normal life. During the mourning there is no dancing or singing, no wearing of new clothes, little moving in and out of the village. The seance lasts for at least three nights. On the first night there is a special meal, and new sarongs are given to those who are not of the village and not connected with the deceased. Relatives still wear the old clothes that they wore throughout the mourning period. After the gifts and the presentation, the shaman leads the singing and asks the dead spirit to leave them in peace and not to bother them. The songs are all sung in a minor key and are considered the most beautiful of Temiar music. Close relatives spontaneously trance and express strong emotion, stumbling and calling out. There is no dancing on the first evening. Subsequent evenings follow the pattern of the planned dance and trance sessions, everyone wearing their better clothes and thus completing the transition back to ordinary life.

The Temiar explain their trance with relation to their concept of the head soul, which is more important to them than 'souls' associated with other parts of their body. Babies are seen as having weak, unformed head souls, which is why their heads are constantly protected and massaged. As well as the notion that babies must not go on the ground until they can walk because the ground is dirty, there is also the idea that by leaving the house the baby's head soul could be endangered. As a child matures and its range of forbidden food decreases, the head soul is seen as becoming stronger. During times of illness, the head soul is felt to be in danger, and finally it leaves the body altogether at death. During trance or sleep, the head soul is thought to go on a journey and meet other head souls. If someone takes time to come round from a trance, the shaman will say that he has to send his own head soul to find it. The reason given for forbidding photographs during trance is that the bright light might wake a trancer while he or she is without head soul, and it might then not have time to return to the trancer's body. This appears, however, to be an aspect of a general unease regarding photography during a state of ritual danger. After childbirth, for instance, there is a general ban on photography until the food taboos are relaxed and also at times when mother or child are unwell. It is consistent with this cluster of beliefs that trance is held to be dangerous for younger children, who should not risk losing their weak head souls. Even their parents should avoid trance and the associated risk to their children's head souls.

It would not be appropriate here to develop an exposition of Temiar shamanism in all its complexity. Interested readers should refer to the analysis by Benjamin (1968:ch.5). However, it is important to clarify the relationship between the shaman and the dance and trance. Although the Temiar do not have a notion of headmanship, it is obvious to the observer that the shaman is in control of the seances, and is referred to for advice and healing powers outside the context of the seance. The shaman, as well as having skills of healing, can be seen as the mediator between people and the world of danger. He is responsible, with the aid of his spirit helpers, for the loss and recovery of head souls in the seance, which is, as we have seen, a state of great ritual danger. Men become shamans by dreaming about their spirit guides. The Temiar differentiate between greater shamans and lesser shamans by whether their spirit guide belongs to 'on the ground' (lesser) or 'off the ground' (greater) categories.

Just as the shaman is the mediator through whom ordinary mortals 'fix' the psychic world of their head souls, so the river is the mediator through which the Temiar fix themselves in their physical world. If one takes a Temiar away from the river he becomes disorientated in space and he becomes anxious. When talking about where people are, for example, he will use river terms to give a sense of direction – 'up-river', 'down-river', 'across river'. All Temiar villages are built on the banks of rivers and of course the river is the main line of communication between villages. People will travel out of preference on the river rather than take dangerous routes through the jungle. Whole families will travel quite freely on the river where they would not in the jungle. One must remember that fish from the river is the one food everyone can eat.

An analogy may be perceived between the communication link in the physical world and the physical resource that the river provides, and the communication link in the metaphysical world and the psychic resource that the shaman provides. Both constitute a cosmological anomaly. The river is both of the village and of the jungle in that it flows close to both; and it is neither quite on the ground nor off the ground, but somewhere in between. Similarly, the shaman is tied to the village through his body like other men, and yet he has the ability to visit distant places through his control over trance. It is this element of ritual control that places him slightly apart from other men, and the more powerful he is as a shaman, the greater this difference. Ordinary people enter the realm mediated by the shaman at times of life crisis, and also through dancing, when they can enter into trance. Thus dance is an activity that in itself bridges the gulf between the physical world, to which the body is tied, and the metaphysical, through which the head soul is released. The contrast in movement between the lower and upper body in dance has its counterpart in cosmological beliefs.

Conclusion: Temiar cosmology and dance

The Temiar see themselves as a peaceful people living within a world that is hostile and chaotic. Possibly they see peace and order within their villages and the distancing of danger (both mortal and cosmo-logical) as the best guarantee for survival.

With the Temiar emphasis on generosity, it is very difficult to be competitive about possessions. The Temiar believe that if someone asks for something then there is a moral imperative to give it, oth-erwise misfortune will come to the person who asked. So there is a constant interchange of goods and little hoarding. To be accused of meanness over sharing is the worst possible insult.

The most striking characteristic of Temiar society is the emphasis on the opposition between violence and nonviolence. Dentan describes a similar phenomenon for the Semai (1968:102). This opposition appears to underpin the ways in which the Temiar view themselves and their world, both physical and cosmological, and to permeate every aspect of their lives.

Violence is a quality that belongs to foreigners, outsiders, and the malevolent deity Thunder. The Temiar do not display overt aggression in terms of fighting or squabbling. They do not normally strike their children, and on the very rare occasion that a child is slapped in irritation the parent is usually overcome with remorse. Children do not play aggressive games and, as with the play dances, when games show signs of getting out of control, or becoming too noisy, parents will calm them down. On the two occasions when I observed individuals losing their tempers (on one occasion a child and the other a young adult) other people around quietly went away and the person in question was left entirely alone. On both occasions later in the evening one of the older men made a speech about 'the youth of today'.

Violence and anger belong to the malevolent Thunder, who is to be avoided and not provoked. Conversely the spirits, who have a benevolent attitude towards the Temiar and bring their positive power to help the shaman in trance and in healing, are small, shy sprites who need to be coaxed into the village and are easily frightened away. Thunder is a constant reminder to the Temiar of anger and disorder. Tropical thunderstorms in their area are frequent, displaying the main force of the northeast and the tailend of the southwest monsoons, so there are few times in the year that are storm-free. During such storms, babies have their ears covered by parents who say 'fear, fear', while the thunder is very loud. Later, young children's ears will be covered by older siblings or grandparents. The Temiar see thunderstorms as Thunder's punishments for the breaking of certain rules. We have already mentioned that one does not trance, dance or play too loudly, and there are other rules concerning mocking, pointing at or mimicking particular animals. Also punishable by Thunder is the breaking of the incest rule, which includes mother- and father-in-law avoidance, both in speech and space. Such rules place the individual under constant constraint and ritual control. He must avoid the state of ritual danger that might bring him to the attention of Thunder.

Here lies the contradiction that is at the root of the socialisation of children and the maintenance of social values among adults. Overtly, the Temiar shun violence and any direct attempt to impose their personal will on one another, consistent with their outwardly peaceful, generous, and nonviolent way of life. Yet at the same time, by constantly reaffirming their fear of Thunder as a ritualised punishment, they are in a sense projecting violence and aggression on to a metaphysical plane, outside society and yet directly threatening them. Here it is not the individual who is imposing his will but society, as a set of beliefs and associated avoidances: thus it is society that is by turns both oppressive *and* libertarian while the individual within that society always retains both his personal autonomy and group identity.

When there is thunder it is not something one can ignore. Even a small clap can produce worried looks and the Temiar may wave a bush knife or a clenched fist towards the sky and mutter 'Go away and do not trouble us.' When there is a major storm there are ritual procedures that must be followed in order to placate Thunder. Usually the women gather with children and younger people of both sexes in one house and there is discussion as to who may have broken an important rule. A senior woman in the village, sometimes the midwife, snips a piece of hair from the heads of those thought to be offenders. She takes a burning log from the fire and places it in the doorway of the house and burns the hair on the log. While so doing she blows the smoke through a loosely clenched hand towards the direction of the thunder and implores thunder to go away and not trouble them, making excuses for the breaking of the rules – for example, 'they are young', or, as in my case, 'they do not know your ways'. I have been told by the Temiar that for the severest thunderstorms the women will go into the open space in the centre of the village, cut their legs with bush knives and throw the blood towards the thunder (Dentan 1968:23). The worst thunderstorms that I encountered produced enough anxiety for women with very young children to leave the house, and for the young people to cluster under the house as there was a real fear of trees crashing down or lightning striking the house. We can see another opposition in terms of upper body (hair) and lower body (blood) in these rituals, which mirrors the distinction in the dance.

Tiger is also thought to be a manifestation of evil, and the other dominant symbol of aggression and anger. Tiger is perceived as all powerful, all knowing and able to change into other beings. Therefore, to try and mislead Tiger, the Temiar will lie; for example they will not say they are about to go out hunting in case Tiger hears them and will be waiting to attack them. The actual dangers are few as the tiger population has been greatly reduced. However, on the one occasion when a tiger visited the village where I was staying, the level of anxiety it created was out of all proportion to the actual danger.

As with Thunder, Tiger is so much to be feared that it will not be referred to by its real Temiar name, and instead a euphemistic term or the Malay word will be used.

The greatest shamans of all, and the Temiar say that there are very few left now, are the tiger shamans. These shamans, by their experience, power, and control, are able to have Tiger as their spirit guide. The tiger seance is quite unlike any other seance and is characterised by no dancing at all, and complete physical control. The shaman himself is the only person involved, trancing in a palm shelter built in the centre of the dancing area. There is no lighting and the Temiar believe that the shaman changes at least partly into a tiger while in trance and are convinced that they have seen claws disappearing from the fingers as the lights come up after a seance. Benjamin (1968:266) describes this type of seance as 'ascetic rather than ecstatic'.

Strictly speaking, then, Thunder and Tiger have no direct relevance to the Temiar dance. But they do have a direct relevance to the shaman in his most extreme form. They too are transcendental beings, Tiger perhaps dominating the ground and the jungle, and Thunder the air. Other shamans may not have the excessive power of the tiger shaman or the control over such awe-inspiring metaphysical forces, but they have nevertheless developed skills in this direction, and these are exercised through their ability to control the trance dance. Thus one may regard this dance as a step tinged with danger which leads logically towards the realm dominated by the violence of Thunder and Tiger. The relation of dance, trance, and shamanism is represented diagrammatically in Figure 1.1. The essential feature of this figure is that trance, which is induced among younger people with so much expenditure of energy in dance, can be self-induced by the older men almost at will during a trance dance, with minimum movement. At the extreme, trance can be induced in the tiger shaman's seance without any dance at all.

Given, then, this contradiction in Temiar society, in which non-violence is displayed although their system of beliefs is dominated by the notion of aggression on a cosmic scale, poised to punish them for minor breaches of their ritual avoidances; given also the place that dance has as a catalyst that can release the head soul in a healing trance, one is led inevitably to consider the cathartic effect of these dances. The events that precipitate a trance dance and especially a healing seance are accompanied by a visible display of unease and a general sense of tension that contrast with the feeling of relaxation and ease that permeates the village afterwards. This is true for those who had watched as well as for those who tranced.

61

Sue Jennings

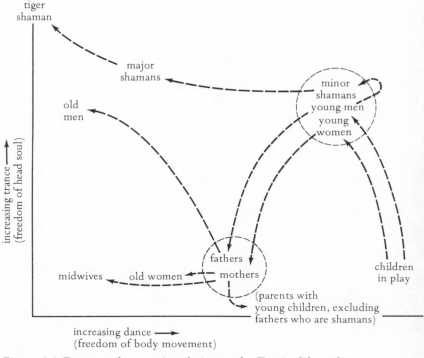

tiger
shaman

major
shamans

minor
shamans
young men
young
women

old
men

increasing trance ⟶
(freedom of head soul)

fathers

midwives   old women   mothers

children
in play

(parents with
young children, excluding
fathers who are shamans)

increasing dance ⟶
(freedom of body movement)

Figure 1.1 Dance and trance in relation to the Temiar life cycle

There is an alternative explanation. The suggestion that Temiar dancing is a mechanism that releases tension is contradicted by the fact that those with most to be anxious about are precisely the ones who must observe the most rigorous avoidances and are prohibited from entering trance; to release their head souls might be too dangerous for them or their children. It is here that it is important to stress that the dances are felt to relax tension for *everyone* and not just those who have entered into trance. The trance dance builds up through a spirit of elation that is infectious, and the spectators play almost as important a part in engendering it as the dancers themselves. Thus those who are prohibited by their condition from a full social existence are at least permitted to enter the dance vicariously, and the joint occasion that brings the village together as a group has the effect of drawing in the more marginal members, dispelling their anxieties. Their cure lies less in permitting them to release their head souls – in their weakened state, this might be irreversible – than in binding them firmly into the peaceful, ordered world of the village and into the rejuvenation of the entire life of the village.

In this way, Temiar society, which cultivates belief in Tiger and Thunder, also provides the mechanism whereby these fears of cosmic threat can be assuaged. If one is led to accept a theory of 'tension release' as the most logical explanation of Temiar dance, then this should be coupled with an understanding that this operates at the level of the group rather than the individual, and serves at the same time to reinforce those beliefs that together form the Temiar cosmos.

NOTE

This material is based on research I carried out with my three children amongst the Temiar from 1974 to 1976. The research was made possible by funding from the Evans Trust in Cambridge, and by the cooperation of the Department of Aborigine Affairs, Kuala Lumpur. I would also like to thank Paul Spencer for his help in the preparation of this chapter.

REFERENCES

Benjamin, G. 1968, 'Temiar religion', Ph.D. dissertation. Cambridge University.
Dentan, R. 1968, *The Semai, A Non-violent People of Malaya*. New York: Holt, Rinehart & Winston.

2 Movement, dance, music, and the Venda girls' initiation cycle

JOHN BLACKING

Social anthropologists are heirs to a long tradition of examining general human problems in the most specific and limited of contexts. But their enthusiasm for a properly constituted science of culture and society has often led them to contradict their traditional method of enquiry by writing in the ethnographic present and explaining social action as the result not of individual decisions made in historical situations, but of factors such as social and economic forces and cultural imperatives. This mode of analysis asserts that what the anthropologist observed has stability and continuity well beyond the limited period of time during which the data were collected, and claims that an analyst may understand better than the actors the motivations and constraints that influence individual actions. Thus the actual reasons why people choose to bring about a specific situation may be overlooked in the interests of a more comprehensive explanation that seems to have greater analytical power.

The tendency to generalise too quickly has its academic rewards and often moves further enquiry into useful directions, but it can betray the aims of social anthropology. The very particularity of anthropological data holds out the greatest hope of establishing a verifiable human science, for a valid theory of human social behaviour must be able to account for the variety of individual decisions and of shared perceptions and interpretations of the world, as well as the continuity of institutions and the recurrence of familiar social and cultural patterns.

Although there is evidence of institutional stability even in a society that has been changing as rapidly as Venda, I prefer to restrict my account to the period when I carried out fieldwork, 1956–8. However, this chapter goes beyond the description of Venda actions and conceptualisations during a particular period of their history, because it also carries an underlying view of dance and movement that is only suggested by the facts, and not fully worked through.

Movement, dance, music, and ritual can usefully be treated as modes of human communication on a continuum from the nonverbal to the

64

verbal. All four modes can express ideas that belong to other spheres of human activity: social, political, economic, religious, and so on. What is anthropologically interesting about dance and music is the possibility that they generate certain kinds of social experience that can be had in no other way, and that they constitute a link between the behavioural and biological aspects of movement and the social and cultural aspects of ritual. Perhaps, like Lévi-Strauss's 'mythical thought', they can be regarded as primary modelling systems for the organisation of social life, so that we should look to dance and music for the more fundamental explanations of ritual.

The chapter will explore the notion that ideas and feelings can be expressed collectively through dance and music before they are articulated in speech, although the associated ideology and verbal explanations of ritual action may express a false consciousness. That is, ritual may be enacted in the service of conservative and even oppressive institutions, as Maurice Bloch suggested for the Merina (Bloch 1974); but the experience of performing the nonverbal movements and sounds may ultimately liberate the actors (cf. Blacking 1981). Performances of dance and music frequently reflect and reinforce existing ideas and institutions, but they can also stimulate the imagination and help to bring coherence to the sensuous life, the 'intelligence of feeling' (cf. Witkin 1976), which in turn can affect motivation, commitment, and decision making in other spheres of social life. It is the 'effectiveness of the symbols' (cf. Lévi-Strauss 1963, ch. 10) of dance and music that is of prime concern to social anthropologists, their sensuous meaning to the human bodies that become involved in their sequences of nonverbal action.

There is a methodological problem that cannot be avoided: aspects of dance and musical communication cannot be translated into other modes without distortion of meaning. Discourse about dance, as about any nonverbal communication, really belongs to metaphysics, because it is, strictly speaking, an unknowable truth. Without verbal language we cannot transmit a truth. But the words required to explain anything that makes a claim to being verifiable truth belong to a realm of discourse that is different from the subject of enquiry – dance. This does not matter so much in the natural sciences, where truths about processes can be demonstrated without words, and the words that are used need only be approximate. Substances can be objectively seen to react, a catalyst can be seen to hasten a process without altering the result, and so on. In dance this is impossible, because the 'substances' are not inert: each human being reacts individually.

Nevertheless, we need not worry too much about using one language to describe another, and we need not despair of verifying truths

John Blacking

about dance, provided we recognise that verbal language is approximate and objectivity impossible, and we build subjectivity into the model of investigation. That is, since an unknowable truth can only be approached obliquely or indirectly, the subjective verbal accounts of individuals have a special status as data in the search for meaning in what people believe to be dance. The processes by which the content is formulated may reveal as much about the subjective dance experience as the content itself.

I suggest, therefore, that a way forward in the anthroplogy of dance lies not so much in developing a metalanguage for cross-cultural study, or analysing movements in terms of a standard set of parameters, as in asking dancers and spectators from the widest possible range of societies and social situations what they think *they* are doing and experiencing, and looking for patterns of coherence in their explanations. The very language and metaphors that people use, and the analogies that they draw in talking about dance, may ultimately be more scientific than any 'objective' analyses of their movements. Films, videotapes, and various notations such as Laban and Benesh are all useful tools for referring to the object of study, but they cannot describe or explain what is happening as human experience, because dance, as a topic of anthropological study, is about subjective action and conscious human intentions, and not only about observed behaviour. Moreover, there is no such thing as '*the* human body': there are many kinds of body, which are fashioned by the different environments and expectations that societies have of their members' bodies. There can, of course, be unintended consequences of actions, and people can have difficulty in verbalising their intentions. But this does not give anthropologists a licence to invoke psychological explanations of movement sequences and dance motivation in terms of the unconscious or the subconscious. When people talk about 'being danced' or claim that their movements are directed by internal or external 'forces', they are obviously not describing unconscious states: nor are they necessarily reporting altered states of consciousness. They are trying to describe nonverbal modes of discourse, whose logic and forms can be precisely expressed and understood, but not always clearly articulated in words.

Behavioural analyses of movement and dance can usefully be contrasted with social anthropological analyses, provided it is remembered that they are mediated with the categories of the cultures of the analysts and of their disciplines, and do not necessarily reflect the intentions and meanings of the actors. For example, Pitcairn and Schleidt (1976) inferred decision making in the Melpa courtship dance from a careful ethological analysis of the mutual head movements of girls and youths observed on a film. The actual moments of decision of the actors could have been made well before the movements, or as the movements began, or even after the movements were observed to begin. (The beginnings and ends of movements, as of musical phrases, can be difficult to establish precisely.) Moreover, different individuals could have had longer or shorter delays between decision and movement, and pairs of dancers whose movements appeared to be synchronised need not necessarily have had synchrony of decision making. Contrasts between the timing of the actors' decision making and of their observed movements would be difficult to establish and analyse. But such work must be attempted, because it is at this level of analysis that we are most likely to be able to determine when and how the performance of dance affects the quality of social interaction, and perhaps influences thought and decision making in other spheres of social life. That is, differences in timing between intention and movement, and between the intentions and movements of different people, could be crucial factors in the communication of experience through dance.

Instead of invoking the subconscious to explain dance experiences and the performance of patterns of movement whose logic seems to defy verbal description, even by participants, we should recognise that there are coherent, structured languages of dance, and that the transfer of decision making from verbal to nonverbal discourse constitutes the core of the dance experience. It is not that people abandon reason for emotion when they dance, but that they often introduce another kind of reasoning, whose grammar and content are most effectively, though not exclusively, expressed in nonverbal language. Thus, the dancing of the Melpa couples could be seen in relation to a continuum from verbally to nonverbally dominated communication, in which the transformation is achieved by the performance of the dance, and the relative position of individuals on the continuum is measured by the narrowing of the time gap between deciding to move the head as a culturally specific social action, and deciding and moving the head simultaneously as part of a sequence of movement. The desired harmony of movement between pairs of dancers probably coincides with synchrony of the second kind of decision making, so that the experience of 'being danced', far from being a passive reaction to external forces, is a consequence of actively sharing a nonverbal mode of discourse.

Dance forms and contrasting modes of expression

It should be clear that I am not simply asking for more data on the uses and functions of dance in different societies. There have been many

John Blacking

good anthropological reports of this kind, and such data are a necessary first step towards analyses of what is unique about dance as a
symbolic form and dancing as a special kind of social action. The kinds
of data that are most needed are people's perceptions and conceptions
of how their dances are structured, and what they mean to them and
to others, how decisions were made in particular dance situations, and
how dance experience affects social life. The emphasis must be on the
languages of dance as means of human communication, on the grounds
that dance may be a special form of knowledge, derived from a particular repertoire of species-specific characteristics, whose practice can
have implications for action beyond its immediate social uses and assigned meanings. In other words, although the meanings of different
dance styles are, as symbol systems, intimately associated with social
and cultural systems, the act of performing the movements can generate somatic experiences that are detached from those specific meanings and can be reinterpreted in a variety of ways. This was the case
with the Venda *domba* and *tshikona* dances, which were often described
without reference to their social use and particular symbolism.

It is the forms of dance, as a medium of nonverbal communication,
that make it interesting to anthropologists. In his *World History of
Dance*, Curt Sachs wrote:

If the dance, inherited from brutish ancestors, lives in all mankind as a
necessary motor-rhythmic expression of excess energy and the joy of living,
then it is only of slight importance for anthropologists and social historians.
If it is established, however, that an inherited predisposition develops in
many ways in the different groups of man and its force of direction is related
to other phenomena of civilization, the history of dance will then be of great
importance for the study of mankind. (Sachs 1937:12)

Sachs was looking at dance as a historian of culture, but his words
are no less relevant for social anthropologists. The study of dance in
society involves not only the uses of dance in different social contexts,
but the study of what is used and how a dance event can differ
qualitatively from other social events.

It has become common practice to look at developments in dance in
historical contexts as reflections of trends in economic and social life,
as well as products of the psychology of individual artists. This has
been a step in the right direction, provided we remember that trends
in economic and social life are the result of individuals' decision making; before decisions are crystallised in words that relate to specific social and economic problems, the attitudes that influence them can
sometimes be felt and expressed through forms of nonverbal communication concerned primarily with the expression of feelings. The

68

sources of social change, as indeed the infrastructures of societies at particular periods of their history, are not determined by universal laws but by the individual human decisions made in the course of communities' adaptations to their environment. Contradictions and social forces do not cause social events, except in so far as human beings invoke them as reasons for intentional action. Similarly, individuals are not cultural dopes who react to pressures and structural imperatives no less mysterious than fate, witchcraft, or the will of God: they are constantly interpreting, invoking, and reinventing the notions and institutions that we call culture, in the context of different social situations.

I am not suggesting that dance experiences in themselves can change someone's political attitudes, because it is what people make of their experience that counts; but I argue that in particular contexts some *forms* of dancing are more likely than others to stimulate people's imagination and expand their consciousness, because of what they involve in terms of body movement, social interaction, and a challenge to previous experience. Just as some dance teachers insist that one moves as one thinks, so a change of movement may generate a change of mind. That was the stated intention of the change in Venda movement styles from the *ndayo* of *vhusha* after puberty to the premarital *domba* dance, and a similar view of the interrelatedness of movement and thought has been the basis of the practice of the Alexander principle, that use affects functioning (Barlow 1975, passim).

The biologist Professor J.Z. Young has argued that the capacity to create new aesthetic forms 'has been the most fundamentally productive of all forms of human activity. Whoever creates new artistic conventions has found methods of interchange between people about matters that were incommunicable before. The capacity to do this has been the basis of the whole of human history' (Young 1971:519). The argument for the primacy of formal invention was also put forward at the turn of the century by Karl Bücher, who is well known for his theory, in *Arbeit und Rhythmus* (1896), that music had its origin in the rhythms of work. What is often forgotten is that four years later, after reading Karl Groos's book on play amongst animals, he rejected his theory and proposed, 'It is accordingly in play that technical skill is developed, and it turns to the useful only gradually. The order of progression must therefore be reversed: play is older than work, art older than production for use' (Bücher 1901:28–9).

Communal dancing could be described as a form of play that is more positively adaptive than any observed amongst nonhuman primates: In addition to 'motivation for exploration' and a 'context for learning locomotor and manipulative skills' (Dolhinow and Bishop

69

1971:193) dancing requires a much higher degree of social interaction and interpersonal coordination than play, and therefore 'selects' for the maximum of cooperative behaviour (see also Blacking 1976b:7ff.). The invention of new forms is not just the work of a few talented individuals. It is only possible because of the discovery and application of the forces of production within the body in community. Creativity in dance is the rule rather than the exception: it is as basic a capability of the human body as creativity in speech. Whether or not, and how, the enormous creativity of small children is matched by creativity in adults depends on the scope that different political systems allow for the development of rich human relationships and of each individual's human potential. Andrée Grau, who is a dancer and choreologist trained in anthropology, has reported (1983) that many Tiwi in northern Australia are ceaselessly creative in their invention of new dances.

A crucial analytical problem is how to make sense of the numerous different forms of dance in a way that adheres to the definitions of the signs that are given by the 'emitters' and 'receivers' of the 'medium of transmission', but does not lose sight of the important broader issues raised by Curt Sachs. I suggest that the contrast between verbal and nonverbal modes of discourse, which I discussed earlier, provides a useful model for approaching the forms and meanings of dance in a variety of social contexts. It is an approach that has been widely used in folk evaluations and classifications of dance, and more recently it has been given significance by psychologists and considered to have sociological relevance (for example, Bloch 1974).

I prefer this to the more conventional division between form and function, not only because form and function are closely related in living organisms and it is not helpful to assign a causal status to the one or the other, but also because it emphasises the creation and interpretation of dance as an ongoing *process* in which the intentions of the actors are of crucial importance: different modes of discourse can sometimes be used to achieve the same ends, while different ends can be attained with the same mode. Since contrasting modes of discourse are probably the most significant elements affecting the quality of human relationships in the context of different societies, I choose them as a model for analysis.

Most cultures lack an adequate set of labels to describe in words the experiences felt and the decisions made by individuals in the performance of dance, but classifications of style are not uncommon and they often reveal what kinds of experience are expected in different dances and how the forms of dance contribute to this. One of the most ancient treatises on dance and theatre, the Indian *Bharata Natya Sastra*, serves as a useful starting point for developing a model that can be applied as much to European ballet as to Venda initiation dances.

Natya (dance and/or drama) is sub-divided into *Nritta*, which might be translated 'abstract' or 'expressive' (performative) and *Nritya*, which is 'discursive' (propositional). In the latter class are the face and hand movements (*abhinayas* and *mudras*), which convey specific messages and enable the dancer to tell a story. In the former class are the 108 body postures (*karanas*), which could be compared with the five basic positions of European ballet, together with all the pirouettes, arabesques, entrechats, etc. The contrasts between *Nritta* and *Nritya*, either of which may dominate in the dance *Bharata Natyam* or both of which may be combined, can be compared with the emphases on movement and on story or plot in European ballet. At the end of the seventeenth century, the *ballet à entrée*, the entr'acte, predominated as an interlude in theatre, with emphasis on virtuosity and technique. In the eighteenth century, the *ballet d'action* became more popular, stressing dramatic unity. This survived into the nineteenth century, with ballets such as *La Sylphide* and *Giselle*, only to be superseded by the reintroduction of virtuoso technique by choreographers such as Marius Petipa.

The *mudras* (or *hastas*) of Indian dance have been compared with the Chinese sleeve gestures (*hsiu*) by Gloria Strauss (1975). Both are denotative systems, but they work differently. *Mudras* can relate an entire narrative, with gestures that act as nouns, verbs, and modifiers; but *hsiu* can only embroider the narrative with 'gestures that act as verbs or modifiers, directing people or indicating how they feel' (Royce 1977:195).

The most obvious comparison with the *mudras* is that of classical mime, which plays a considerable role in many ballets. It is important to remember that the gestures were understood by the audiences. But what is interesting (and I have not found this mentioned in what I have read on mime) is that the gesture order still follows the French language. Thus the order of movement is

	1	2	3
(i.e. *Je t'aime*)	I	you	love
and not	I	love	you

The contrast between discursive and expressive movement, or, in this case, between mime and dance, is particularly important in view of the expressed transcendental aims of dance; it is therefore necessary to see when and how it is used and who executes it. Discursive movement would, for example, be quite out of place in a Venda dance

71

John Blacking

of spirit possession, but such interludes occur in their major dance, *tshikona*, and the the *vhusha* and *domba* initiation dances. Moreover, as in the European ballet, discursive movement is generally executed by principal dancers, while the corps de ballet reacts collectively.

I suggest that these contrasts are compatible with the transcendental aims of dance. To be effective in society, dance must mediate between nature and culture in human existence and so be transcendental in context. The intelligence of feeling should inform all action, and the insight and intuition that are nurtured by 'artistic' experience are essential for the quality of life; but sequential, linear processing of information is required for many of the techniques of living. Discursive or linear elements in dance, such as mime, relate the transcendental to the practical, and the principal dancers are the most appropriate people to perform this act. For they are principals largely because they have experienced transcendence most frequently through perfection of movement, and indeed they can be *seen* to be transcendent – witness how frequently outstanding dancers seem to 'be danced'.

The meaning and impact of dancing do not necessarily correspond to the context of the dance event, and changes in the social organisation of dance may not immediately affect its forms. Dance forms generally relate to the society as a whole, whilst the administration and organisation of dance varies with the changing role of dance in society. In the New York City Ballet, for example, this area of change was the concern of Lincoln Kirstein and the administrators of the company. Change in the forms of the dance were related more to the general culture of the society. Thus Balanchine, as choreographer of the New York City Ballet, could be said to have reflected the American life in the amazing speed of his ballets, and he has in fact been called the founder of American ballet.

In dance, as perhaps in all aspects of life, the problem of creation is to capture the force of an idea with form, and so the pieces are put together after the whole is conceived (cf. Susanne Langer in *Feeling and Form*). This applies not only to the mimetic or discursive interludes in expressive movement, but also to the creation of new patterns of movement. Technological changes and urban living, for example, clearly bring about new patterns of movement in a society (urban Africans in Johannesburg say that they can always detect rural persons by their walk, no matter how sophisticated their clothes). Such changes may also disturb the quality of bodily experience and of social relationships, and so precipitate new expressive movement to achieve a new synthesis.

What are constant in different societies are the basic processes by

72

which the content is formulated, no matter how varied are the social situations or the modes of thought prevalent in a cultural system. Whether or not there are biological foundations of dance (cf. Hanna 1979), as there are of speech (cf. Lenneberg 1967) and whether or not the postulated characteristics of the two hemispheres of the brain will survive thorough testing, all feeling and thinking consist of movements of the body and begin with movements of the brain and central nervous system. Because the theory of cerebral specialisation happens to coincide with a number of different folk theories of dance, it may be useful to adopt the contrasting functions of the left (discursive and segmentary) and right (expressive and holistic) hemispheres of the brain as a model for dance analysis.

Table 2.1 lists some contrasting (but not conflicting or opposite unless human beings wish to make them so) processes of action which can be expressed in dance movements. It also includes an alternative view of Artaud (1958), who places different arts in a hierarchy in relation to their exploration of time and space. Dance is the only one that belongs to both. Richard Waterman (1962) classified dance as a mode of communication, while Hanna (1979) was concerned with its functions. Wundt's (1900) dichotomy combined form and function. The table could have included many other similar classifications, but these were considered sufficient to make the point and apply the principle to the Venda data.

Dance and music in Venda (1956–8)

The Venda of the Sibasa district live in a lush, mountainous part of southern Africa, directly south of Zimbabwe. In 1956 many lived in cities, though they maintained contacts with the country. This did not mean that traditional dances died out. On the contrary, some of the best dance teams could be found in the urban areas, and especially in Soweto, where they met once a week and rehearsed their steps. Dance had become a focus of social activity, and no longer had to be sponsored by a chief or headman as in the rural situation.

All dances were accompanied by music, whether it was a guitar for jive, drums for a possession dance, or handclaps and voices for a *malende* beer dance.

The organisation of dance teams and dance performance was similar in rural and urban areas. Every team had a manager (*nduna*) an assistant manager, a musical director (*malogwane*) and assistant, and a dance director (*maluselo*) and assistant. An assistant was referred to as 'the hand of' (*tshanda tsha*) the director. Music and dance for communal rites

73

John Blacking

Table 2.1. *Contrasting modes of thought and action*

1. The brain (cf. Ornstein 1974)	Left hemisphere	Right hemisphere
	Analytic thinking	Orientation in space
	Language and logic	Body awareness
	Linear processing	Simultaneous processing
	Verbal	Nonverbal
2. Dance	*Nritya*	*Nritta*
	Ballet d'action (story)	*Ballet à entrée* (movement)
	(Waterman)	
	Denotative (as a mode of communication form)	Subliminal
	Mimetic	Abstract
	(Hanna)	
	Cognitive (socio-psycho functions)	Affective
	(Wundt)	
	Magical/socially functional	Ecstatic/personal
	Content	Expression
	Business of living	Quality of life
3. Time and space (Artaud 1958)	Time	Space
	music	dance and mime
	song	theatre
	literature	painting
	dance	sculpture
	opera	

of passage were directed by ritual specialists, who above all had to be good musicians and dancers. The men in charge of the girls' and boys' *domba* were called *Nyamungozwa* (*Nya* was normally a female appellation), and the women in charge of the girls at *vhusha* and *tshikanda* were called *Nematei* (*Ne* being normally a male appellation).

Communal dances were classified as either *ngoma* (literally 'drum', hence sacred or important), or *mutambo* (game, play). The most appropriate translation of *ngoma* is probably 'rite', although it must be emphasised that the music and dance were indispensable and usually the most important elements. The principal *ngoma* dances were:

Tshikona, a dance accompanied by reed-pipes played by men and youths with drums played by women and girls. Its performance was essential at the installation of a ruler, the commemoration of a dead ruler, sacrifice of the first fruits, the inauguration of *domba* initiations, and other state occasions.

Vhusha, tshikanda, and *domba*, the three-part initiation of girls between puberty and marriage, and these terms also referred to the dances of each part. They too could only be sponsored by rulers.

Sungwi, a girls' initiation school organised by doctors, adopted more recently by the Venda in the latter part of the nineteenth century.

Ngoma dza midzimu (literally, 'drums of the ancestor spirits'), one of a number of types of possession dance organised by different cult groups and also acquired more recently.

The principal *mitambo* play dances were included in the *domba* initiation and were adapted choreographically to the *domba* context as a kind of link between the worlds of childhood and adulthood. They were:

Tshigombela for girls and *tshikanganga* and related reed-pipe dances for boys and girls that were generally organised under the auspices of a ruler and rehearsed for several weeks at his home.

Dzhombo, an ad hoc arangement of young people that was performed on moonlit nights in flat, open spaces.

There was also a quite separate category of solo dancing by men and women: the *malende* beer dances, which accompanied the singing of *malende* beer songs and could be organised at any home where someone had bought or brewed beer.

Most Venda dances were circle dances and the general movement was counter-clockwise. This was appropriate for the restricted dancing space that was common in the mountainous Venda countryside, but it could also be related to the symbolic significance of the circle in Venda thought.

In the *domba* dance, for example, the circle of dancers enclosed a space that symbolised the womb (see Figure 2.1). Their feet made 'python tracks' on the ground – though Venda were careful to point out that pythons do not move in circles. Their movements, and the accompanying music, symbolised an act of love. The ashes of the fire symbolised the semen that was said to build up the foetus in the womb, and the bass drum was the unborn baby. By regular performances of the *domba* dance (that is, repeated acts of love), a baby would be symbolically created and finally born in the last hours of the initiation.

In *domba*, as in the Venda national dance *tshikona*, there was no

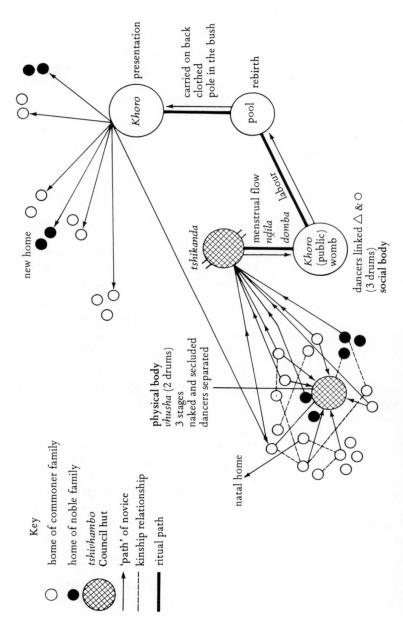

Key

○ home of commoner family

● home of noble family

⬡ *tshivhambo*
Council hut

→ 'path' of novice

---- kinship relationship

━━ ritual path

---

presentation

Khoro

carried on back
clothed
pole in the bush

pool rebirth

menstrual flow
ndila labour
domba

Khoro (public)
womb

dancers linked △ & ○
(3 drums)
social body

tshikanda

physical body
vhusha (2 drums)
3 stages
naked and secluded
dancers separated

new home

natal home

Figure 2.1 *Domba* – movements of novices

organised solo dancing. The dancers were a united body – the girls being physically linked in *domba*, while the men in *tshikona* were separate but linked by the music that they played on pipes and the steps that they performed in consort.

There was a general term *utshina* that referred to all kinds of dancing, but particularly to communal dancing. In the play dances *tshikanganga* and *tshigombela*, a period of communal circle dancing round the drums was followed by a period of *gaya* display dancing, solo in *tshikanganga* and in twos and threes, forwards and backwards within a limited space in *tshigombela*. A similar alternation between circular and display movements was observed by each solo dancer in the possession dances.

Men's communal dancing was more 'airborne' and flowing than the dancing of women, which was 'earthborne', with the hips set low, and meant to be kept on a plane, while the knees were bent and the feet dug vigorously into the ground.

There were other recognised styles of dancing. Old ladies danced in a stately way (*tanga*) on important occasions, or sometimes danced with joy (*-pembela*). At *vhusha*, nubile girls performed special dance exercises (*ndayo*), whose characteristic movement was called *-thaga*. All of these terms referred to styles of movement that had some ritual or transcendental purpose and were distinguished from movements such as walking (*-tshimbila*), running (*-gidima*), sitting (*-dzula*) and standing (*-ima*).

If we apply the principles of Table 2.1 and the segmentary (propositional, discursive)/holistic (performative, expressive) dichotomy to Venda dance events, it can be seen that most of them incorporate both elements. Segmentary forms (as in the *ugaya* display of *tshigombela*) could be used to produce something approaching an ecstatic state in each individual, after all members had participated in sweeping, corporate movements (*-tshina*) that were more likely to induce transcendence. In *vhusha*, on the other hand, the segmentary forms of *ndayo* exercises were intended to teach lessons and stretch the body, and I never heard anyone describe them as exciting or transcendent: they required much self-critical concentration, and girls often broke down in the middle of them, after making a mistake or losing balance. But in *domba*, performance of the segmentary forms of play songs could be positively transcendental on some occasions, such as the final days of the ceremony.

Table 2.2 is an attempt to summarise contrasting features of Venda dance events. Contrasts *between* events (A) are distinguished from contrasts *within* dance events (B). Where there are intended variations

John Blacking

Table 2.2 *Contrasting features in Venda dance events, 1956–8*

==

A. Contrasts between events

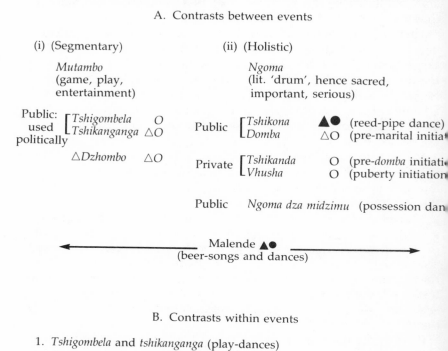

(i) (Segmentary)

Mutambo
(game, play,
entertainment)

Public:
used
politically
⌈*Tshigombela* O
⌊*Tshikanganga* △O

△*Dzhombo* △O

(ii) (Holistic)

Ngoma
(lit. 'drum', hence sacred,
important, serious)

Public ⌈*Tshikona* ▲● (reed-pipe dance)
⌊*Domba* △O (pre-marital initia▮

Private ⌈*Tshikanda* O (pre-*domba* initiati▮
⌊*Vhusha* O (puberty initiation▮

Public *Ngoma dza midzimu* (possession dan▮

◄────────── Malende ▲● ──────────►
(beer-songs and dances)

B. Contrasts within events

1. *Tshigombela* and *tshikanganga* (play-dances)

Ugaya (dance for 2 or 3 by
drums)

Utshina (dance for all in circle
formation)

Luimbo (song continuing
through performance)

individual experience ──────►

2. *Vhusha* and *tshikanda* (initiations)

Ndayo (*uthaga* for
individuals, or 2 or 3
together)
Nyimbo (songs)
Milayo (spoken 'laws' of
school)

Vhusha (dance for all present)

78

3. *Domba* (initiation)

   Nyimbo dza (songs of . . .   *Domba* (dance for all novices and
    (a) *Ngoma* (rites)   sometimes married
    (b) *Matano* (shows)   women and men present)
    (c) *Mitambo* (games) ————————————▶

   Milayo (spoken 'laws' of school)

4. *Ngoma dza midzimu*   *Utshina* (dance for individuals
   (possession dance)   surrounded by cult
                            members and audience)

                   Luimbo   (song throughout
                            performance)

5. *Malende* (beer songs)
  Utshina (dance for all, individuals surrounded by friends)

  ＼   Individual experience ————————▶

6. *Tshiknona*   *Utshina* (dance for all members
   Different dance steps   of team)
                       Same music played in
                       hocket style on reed-
                       pipes

Notes: The lines and arrows indicate the directions in which dance experiences tend to go: i.e., *Ugaya* of *tshigombela* can become 'holistic' or 'transcendent', while the dance steps of *tshikona* provide the segmentary contrast to the music of the pipes. *Ngoma dza midzimu* was 'transcendent' only for members of the cult. *Mitambo* (c) were 'transcendent', if at all, for performers. *Tshikanda* and *vhusha* were attended and performed only by novices and former initiates. ▲● indicates events intended for men and women. △○ indicates events intended for youths, girls and children (in the case of *dzhombo*).

John Blacking

within a single performance, as in the dances *tshigombela* and *tshikanganga*, the segmentary (*ugaya*) element is achieved by changing rhythms, while the vocal or instrumental base remains constant. Where different kinds of dance or rite were incorporated within a single general category, such as *domba* or *vhusha*, they were linked by a common musical system. The contrasts between variation and thematic unity in the music of *vhusha*, *tshikanda*, and *domba* were analysed in Blacking 1970 (see also Blacking 1977b).

The contrasting unity and variety of the music was related to the unity and variety of the associated dances and ritual symbols. There was one overriding principle of musical organisation that applied with increasing intensity as the social and political importance of the dances progressed from the *tshigombela* and *tshikanganga* of childhood to the *tshikona* of adult life, the dance rite that linked the worlds of matter (for example physical bodies, plants, animals) and spirit (ancestor spirits and other spiritual beings): this was the principle of developing individuality in community. Thus, as more and more people became involved in dancing and music making at the same event, the increasing uniformity of dance steps was balanced by the completely individual contributions of each dancer to the accompanying music, by application of a hocket technique in *tshikona* and the *tivha khulo* singing of *domba*, and also by various forms of polyphonic elaboration of vocal parts and drum accompaniments in other classes of music. The most striking contrast was perhaps between the *ndayo* exercises of *vhusha* and *tshikanda* and the *domba* dance: music was provided entirely for the dancers of *ndayo* exercises who had to concentrate hard on the complex sequences of movement, but in *domba* girls danced and sang at the same time.

In *tshikona*, men danced and played reed-pipes at the same time. The hocket style of performance provided a dynamic ground which contrasted rhythmically with the variations of the dance steps. *Tshikona* embodied the maximum of individuality in the largest possible dancing and music-making community, so that an intention to perform the dance properly was, as the Venda regularly insisted (cf. Blacking 1976a passim), more likely to increase people's individual awareness than to anaesthetise them, and the polyphonic structure of the music was an essential ingredient in the social experience, because of the tension of cooperation that it maintained between dancers.

Vhusha, tshikanda, and *domba*: the three-part initiation of girls

In the past there were schools for youths corresponding to *vhusha* and *tshikanda*, but by 1956 these had been superseded by mission and state

80

school education and by the imported circumcision school, *murundu*. *Domba* was still officially a school for youths and girls, but few youths danced at the schools I attended because they were working on white-owned farms and in cities, or studying at state schools.

The cycle of initiation could last from between one and four years for any girl who attended. *Vhusha* was held regularly in the council houses of local rulers whenever a commoner girl in the district began to menstruate and her family asked for her to be initiated. *Domba* was held every four or five years in the capitals of chiefs and of important rulers, and it was preceded by *tshikanda*, which was generally held in the same places as *vhusha*. *Tshikanda* was a month-long school whose main purpose was to rehearse the songs and dances of *vhusha*, with girls of ruling and commoner families on an equal footing. *Vhusha* was an ancient Venda rite, which the ruling families had found when they arrived in Venda in the eighteenth century. Their girls did not have to attend it, but the wives of rulers had to supervise it. Thus it was necessary for potential rulers' wives to learn what they might one day have to teach. They were able to do this at *tshikanda*, after they had attended their own (nobles') *vhusha*, at which there was no music or dancing, merely verbal instruction and ritual washing and beating.

When *domba* was held in a district, performance of all other communal music, except *tshikona* and *malende* beer songs, was suspended. If a girl reached puberty during this time, she was allowed to join *domba* immediately, and attended *vhusha* when it had been 'burnt' – the term for the end of *domba*. She might have to wait some years before she could attend *tshikanda*, and so it was not uncommon to find one or two married women at *tshikanda*. Married women also attended the final rites of *domba*, if for some reason, such as living in town, they had missed the initiation before marriage. But these were exceptional situations which most non-Christian girls, and even many Christians, tried to avoid.

Domba was not only an institution in which girls 'learnt the laws' (*uguda milayo*) of childbirth, of certain rituals, marriage, and motherhood: its steady crescendo of daily music and dance, reflecting the increase in the number of recruits (sometimes up to more than two hundred novices) and in their musical expertise, and the concentration of more and more people in one part of the countryside, provided most novices with an unforgettable, sustained experience of high living, which was shared by others in the district who had been to *domba* in their youth. Even though the quality of this experience was not often expressed in words during the course of *domba*, and though the idle chatter and schoolgirl jokes before, after and between dances

81

John Blacking

and rites was not exactly uplifting, everyone was acutely aware of what they had felt throughout *domba* when it was finally concluded after at least twenty-four hours of almost nonstop music and dancing. The contrast between periods with and without *domba* in a district illustrated perfectly what Durkheim meant by cycles of more and less intensity of social interaction. At the end of *domba*, when novices and their families dispersed to their homes, even a well-populated ruler's capital felt like a deserted place.

Although numerous different dances, songs, and rites were performed throughout the cycle of initiation, it is important to see it as the Venda themselves saw it: as one extended event, as a huge drawing of breath of the whole countryside, achieved by the coordinated movements of human bodies in space and time.

In the *milayo* laws of *domba*, natural features of the countryside were renamed as parts of a human body, which was animated by the dancing, drumming, and singing. From the beginning of *vhusha* to the end of *domba*, we moved from the initial climaxes of individual girls experiencing the first signs of sexual maturity through a series of measured stages, to a final, massive climax in which the community participated in the symbolic rebirth of itself through the corporate rebirth of the novices.

Vhusha, tshikanda, and *domba* consititued a single dance–music–drama, an extended multi-media event comparable in scope and imagination to the Ring cycle, but shared and performed by all members of the community and not only by an artistic élite. What was even more remarkable was that all the parts were interrelated and they expressed the intentions of the whole performance. Even the varied music of the didactic *ndayo* exercises of *vhusha* was related to the other music of initiation (Blacking 1970), and the girls' *tivha khulo* of *domba* was a transformation of the men's music of the sacred dance, *tshikona* (Blacking 1976a;88ff), with which every *domba* had to be initiated. The contrasting styles of dance movements in *vhusha* and *domba* expressed precisely the symbolic content and educational intentions of the initiation schools.

Figure 2.1 illustrates the ideal passage of girls from their natal to their marital homes. The purpose of the cycle of initiation was to bring about symbolically a transformation of the physical bodies of young girls into the social body of the adult community. This transformation was achieved by three elements in the initiation cycle: movements of bodies in space and through time, a corpus of songs and dances, and a series of spoken pairs of concepts.

Movements of bodies in space and through time marked a transition from the scattered natal homesteads in which individual families lived (bottom left of diagram) to the political centre of the community, and then on to new homesteads; from individual dance movements that were physically difficult to do and so emphasised the new complexity of the body (*vhusha* and *tshikanda*) to corporate dance movements that were easy to do but difficult to coordinate with others (*domba*) and so emphasised the complexity of social life; from the private seclusion of the first six days, with naked, completely shaven, unwashed bodies (bottom left), to the public presentation of a large group of washed, finely dressed bodies, with the long, specially cut hair of a pregnant woman, the clothes of a new bride and the ornaments of *domba* (top right of the figure).

The movements were cumulative, gathering in momentum and intensity as the cycle progressed. First one novice in a ward was taken for the first stage of her initiation and remained in seclusion for six days; then another novice in the same or another ward was taken and the first girl was recalled for the second stage of her initiation. Meanwhile, in the headquarters of another headman, the same process was taking place. After a year or two, there were several girls in a number of related districts who had passed all three stages of *vhusha*. The number of sessions that had been held depended on the number of new novices, for the first stage of each novice's initiation was automatically the second and third respectively of two or more other novices, and an occasion for a reunion of all who had passed their three stages but had not yet been to *domba*. During the six nights of each session, all novices and recently initiated girls gathered in the homestead of their headman (bottom left of the figure) to rehearse the *ndayo* dances, perform certain rituals, and learn the 'laws' (*milayo*) of the school.

Girls of noble families were not obliged to attend the commoners' *vhusha*, but all girls in a district had to attend *tshikanda*, and all were treated alike. Thus the council house of each headman became the focus of a great concentration of people and intensity of activity for one month, shortly before the beginning of *domba* at the chief's capital, where the first *tshikanda* of the series was always held. It could happen that *domba* began before each and every *tshikanda* had been 'burnt' in the districts.

As soon as *domba* was initiated at the chief's capital, girls who had passed *vhusha* and *tshikanda* began to join the school. Commoners tended to be reticent about joining before several girls from noble families had been recruited, although there were no visible signs of rank. The only distinction between early and late arrivals was that the former had the longest hair, because all new recruits had to shave completely and could not shave their hair again until graduation.

83

John Blacking

Girls who came from outlying districts often stayed with relatives near or in the chief's capital, at least during the weekends when the most intensive dancing took place, if not during the week, when there was dancing every night and early every morning. Activities took place in the chief's public meeting place, except when it rained and the council hut was used, and performances of *domba* and related dances were often watched, and sometimes joined, by many spectators. As more and more girls joined the school, so the concentration of people in one part of the country increased, and feelings of generalised excitement and satisfaction grew.

Finally, when the last phase of *domba* was reached, people came from all over the country to witness the graduation of their relatives, often to collect a young bride, or simply to join in the celebration. After a long period in which there had been a gradual increase in movement and concentration of people in different districts (bottom left of Figure 2.1), and then a series of almost simultaneous, short intensive months at *tshikanda*, there was a further period of three months to a year, and very occasionally two years, in one centre with different movements enacted publicly (bottom centre of Figure 2.1). This reached a climax of intensity as more and more novices joined the school. Then there was a sharp, dramatic conclusion to the whole initiation: after dancing all night, surrounded by scores of people, the novices went down to the pool, washed, gathered in the bush, dressed in graduation uniform, were carried back into the public place, and danced for the last time before dispersing in the late afternoon (right of Figure 2.1).

The chief's capital was quiet and comparatively empty for the first time in many weeks, and on the following day graduates in different districts began a few days of celebratory visiting.

A corpus of songs and dances, the second element in the initiation cycle, was generally accompanied by drums, and sometimes by shows (*maṭano*). During the first phase (*vhusha*, bottom left of Figure 2.1), there were special songs to mark events such as the removal of each novice from her home, or the passage of a group of novices from the council house to the river and back. But most of the time was spent rehearsing the physically difficult *ndayo* dances. The communal dance of the school was performed two or three times every evening, and for this novices and instructresses danced in a circle counter-clockwise, without touching each other's bodies as they did in *domba*. There were ritual songs for the end of each phase of *vhusha*, and also at the end of *tshikanda*, after which the story of Thovhela and Tshishonge (the dramatisation of a myth) was enacted before the dismissal of the girls.

84

During *domba* (bottom centre of Figure 2.1), there were songs accompanying rites that every novice had to perform. Although some shows were not presented more than once during an initiation, their accompanying songs were performed regularly, together with the play songs that were interspersed, like episodes in a rondo, with the frequent performances of *domba*, the main dance rite of the school. All dances were communal, in contrast to the pattern of *vhusha*, but variations on the counter-clockwise, circular movement of *domba* were achieved by differences of tempo, by breaking up the long 'chain' into interweaving groups, by stepping backwards as well as forwards, and by varying the arm movements. The only people who were allowed to dance individually at the *domba* were those who had graduated (*midabe*): they paraded in small groups outside the *domba* circle, four paces forward, kick, and four paces backward, with a graceful movement described as *udabela*.

A series of spoken pairs of concepts, the third element of the initiation cycle, was presented formally by the master of initiation, and these related symbolic movements, song texts, and rites to problems of adulthood and married life. They reinterpreted familiar objects (such as houses, paths, sunrise, fire) in a new way by relating them to the objects and concerns of womanhood. In the *milayo* laws that were taught throughout the initiations, many sections began with a sentence that compared their progress to a journey of adventure ('I walked along a narrow path and I came to a place where...'). In Figure 2.1 (centre) *ṋḓila* is the word for path and also for the passage from the womb to the vagina: Everyone used the red path which led to the public *khoro* (meeting-place) where *domba* was danced, but it was also the place where the novices performed special action songs about the menstrual flow and the pains of labour. When they danced *domba*, the *khoro* became a womb in which a foetus (the bass drum) was nourished by the intercourse (regular dancing) of the girls and semen (the ashes of the fire). After several months, the novices left the *khoro* by the path into the bush. Their journey (labour) was made painful and hurried on by a stinging potion that was splashed on their backs. They were then ritually washed in a 'pool', from which all babies are said to come. The subsequent rites repeated the rituals surrounding the presentation of a newborn baby (the novice emerging from the seclusion of initiation). The final *milayo*, which were recited in the master's home, were about the leather skirt of married women, and the other decorations that the girls wore as part of their graduation dress.

The initiation cycle was a system of formal education designed to follow the informal education of childhood (Blacking 1964). But it was

John Blacking

also a sensuous bodily experience that was considered essential for the well-being of each individual body and the whole human and natural environment. It was a productive technique of the body (cf. Marcel Mauss) for the purpose of reproduction. But although there was much explanation of sexual matters, it was not a system of education primarily concerned with the actual techniques of reproduction. The most important lesson of *domba* and of the other initiation schools was the instruction about the institutions and responsibilities of motherhood, fatherhood, and marriage. Thus, if a girl became pregnant during *domba*, she was not praised for succeeding in what the school might have seemed to be teaching: she was thrown out in disgrace!

The symbolic relationships expressed with the physical environment were concerned not only with the fertility of the earth and of women, but also with the role of the ancestor spirits as guardians of the countryside and the source of life. Every birth was a rebirth, a recycling of a spiritual being. In *tshikanda* and *domba* distinctions of rank were obliterated, although girls of noble rank tended to be rather more noisy than commoners: the length of girls' hair and where they stood in the dance were signs of how long they had been in the school. Throughout the initiation, the unity of the community and the equality of its members were emphasised.

The future of the cycle of initiation is hard to predict. At the beginning of the century, the missionaries claimed that *domba* was a thing of the past. By 1956-8, it had been adjusted to suit changing conditions, with a concentration of activities at weekends. If anything, interest in *domba* was increasing, because of its significance as a symbol of Venda and African identity in an intolerable political situation. The little that Andrée Grau saw of it in 1977 suggested that its appeal had diminished, though one tiny section of it, the main *domba* dance, was regularly presented as a tourist attraction.

The corporate education of the emotions and of social skills, and the aesthetic experience of music and dancing that the cycle of initiation provided, are not incompatible with the aims of a modern society. Perhaps Venda musicians, dancers, and educators will develop at least some of this rich tradition to suit the needs of their rapidly changing society, as their ancestors successfully did in the past. The dances could be given new social meanings, while retaining their essential choreographic appeal.

In 1956–8, all who had taken part in the cycle of initiation were agreed that the most important element was the *domba* dance. Concern for the dance outweighed consideration of its extra symbolic significance. Women who had forgotten most of what they might have learnt

86

about the associated symbolism had not forgotten the experience of dancing: they talked of problems of coordinating movements and music, the closeness of others' bodies, the excitement when the dance went well, the transcendence of altered time schedules and the sense of transformation from the physical to the social body that was experienced through contrasting movement styles.

Similarly, *tshikona* was invariably described and discussed in terms of its expressive power rather than its social and political uses. Although its performance was often an expression of the political power of its sponsor, the experience stimulated individuality as much as a strong sense of community, and people talked more of the refreshment that it brought to their lives rather than the adherence to a political order that it was supposed to consolidate. I suggest that they talked in these ways not because they were well indoctrinated and complacent, but because the forms of the dances and music were such that they could not be satisfactorily performed by complacent, unthinking, insensitive human beings.

What would happen if they ceased altogether to be performed? Would the Venda create substitutes within the same stylistic range? Or could some radical changes of movement style affect the character of Venda culture and society, as the Alexander principle suggests? In 1977, *tshigombela* was little danced, and then mostly by married women who had learnt it as girls, because the spread of school education had taken away the occasions for performance. Disco and modern African styles of dancing were common among young people, but the questions remain. What will they dance, if anything, when they grow up? Are they finding a new identity through the corporate practice of new styles? Will Venda gain or lose its political vigour and flexibility if there is less adult dancing than in the past? Will tomorrow's urban workers be dancing *tshikona* or condemning it as reactionary and irrelevant? The situation has been complicated by the fact that in the South African context performance of traditional styles, which elsewhere in Africa could be seen as aids to shaking off European domination, can be interpreted as accepting apartheid. The future of dance in Venda cannot be separated from the political values that are given to different styles and the political uses to which dance is put. The traditions of *tshikona* and *domba* were ancient practices of the indigenous inhabitants. Thus it is hard to envisage that they may disappear altogether in the next half century, although this might happen to dance forms that have been adopted in the last hundred years, such as *tshigombela* and *ngoma dza midzimu*. The power of *tshikona* and to a lesser extent *domba*, as symbols embodying Venda society, has been so great that they have survived

John Blacking

many fundamental social and economic exchanges. By 1956, *tshikona* was already being danced in contexts and for purposes other than its original political and ritual uses. Performance was in itself a satisfying experience, and of more significance to people than the extramusical meanings that were assigned to it.

Conclusion

As I argued in the first paragraph of this chapter the aims of social anthropological analysis are in some respects at odds with the kinds of data generally available in the field. The task of interpreting the pervasive patterns of social life cannot be based solely on even the most meticulous analysis of individual decisions made during the period of fieldwork, because an understanding of choices made and of the the the cultural material that is invoked requires knowledge of the past that is generally not available. Not even a twenty-five-year field study of the genesis and expansion of Nazi culture could have provided all the information needed to account for the transformations of German social and cultural life that affected the decision making of millions of individuals.

The most daunting task of social anthropology is to explain the emergence and survival of the distinctive sets of ideas and institutions that influence decision making, in so far as people consistently choose to invoke them rather than alternative courses of action. This involves an analysis of the effectiveness of symbols and of the quality of experience that people derive from using them. For it is experience, or expectation based on experience, that motivates people to invent and use different modes and patterns of communication.

Dance and the performing arts are especially interesting because they are areas of human life in which the most individualistic people are willing to suspend the sort of decision making that they use for most tasks, and because they seem to express, and are invariably claimed to express, the ethos of a society's collective life.

In Venda, between 1956 and 1958, performance of various styles of dance provided opportunities for different kinds of interaction, different kinds of experience, and different kinds of social and political use; there is little doubt that when some styles of dancing were invoked, the conditions of their performance and their contrast with the movements of daily life affected people in ways that influenced their decisions outside the immediate dance situation, and regardless of their interest in the social context of the dance. For instance, many people enjoyed dancing *tshikona* even though they cared little about the chiefs who sponsored it, were not Venda chauvinists, and did not expect it to have therapeutic powers.

The interest in dance as a special kind of knowledge was reinforced by the greater concern often shown for the language and technicalities of dance than for the symbolic context of the action. Although many girls at *domba* did not know, or could not remember, the verbal symbolism referring to the dance, they were able to perform efficiently, criticise their own and others' performances intelligently, and describe the feelings evoked by their dance experiences. Thus they were fully aware of the need to lean the body slightly backwards when in front of the *domba* 'chain', as they had appreciated the correct tilt of the body for the movements of *tshigombela* and grasped the kinetic principles of the complex *ndayo* movements. They realised that unsteady or too fast tempi could make smooth, accurate step dancing difficult and aesthetically displeasing, and in the *ngoma dza midzimu* defeat the transcendental aims of the dance. They enjoyed putting on the special costume for *tshigombela* as much as they liked undressing for *domba* (provided it was not too cold!), and they regarded these acts as essential for good, satisfying performances. There was an interesting contrast between their attitudes to nudity in *vhusha* and *domba*: in *vhusha*, nudity emphasised the humility of the novices, whereas in the latter stages of *domba* it became a source of exhibitionism and mutual satisfaction. Girls spent a great deal of time washing and oiling their bodies, so that they should be smooth and shine in the sun, and they enjoyed leaning on and feeling each other.

I hope that I have made it clear that if my main purpose had been to study the anthropology of dance, I spent too much time collecting the wrong kind of data! The kinds of data that are necessary for understanding the context and assigned meanings of dance are necessary but not sufficient for the study of dance itself. Standard anthropological questions about the symbolism and technical terms do not go far in describing and explaining structures of nonverbal communication and their meaning for the actors.

Above all, I hope that this chapter has shown that much can and must be done in the analysis of dance without invoking psychological explanations. Dance is a social fact, but it eludes straightforward sociological explanations because its structures are conceived nonverbally. In particular, it is unnecessary and unacceptable to drag in the unconscious to explain what happens in dance. Not only is the notion of making an unconscious decision absurd, it diverts attention from the serious analysis of the processes of intuition and unpremeditated decision making, and the structure of nonverbal communication. For

John Blacking

example, people spend a lot of time repeating to themselves ideas or tunes, especially when at rest or during physical labour. They are conscious of this but do not pay attention to it. Sequences of thought (or of melody) can undergo many transformations and then disperse as attention is given to a new task, or they can lead to what could be described as an unpremeditated decision, as attention is given to the train of thought and a new idea is picked up from it.

Finally, one of the important lessons that the study of dance may have for general anthropology is that people's perception and experience of structural coherence can be intensely satisfying and motivate decision making in fields not necessarily associated with the source of the experience or the social and symbolic foundations of the structures. This is why I found the model of the cognitive and affective structures of the activity useful as a basis for analysis. Study of the emergence and spread of a dance style can be a microcosm of the growth of a culture, containing its first principles and constituting a primary modelling system for thought and action.

REFERENCES

Artaud, Antonin. 1958. *The Theater and Its Double*. New York: Grove Press.
Barlow, Wilfred. 1975. *The Alexander Principle*. London: Arrow Books.
Blacking, John. 1964. *Black Background*. New York: Abelard-Schuman.
    1969. 'Songs, dances, mimes and symbolism of Venda girls' initiation schools', parts 1–4. *African Studies*, 28.
    1970. 'Tonal organization in the music of two Venda initiation schools'. *Ethnomusicology*, 14 (1): 1 – 54
    1971. 'Music and the historical process in Vendaland'. In Klaus P. Wachsmann (ed.), *Essays on Music and History in Africa*. Evanston, Ill.: Northwestern University Press.
    1976a. *How Musical is Man?*. 2nd ed. London: Faber & Faber.
    1976b. 'Dance, conceptual thought and production in the archaeological record'. In G. de G. Sieveking, I. H. Longworth and K. E. Wilson (eds.), *Problems in Economic and Social Archaeology*. London: Duckworth.
    1977b. 'An introduction to Venda traditional dances'. In Roderyk Lange (ed.), *Dance Studies*, 2.
    1981. 'Political and musical freedom in the music of some Black South African Churches'. In Ladislav Holy and Milan Stuchlik (eds.), *The Structure of Folk Models*. ASA monograph no. 20. London: Academic Press.
Blacking, John (ed.). 1977a. *The Anthropology of the Body*. ASA monograph no. 15. London: Academic Press.
Bloch, Maurice. 1974. 'Symbols, song, dance and features of articulation: is religion an extreme form of traditional authority?'. *Archives Européenes de Sociologie*, 15:51–81.
Bücher, Karl. 1896. *Arbeit und Rhythmus*. 6th ed. 1924. Leipzig: Emmanuel Reinicke.

1901. *Industrial Evolution*. Trans. S. Morley Wickett. London: George Bell & Sons.
Dolhinow, P.J. and N. Bishop. 1971. 'The development of motor skills and social relationships among primates through play'. In J.P. Hill (ed.), *Minnesota Symposia on Child Psychology*, 4:141–98. Minneapolis.
Gell, Alfred. 1979. 'On dance structures: a reply to Williams'. *Journal of Human Movement Studies*, 5:18–31.
Grau, Andrée. 1983. 'Dreaming, dancing, kinship: a study of yoi, the dance of the Tiwi of Melville and Bathurst Islands, North Australia'. Ph.D. thesis, Queen's University of Belfast.
Groos, Karl. 1896. *Die Spiele des Tiere*. Jena: G. Fischer.
Hanna, Judith Lynne. 1979. *To Dance Is Human: A Theory of Nonverbal Communication*. Austin: University of Texas Press.
Langer, Susanne. 1953. *Feeling and Form: A Theory of Art*. London: Routledge & Kegan Paul.
Lenneberg, Eric. 1967. *Biological Foundations of Language*. New York: Wiley.
Lévi-Strauss, Claude. 1963. *Structural Anthropology*. New York: Basic Books.
Mauss, Marcel. 1936. 'Les techniques du corps'. *Journal de la psychologie*, 32.
Ornstein, Robert. 1975. *The Psychology of Consciousness*. Harmondsworth: Penguin.
Pitcairn, Thomas K. and Margaret Schleidt. 1976. 'Dance and decision: an analysis of a courtship dance of the Melpa, New Guinea'. *Behaviour*, 58 (3–4):298–316.
Royce, Anya Peterson. 1977. *The Anthropology of Dance*. Bloomington: Indiana University Press.
Sachs, Curt. 1937. *World History of the Dance*. New York: Norton.
Strauss, Gloria. 1975. *The Art of the Sleeve in Chinese Dance*. New York: Marcel Dekker. *Dance Perspectives* no. 63.
Waterman, Richard A. 1962. 'Role of dance in human society'. In Bettie Jane Wooten (ed.), *Focus on Dance 2: An Interdisciplinary Search for Meaning in Movement*. Washington DC: American Association of Health, Physical Education and Recreation.
Witkin, Robert W. 1976. *The Intelligence of Feeling*. London: Heinemann.
Wundt, W.M. 1900. *Völkerpsychologie*. Leipzig: W. Engelman.
1928. *Elements of Folk Psychology: Outlines of a Psychological History of the Development of Mankind*. Trans. E. L. Schaub. New York: Macmillan. Originally published 1912.
Young, J.Z. 1971. *An Introduction to the Study of Man*. Oxford: Clarendon Press.

3 Structured movement systems in Tonga

ADRIENNE L. KAEPPLER

Cultural forms that result from the creative use of human bodies in time and space are often glossed in English as 'dance'. These cultural forms can be said to formalise human movement into structured systems in much the same way that poetry formalises language. Such forms, though transient, have structured content, are often visual manifestations of social relations, and may be part of an elaborate aesthetic system. In many societies, however, there is no indigenous concept that can adequately be translated as 'dance'. These formalised movement sequences, in which human bodies are used or manipulated in time and space, may be considered by the society as different when performed for the gods from when performed for a human audience. Structured movements when performed as presentation pieces (for an audience) may be viewed as quite distinct activities from performances that are primarily participatory. Or social activities and social duties that include similar structured movements may be categorised quite differently from an indigenous point of view.

Western notions tend to classify all such movement dimensions together as 'dance', but culturally it would seem more appropriate to analyse them more objectively as movement dimensions of separate activities. The concept 'dance' may be masking the importance and usefulness of analysing human movement systems by introducing a Western category. From a more holistic and objective point of view the movement dimension of various activities should be recognised as an integral part of that activity. They should be described, analysed, and used in formulations about the form, function, and meaning of the activity, as well as in constructs about cultural philosophy and deep structure.

Much social or religious ritual includes the manipulation of human bodies in time and space and may have a similar kind of structured content. Trance or other altered states of consciousness are often associated with structured movement systems. Indeed it seems almost impossible (and perhaps culturally inappropriate) to separate dance from other structured movement systems except by native categories. The Tasaday of the Philippines apparently do not have what would be categorised as dance from a Western point of view. Yet when they sing they usually strike a pose with one hand placed to the side of the head. What are the components in our society that make it possible to classify together ballet, rock and roll, square dancing, and the waltz but separate them from ice skating, cheerleading, and a church processional? Is the concept 'dance' useful in studying either our own culture or others?

Every society has cultural forms in which human bodies are manipulated in time and space. How these forms are regarded by the society itself seems a crucial question for an understanding of that society. Can we isolate components that will either group or separate the various movement dimensions or the activities they project into visual form? An ideal study of a movement system would analyse the cultural forms in which human bodies are manipulated in time and space, the social processes that produce them according to the aesthetic precepts of a specific group of people at a specific point in time, and the components that differentiate activities that include movement. Discovering the structure and content of such forms, as well as the creative processes and philosophies from the indigenous point of view, are difficult tasks, but detailed empirical studies of movement systems including both etic and emic analyses will be necessary both for significant cross-cultural research and for understanding the deep structure of a society.

The concept 'dance' appears to be an unsatisfactory category imposed from a Western point of view because it tends to group together diverse activities that should be culturally separated. Yet a number of activities in many societies have enough common characteristics that outside observers describe certain sets of movement dimensions as dance. Many observers will describe dance and then describe other movement sequences as being 'like dancing'. Supporters of the idea that ice skating is dancing will agree that there is a difference between simply ice skating and dancing on ice skates; on the other hand, some purists may not agree that even dancing on ice skates is dancing. What is it that we have in our heads when we decide if something is dancing or not? I have not yet found a definition of dance that satisfies me.[1] Apparently it has something to do with structured movement that is somehow further elaborated – perhaps by something as simple as having a definite beginning and ending.

I propose that one of the tasks of an ethnographer is to study all human movement that formalises the nonformal and to elucidate

93

Adrienne L. Kaeppler

what the movement dimensions of various activity systems are communicating and to whom. Such an analysis could delineate similarities and differences in the movement dimensions and their contexts as well as how these are regarded and categorised and the components by which they are grouped or separated. It might then be possible to illuminate cultural constructs that produce a cultural conception of dance.

This chapter will explore some aspects of the movement dimensions of various activities in Tonga and I will attempt to delineate cultural constructs that might produce a cultural conception of dance for that society. In previous articles on Tongan dance I have examined kinemic and morphokinemic structure, change in form and function of dance forms, aesthetics, underlying principles, and the communication of social values (Kaeppler 1967b, 1971, 1972, 1976, 1978). I did not, however, really address the abstract conceptualisation of what dance is or whether the varied manifestations I described as dance can be grouped together in a way that implies that they have something in common that separates them from nondance.

Some activities in Tonga today that include structured movement are the ceremonial presentation of pigs; the ceremonial enumeration of pigs, kava roots, and baskets of food; the ceremonial mixing of kava; group speeches with choreographed movements; and movements performed in conjunction with *hiva kakala* (sweet songs), which may have preset choreography or may be choreographed spontaneously. The first four of these activities often occur as part of a larger ceremonial occasion known as *kātoanga* while the fifth is usually part of a less formal occasion. An examination of each of these activities will illustrate some of the important characteristics of the contexts and the movements.

Presentation of pigs

Ceremonial presentation of pigs today is usually part of the prelude to an important kava ceremony, especially the *taumafa kava*, kava drinking in which the king partakes. The drinking of kava, an infusion of the root of a pepper plant (*Piper methysticum*), serves important functions in Tongan society ranging from informal get-togethers to an assembly of all the titled men of the kingdom. The *taumafa kava* is a representation of rank in action. It illustrates the relative ranking of titles and their proximity to the line of the individual holding the ceremony by the floor plan in which the title holders are seated and the order in which they are served. Important ceremonial occasions

94

for the drinking of kava are associated with weddings, funerals, and the bestowal of titles. The actual mixing of the kava is usually preceded by the ceremonial presentation and enumeration of pigs, kava roots, and baskets of food. The largest pigs are pulled on sledges into the ceremonial receiving area. Although these sledges can easily be pulled by a few strong men, a large number of men and women may ceremonially pull the pig. Ostensibly this performance illustrates that the pig is so large that a large group is required to pull it – culturally, of course, it does much more than that. A number of persons dragging the pig distribute the burden and it is appropriate that the movements be coordinated. Sometimes, however, a number of associated individuals make no pretence of pulling but simply move in consort with those who do. Such presentations are done in conjunction with the singing of *tau'a'alo*, work songs. The function of *tau'a'alo* is to lighten the heart and strengthen the muscles as well as to synchronise movements that need to be done together by a number of people, such as rowing a canoe, dragging a canoe, or dragging a pig for presentation. Apparently many *tau'a'alo* traditionally functioned in precisely this way.

Today, however, the pig presentation and associated *tau'a'alo* performed by specific villages (usually the village of Holonga) on specific occasions (such as the validation of the title of the king or crown prince) go far beyond what is necessary for pulling and coordination. This formalised pig presentation has become a *faiva* of Holonga. *Faiva* refers to any kind of task, feat, craft, or performance requiring skill or ability, or anything at which an individual or group is clever. *Faiva* is an important concept because of the cultural implication that some things require cleverness while others do not.

The necessary requirements for the performance of Holonga's *faiva*,[2] which is categorised as a *tau'a'alo* (although in many ways it is quite different from more traditional *tau'a'alo*), are an appropriate ceremonial occasion; a poetic text, either newly composed or a previous text appropriate to the occasion; someone who can add the melodic and rhythmic setting to the poetry – characteristically sung by two groups of men and women, each group having up to six-part polyphony; someone who knows how to do the formalised walking movements; a pig of the largest category (*puaka toho*) for presentation; and a large number of men and women to pull and accompany the pig. The movements are basically formalised walking, pulling, and pushing. The actual movement of the group with the pig into the receiving area may take half an hour. The observers listen to the poetry (which is sung several times), critically analyse who the individuals are and

95

Adrienne L. Kaeppler

what chiefly lines they represent, and, most important, note the presentation.

The most important element in this ceremonial pig presentation is the poetic text. The poetry conveys information through metaphor and allusion interwoven with the Tongan aesthetic principle *heliaki*. This concept, usually translated as 'not going straight' or 'to say one thing and mean another', is characterised by never going straight to the point but alluding to it indirectly. *Heliaki* is poetically realised through the Tongan literary device of alluding to people and their genealogical connections with place names, flowers, and birds, metaphorically making reference to the occasion and those honoured by it. By formalising the walking movements, the movement dimension itself becomes public and an appropriate medium for communicating the poetic information to the observers. Thus the presentation publicly acknowledges the occasion and the status of the receiver, and proclaims that the presentation should be noted as a symbol of support for the established social order by the audience as well as by the receiver. Although this formalised presentation is made by only one village, it is in effect symbolic for the presentations of all the villages. The formalised movements underscore and emphasise what is being communicated by the text in a direct (rather than abstract) manner.

Enumeration of foodstuffs

The prelude to the kava mixing during which the pig presentation takes place also includes an enumeration of the foodstuffs presented, including pigs, kava, and baskets of *ufi* (yams). This enumeration is done by designated men as a stylised oral proclamation while touching the foodstuffs, which are counted with formalised movements. The movements include bending the knees, touching the object or the basket with the right hand, raising the head to look at the person being honoured or the *matāpule* (a special ceremonial attendant who directs the proceedings), and shouting the number. The counter then moves to the next basket, bends, touches the basket with the left hand, looks, and shouts the next number. After counting each ten a second man holding a long stick shouts 'one' and keeps track by tens. This counting is done for each category by foodstuff and size. Some of the subtle, but important, movements include raising the head to look at the person being honoured or the *matāpule*, as if for acknowledgement, and which hand is used to touch the baskets. For example, one method is right, left, left, right, left, left, right, left, left, right.

96

While touching a basket with the right hand the left hand touches the right thigh and vice versa. If the *matāpule* does not like the way this enumeration is carried out – that is, if the oral counting or the movements are not to his liking – he will command them to stop. The counters will then sit down, the *matāpule* will chastise them, and then the counting begins again. It can therefore be said that the movement dimension of enumerating foodstuffs has formalised the nonformal into a structured system, and this system differs according to the line of chiefs honoured. Like ritualised pig presentation, ritualised food enumeration communicates support for the occasion by proclaiming it publicly in a direct (rather than abstract) manner.[3]

Kava mixing and drinking

The main part of the kava ceremony is the kava mixing and drinking itself and is the most important institution in Tongan society. It is the Tongan public occasion where various dimensions of rank are proclaimed, legitimised, and solemnised; where deviations involve calculated manipulation of chiefly lines; and where rites of passage of societal importance are celebrated. The most dignified and formalised rendering of the kava ceremony is the *taumafa kava*, which takes place as part of certain state *kātoanga*, especially those associated with the bestowal of titles of nobility. During these occasions elaborate formalised movements are performed in a precise order in response to directions of the officiating *matāpule*. During less formal kava mixing, the movements are less elaborate, less verbose, less structured, but use similar movements – often in a nonformalised manner.

There are different styles of mixing kava depending on which major chiefly line is being honoured. The right and the duty to prepare kava for these chiefly lines is inherited. For example, the right to prepare kava for the Tuʻi Kanokupolu line (the line of the present king) is held by certain individuals of the Haʻa Ngata chiefs. Thus when a ceremony requiring *taumafa kava* is planned, the king must ask the appropriate mixers, often associated with Vahaʻi, the chief of the village of Kolovai, to carry out the mixing for him. In the unlikely event that they should refuse, it would be unthinkable to assign this task to someone else. In many ways the mixers are as important as the receivers. Often the mixers come in their own good time, especially if they think they have been slighted for some reason. For example, the *taumafa kava* for the public validation of the title of the

Adrienne L. Kaeppler

present king had to be delayed for several hours because the mixers did not come.[4]

The two main styles of kava mixing still in use are the styles associated with the Tuʻi Kanokupolu and the Tuʻi Tonga (the original line of chiefs of celestial origin and from which the Tuʻi Kanokupolu line is a second segmentation). The differences are minimal, including such refinements as whether the lug of the kava bowl faces the mixer (for the Tuʻi Kanokupolu) or the person being honoured (for the Tuʻi Tonga), as well as differences in the movement motifs. The mixing is considered a *faiva* and it is recognised that skill is a necessity, especially for performing the *haka* – arm movements combined into recognised sequences.

Tongans are well aware of the differences between similar activities when performed in public or nonpublic venues. Nonpublic activities are not necessarily private, but rather have a restricted sphere of recognition. That is, they are of relevance primarily to the actors and not to an audience. Such nonpublic activities, although they are expected and may be observed, are not formalised into a public display. Thus although the preparation and drinking of kava is an everyday activity, it is usually an event of participation. Only on certain occasions does the ceremony become primarily an event of presentation to an audience. To be more precise, the participants perform primarily for each other and by extension to announce to any observers that they are carrying out the ritual and acknowledging each other's participation. It thus becomes public, for what the titled men are communicating to each other is relevant to the entire society or specific portions of it. The very act of participation communicates the support of each individual concerned for the individual holding the kava ceremony and illustrates the social solidarity of those participating. It does this publicly with formalised movements and therefore is expected to be acknowledged by those for whom it is relevant. Thus the bestowal of Catholic priesthood on a man from the village of Lapaha is of relevance to his family, to his friends, to the village of Lapaha including its chiefly lines, and to the Catholic church in general. The bestowal of a title of nobility on the crown prince is of relevance to every Tongan individually and collectively, at home or abroad. The kava ceremonies in both cases, however, are public because they do not simply concern those partaking of the kava. The differences between the two ceremonies are in style and degree rather than kind.

For the kava ceremony titled men (chiefs and *matāpule*) or individuals who are included for some other reason are seated in an elon-

98

gated, broken, near rectangular ellipse, the mixer and associates (and designated titled men) sit at the far end (*tou'a*) and face the person of honour who sits at the midpoint of the opposite end flanked by two *matāpule*, who call the commands and direct the proceedings.

The mixing of the kava entails a series of movements.[5] The mixer and his helpers enter and are seated cross-legged with the bowl placed behind the mixer. A large kava root is brought to the front and broken up by striking it with a large sharpened stake. The movements are quite straightforward, except that a side head tilt (*fakateki*) is added, which in effect formalises the striking movements. The pieces of kava root are placed on a pandanus mat along with two stones. Pieces of the root are then placed on the larger stone and the mixer raises the smaller stone in his right hand to the right side high above his head and looks at the officiating *matāpule*. The root is then pulverised, accompanied by judiciously placed *fakateki*, which again formalise the movements into a structured sequence.[6] The bowl is placed before the mixer, the pulverised root and water are placed into it, and the mixer performs a series of arm movements (*haka*) above the bowl. These movement sequences are form motifs, some of which are named, and are punctuated by *fakateki* side head tilts. The mixer kneads the pounded kava root fragments with water, and is then handed a *fau* fibre strainer, with which he performs movement sequences. He clears the liquid of the pieces of root by entrapping them in the *fau*, and with a studied movement flings the *fau* to one of the helpers, who shakes out the kava bits. The *fau* is given back to the mixer to remove more pieces of the root. On occasion the mixer holds the *fau* at shoulder level, poses, looking at the honoured end of the kava circle, and does a *fakateki*. There are two named styles in which the wringing of kava with the *fau* may then be carried out, *milolua* and *fakamuifonua*, which emphasise different movement motifs.

When all bits of kava root have been removed, one of the men or women who will serve the kava brings a coconut-shell cup, stoops to hold it over the kava bowl, and the liquid is wrung into it with the *fau*. The mixer then proclaims '*koe kava kuo heka*' (the kava is lifted) in a stylised call and the *matāpule* answers '*ave ia ma'a X*' (carry it to X). The person called claps his hands in acknowledgement, and the server carries the cup of kava to him. By drinking the kava the drinker acknowledges to himself, to those in the kava circle, and to any other onlookers that he is indeed the holder of that title. The next cup is lifted with the mixer calling again '*koe kava kuo heka*', and the *matāpule* calls the name of the next person authorised to drink, following a specified order. This is repeated until each person in the circle is

99

called, claps, is served the kava, drinks it, and hands the cup back to the server. These serving movements are done in a prescribed manner. For example, the server carries the cup with both hands and, stooping, hands it to the drinker; the drinker takes the cup and drinks while the server turns away from the drinker and takes a few steps as if to go back to the *tou'a*, but instead turns back again to the drinker (who has by this time drunk the kava), takes the cup, and returns to the *tou'a*.

Meanwhile, during the straining of the kava, one of the large pigs is removed, cut up, and a piece distributed with yams to each person in the kava circle as a 'relish' (*fono*) to be eaten with the kava. They do not, however, eat the *fono* but it is ritually taken away from each one by someone (called *kai fono*) who is *'eiki* (higher in rank) to them according to *kainga* rank (that is, rank within his ego-based kindred). Such individuals include children of a sister (especially the oldest female child) or *mokopuna 'eiki* (a grandchild of higher rank because of a son's elevated marriage). This taking of the *fono*, within a formal state ceremony, demonstrates that rank operates on more than one level simultaneously. In this case it shows that every individual regardless of his rank within the overall societal structure is outranked within his *kainga* (see Kaeppler 1971 for details). Although it is forbidden to cross into the kava circle, those taking the *fono* do so with immunity. Their movements are not formalised, they simply enter the circle, take the *fono*, and leave. These movements are not considered public. The observers visually see them, of course, but because they are nonpublic and are not relevant to them, they are not acknowledged: The taking of the *fono* is relevant only to the *kainga* of the individual from whom it is taken. Thus the proscription against entering into the kava circle is not broken because from a societal point of view it is not public and can be disregarded.

In short, the formalisation of movements within the kava ceremony communicates that those movements are public and should be acknowledged as such. Which set of formalised movements is used during the kava preparation indicates affiliation with the lineage of specified chiefs. The clapping of hands and drinking of the kava in a prescribed manner proclaims title and rank publicly and is thereby acknowledged by those to whom the particular kava ceremony is relevant. The occasion is a public and nonpublic event where information is communicated selectively by the movement dimensions of various activities within the ceremony.

Formalised movements in the distribution of kava are also used to communicate other information that cannot be communicated orally.

For example, at the *taumafa kava* that validated the bestowal of the title of the present king, his new title was called and the first cup of kava was taken to him. Without being announced a second cup of kava was taken to the king's younger brother, Tu'i Pelehake. This was said to publicly proclaim that Tu'i Pelehake should be considered as the king's equal because he has exactly the same genealogy and according to the traditional reckoning, the Tu'i Pelehake title (of Tu'i Faleua) is more elevated than that of the Tu'i Kanokupolu.

Movement also indicated visually that the three ranking lines of chiefs were all of importance in the Tongan sociopolitical system and indeed that all three were represented in the genealogy of the king and his brother. This was publicly acknowledged by three mixers preparing three bowls of kava. One of the kava mixers was Hahano, son of Vaha'i, a chief of the Ha'a Ngata – the traditional preparers of kava for the Tu'i Kanokupolu. Another mixer was Sione, the son of Kalaniuvalu – closest ranking chief of the Tu'i Tonga line. Presumably the third mixer represented the Tu'i Ha'a Takalaua line. The Tu'i Tonga and the Tu'i Ha'a Takalaua were defeated by the Tu'i Kanokupolu and no one has been appointed to these higher-ranking titles since that time. However, the descendants of those defeated chiefs live on and their elevated personal rank is acknowledged silently on important state occasions – that is, they are not announced with these titles. Instead they are acknowledged visually by formal movement dimensions in the preparation of three bowls of kava, which illustrates that even these higher ranking lines publicly acknowledge the king.

Formalised movements have yet another function at state kava ceremonies – to emphasise taboos by having someone who is immune break them. For example, when the king is seated in his place in the kava circle it is forbidden for a Tongan to walk behind him. During the *taumafa kava* for the validation of the king's title, a Fijian of the title Tu'i Soso broke this taboo on several occasions during the ceremony while performing formalised Fijian movements behind the small pavilion in which the king sat – a silent reminder that Tongans may not do this. Tu'i Soso also took the *fono* of the king. When he did so, he emerged from the *tou'a* where the kava was prepared and advanced through the entire length of the kava ring performing Fijian dance motifs with spear and fan. He then speared a piece of pig and ate it in front of the king. These formalised movements communicated several sorts of information. They illustrated that Tu'i Soso's actions were public and relevant to all observers. Because no Tongan outranked the king in an appropriate way to take his *fono* this had to be done by a foreigner – not just any foreigner, but a foreigner of rank.

101

Adrienne L. Kaeppler

It also demonstrated a difference between the king and other titled men – the *kainga* rank of the others was nonpublic but the rank of the king is relevant to all.

Group speeches with choreographed movements

The major public activity of a large-scale *kātoanga* in terms of the preparation and involvement of large numbers of people consists of group speeches with choreographed movements. Through these group speeches the same kind of information that is communicated through a kava ceremony is communicated by hundreds of people organised by village. These performances communicate the participants' support for the occasion, while at the same time they glorify their own villages with their histories, traditions, and genealogical lines. One might consider a *kātoanga* as a metaphor of a great kava ceremony in which villages take the place of individuals and in which the act of drinking kava is replaced by what would be called in English 'dancing'.

Large-scale *kātoanga* are rare. The seven given during the reign of Queen Sālote Tupou III (1918–65) were listed in the Tongan edition of the newspaper *Kolonikali* (*Chronicle*) shortly after the queen's death. These were the centennial celebration of the coming of Christianity (1926), the centennial celebration of the installation of Tupou I (1945), the double wedding of the present king and his brother (1947), the golden jubilee of the treaty between Tonga and Great Britain (1951), the travelling of Queen Sālote to London for the coronation of Queen Elizabeth II (1953), the visit of Queen Elizabeth and the Duke of Edinburgh to Tonga (1953), and the centennial celebration of the 'emancipation' (1962). The coronation of Queen Sālote in 1918 was not considered a *kātoanga*, probably because it was held too soon after the death of Tupou II and the kingdom was in mourning, which prohibits festivity. On the other hand, the *kātoanga* celebrating coronation week of Tupou IV in 1967 was primarily a public display. Tupou IV had actually been king since December 1965. The 4 July 1967, European-style coronation on the king's forty-ninth birthday, as well as the 6 July *taumafa kava*, and the group speeches with choreographed movements on 5 and 7 July were a public validation of the title. During this week the king's title was validated by all the titled men of the kingdom (that is, all the chiefs and *matāpule*, not just the nobles) as well as by all the villages and their people. This occasion was meant to be acknowledged by the world.

The 1962 emancipation *kātoanga* was the most elaborate in living memory and included seventy-one group speeches with choreo-

102

graphed movements each lasting fifteen minutes to half an hour. These performances were spread over seven days and took place in three locations in the island group. It was easier to transport the royal party to the central and northern group of islands (Ha'apai and Vava'u), where four days of performances were held, than to bring the hundreds of performers to Tongatapu, where the sovereign resides. The group speeches, rendered melodically and rhythmically and accompanied by choreographed movements, included several types. There is no inclusive term for these performances except *faiva*, which as noted above also includes *tau'a'alo* and other things. If *faiva* is qualified as *faiva* with *haka*, *tau'a'alo* and the enumeration of foodstuffs are excluded, but kava mixing and *tau'olunga* (dance) are included. *Tau'olunga*, however, is considered by Tongans to be something quite different.

The types of choreographed speeches included in the 1962 *kātoanga* were *lakalaka*, *mā'ulu'ulu*, *sōkē*, *taufakaniua*, and *meke*. *Me'etu'upaki* and *tafi* were also included in the 1967 *kātoanga*, and presumably an *'otu haka* could be included but apparently never is. The most important of these types today is *lakalaka*, which can be considered the classic type of this unnamed category of performances.

A *lakalaka* is composed according to the structure of a formal Tongan speech. Formal speeches have an introductory section known as *fakatapu*, which acknowledges the important genealogical lines and in effect asks their permission to speak. Although individuals of each chiefly line may not be in attendance, the *fakatapu* announces to whom this speech is relevant. The body of the speech may include information about the speaker and his comments and attitudes about the occasion. It is usually congratulatory to the occasion, the individual to whom it is addressed, and often to the speechmaker himself. Speeches usually end with a closing statement that expresses thanks to the listeners and again acknowledges the chiefs. Speechmaking is a highly respected *faiva*, requiring a knowledge of history and tradition, of honorific and elegant language, of poetic meter and *heliaki*, and stage presence.

Lakalaka texts follow a similar pattern but depend on the status of the composer and which group is going to perform. For example, if composed by Queen Sālote, the *fakatapu* need not make all the acknowledgements and ask permission to speak, nor would this be necessary if one of the king's children were to perform in it. Nevertheless, there would still be a *fakatapu* that would convey appropriate information and retain the structure.

As an example of a *lakalaka* that would be appropriate to this chapter let us examine a *lakalaka* of the village of Kolovai that deals with *taumafa kava*. The poetry was composed by E. Vanisi in 1931.

103

Adrienne L. Kaeppler

Ko e Lakalaka 'A Kolovai Ko e 'Milolua'

I	1	Ko 'eku tu'u ni ke u fakaha	Here I am standing to show
	2	'A e anga 'o 'eku fiefia	The manner of my happiness
	3	Si'i 'aho 4 e mahina	The dear fourth day of the month
	4	Ne fakakoloa ai ho ta fonua	Our land has been enriched
	5	Fakahifo ai e mo'onia	Giving birth to the *mo'onia*
	6	Ne ngatutu he 'a Natula	The land of Tonga was trembling
	7	Pea me'eme 'e manu e 'ata	The birds of the air were dancing
	8	He kuo huhulu mai e la'a	The sun show forth its light
II	9	'Oi Hala-ki 'umata mo e kolo kakala	Alas, the rainbow way and sweet smelling village
	10	Ne mahikihiki 'a e Taungapeka	Kolovai was overjoyed
	11	'E Tuku mo Tafa he mo 'Ahokata	The boundaries of the happy day
	12	'E Ha'a Havea he mo Ha'a Ngata	Ha'a Havea and Ha'a Ngata
	13	Mo hono kotoa 'o e ngaahi ha'a	And all the other lineages
	14	Kuo lonuku he loto'a maka	Are assembled at the stone fence
	15	Kuo tau fakataha ko e fakana'ana'a	We are coming together to praise
	16	'Aki e faiva ko e lakalaka	With the performance of *lakalaka*
	17	Kae tuku mu'a 'a e fakahoha'a	Please stop the disturbance
	18	Ho'o 'akafisi mo ke 'aka'aka	And your rolling about and kicking
	19	Ka ke 'ilo ko e me'a masila.	And note that it is a sharp thing
III	20	'Oi fanongo e Tonga mo e Ha'apai	Alas, listen to me Tonga and Ha'apai
	21	Kae 'uma 'a 'a Vava'u Lahi	And even you, big Vava'u
	22	Pea 'ilo 'ehe Piu 'o Tafahi	And the Piu of Tafahi knows
	23	Mo e maka ko Finetoupalangi	And the rock of Finetoupalangi
	24	'Alele pea mo motu 'A'ali	The island of Alele and the island 'A'ali
	25	Kuo tau katoa 'i Palasi	We have all gathered at the palace

	26	Ke fakamanatu ʻa e ʻaho lahi	To commemorate the great day
	27	Taʻu taha-tolu kuo ne ʻiai.	Thirteen years he has
IV	28	Ke ʻilo ʻe he sola pea mo e taka	I want the stranger and the roamers to know
	29	ʻAe ʻalofi tapu ke tatala	That the kava ring is forbidden to walking and moving
	30	Kau nofo hifo ʻo ngaohi kava	I will sit and make the kava
	31	Ke vakai naʻa ke laka hala	Beware of any wrong moves
	32	Ka ke nofo pe muʻa ʻo mamata	Be content to sit and watch
	33	Ka mau milolua mo fakamuifonua	We will perform the *milolua* and *fakamuifonua* styles of mixing kava
V	34	He ʻoi, 'Kuo holo', 'tuku atu', 'tuku malie pe kae palu'	It has been pounded, put it down, put it slowly and mix it
	35	'Tafoki kimoua' pea 'ui haʻa mo vai'. . . . 'Vai'	Face inward and call for your water. Water!
	36	'ʻOi vai taha,' 'taʻofi ʻa e vai'	Stop one water, stop the water
	37	'Palu pea fakatatau' pea 'tui haʻo fakama ʻu'	Mix and squeeze – circle and squeeze with one hand
	38	'Palu ki lalo' pea 'ʻai ange ʻa e fau.'	Mix it low and put in the *fau*
VI	39	He ʻoi, pea te u milolua, milolua mo fakamuifonua	And now I will wring the kava in *milolua* style
	40	He ʻoi, mo fakamuifonua He ʻoi mo fakamuifonua	And wring it in the *fakamuifonua* style
VII	41	Ko e ngata e holo taumafa	This is the end of our royal kava mixing
	42	Hiki e touʻa kau foki ange	Kava mixers and helpers move and return
	43	ʻO ʻeva he Fala ʻo Setane	To walk upon the Mat of Satan
	44	ʻO kahoa hono lumaile	And wear the *maile* leaves
	45	Mo ta sei hono lou siale	And our ear ornament of *siale* flowers

46	Mo e kotone ko Fakavale	And the *kotone* trees which bring possession
47	Si'ene maki 'i kae tauele	Her dear giggling and beguiling
48	Fakalavetala kia te koe	Flirting with you
49	Ka ke ha'u kau 'ave 'a koe	You come and I'll take you
50	Ki homou hala ko Fine 'ehe	To our road, Fine'ehe
51	Hala sili mo e tukungapale	Road of fishermen and place of the prize
52	'Uta'anga 'o e manu fefine	The desired place of the females

The first stanza of a *lakalaka* speech is usually the *fakatapu*. Here, however, because of the subject and the performers, this composition does not have a well-defined *fakatapu*, but the first two stanzas serve as one.[7] The body of the text or *lakalaka* proper gives information about the performers and their village, comments on the occasion by alluding to the genealogy of the person honoured and his association with the village of the performers, and conveys other relevant information. The last stanza is the *tatau* – the closing counterpart of the *fakatapu* in which the performers say goodbye and again defer to the chiefs. In addition to the three divisions of a speech, a *lakalaka* text often includes a section known as the *tau*, which contains the essence of the speech. The *tau* is a stanza or part of a stanza which elicits the performers' best efforts and during which the audience is encourged to pay strict attention. The *tau* of this *lakalaka* is stanza six, which formalises the wringing of kava. The wringing of the kava is not only the essence of this *lakalaka* but also the essence of the village of Kolovai, giving them their importance in the Ha'a Ngata. By extension the *taumafa kava* is metaphorically the essence of the sociopolitical system, which cements the relationships between the king, his nobles, the chiefs, *matāpule*, and the people in general. Performance of this *lakalaka* formalises and underscores that relationship for performers and audience, and thereby demonstrates their allegiance to the king and his government.

The translation of the text given here[8] is a quite literal translation in order to illustrate the aesthetic principle *heliaki*, 'not going straight'. Although the *lakalaka* is ostensibly about *taumafa kava* and stanzas five and six reiterate the directions and movements for mixing and wringing the kava, the real object of the poetry to which the *heliaki* alludes in the overall sense is the thirteenth birthday of the present king. This can be deduced from line 3 (he was born on 4 July) and from line 27, referring to the thirteenth year. A line-by-line analysis of the text is not relevant to this chapter, but a few verses are of interest to it. That *lakalaka* is a kind of *faiva* is shown in line 16. The literary device of alluding to people with flowers is found in line 5, where Tupou IV is alluded to by *mo'onia*, a specific way of sewing or stringing flowers. Kolovai, the home of flying foxes, is alluded to in lines 9 and especially 10, as an ancestral place of the Ha'a Ngata. The meaning to which the *heliaki* of lines 17–19 alludes is that it is the duty of the Ha'a Ngata chiefs (to whom the people of Kolovai belong) to protect the king and they will not accept any disturbance. And, of course, it is also the duty and privilege of the Ha'a Ngata to prepare the *taumafa kava*. Stanza four points out that it is forbidden to cross into the kava circle, but the *heliaki* implication is that according to Tongan tradition there are right and wrong ways to do things and one learns the correct way by observing. The last stanza glorifies Kolovai with place names such as the sandy beach called 'mat of Satan'. Plants such as *maile, siale,* and *kotone* and a specific kind of net fishing used in Kolovai are further references to the performers. The *heliaki* contends that Kolovai is such a marvellous place that it can lure one away supernaturally like that specifically Tongan affliction called *'āvanga* in which a spirit calls one to follow and one obeys as if possessed.

The movements that go with such a speech would be choreographed from beginning to end by a specialist (*pulotu haka*)[9] at the request of the chief of Kolovai for performance on a specific occasion. This particular version was performed for the thirteenth birthday of the prince. It could be performed at other times to commemorate that occasion, or by simply changing line 27 it could honor some other occasion specific to the king. Although the poetry should only have minor changes, the movements and musical setting might be changed each time the composition is performed.

Movements for this sort of *faiva* are based on three sections of the body – legs and feet, arms and hands, and the head.[10] *Lakalaka* literally means to keep on walking or to 'step it out' and figuratively means to advance or make progress. Foot and leg movements are basically a continuous walking by stepping to one side, bringing the other foot to touch next to it ('place'), stepping to the opposite side, and touching the opposite foot to place. The function of the foot movements is primarily to keep time. The most important movements in a *lakalaka* are the movements of the arms and hands. These movements form motifs, which are strung together in such a way that they can be said to 'comment' on a word or concept of the verse of poetry that they accompany. In effect, they make visual some aspect of the text by alluding to it – another form of *heliaki*. The arm movements form a secondary abstraction, alluding to selected words of the text that

107

themselves allude to a deeper meaning. Or the arm movements, instead of alluding to the poetry, may allude to the deeper meaning, giving the superficial appearance that they have little if anything to do with the text. That is, the arm movements say one thing, but mean another. In short, the arm movements are the *heliaki* of the poetry while the poetry is the *heliaki* of the text. The third body part important in *lakalaka*, the head, is used primarily in the side head tilt *fakateki*. Although sometimes choreographed, the *fakateki* is usually added by individual performers to attract and hold the attention of the spectators. Aesthetic and decorative, the *fakateki* emphasises the publicness of the performance and proclaims that this presentation is meant for an audience. *Fakateki* is par excellence the movement that compels a Tongan to watch.

Lakalaka is performed by all the men and women of a village who care to perform, often as many as two hundred. The performers are arranged in two or more long rows facing the audience – the men forming the right half, the women forming the left half (from the observer's point of view). Men and women perform two separate sets of movements, illustrating the Tongan view that in public different kinds of actions are appropriate for men and women. Men's movements are strong and virile while women's movements are soft and graceful. Two sets of movements also make it possible to allude to the text or its underlying meaning in two different ways, adding another dimension of *heliaki*.

Next to *lakalaka* the most appropriate performing medium for *kātoanga* is *māʻuluʻulu*, a group speech with choreographed movements performed sitting down. Although *māʻuluʻulu* are often performed on semiformal occasions as a showpiece and need not have a strict formal structure, when performed for a *kātoanga* they too incorporate the formal speech-making divisions of *fakatapu*, body of the text, and the *tatau* closing statement. The overall structure has one of two forms – a through-composed form similar to its *ʻotu haka* prototype or a verse –refrain form adapted from Christian hymn tunes. The latter is now the more usual and in it the refrain or chorus is a *tau* that contains the essence of the composition. During the *tau* the performers do their best in order to compel the audience to pay strict attention. Although strophic in form (that is, verse/refrain, verse/refrain) the verses need not have the same melody or the same number of phrases per verse.

Seated cross-legged in one or more rows or with the rows gradually elevated in various ways – kneeling, sitting on chairs or benches, or standing – the performers are accompanied by one or more skin-covered drums. The arm movements are similar to those used for mixing kava and for *lakalaka* but more varied and precise. The poetry is preceded and followed by *haka fakalongolongo*, silent *haka*, performed in conjunction with drumming but no text. As in *lakalaka* the *fakateki* head tilt rises from inner feelings of exhilaration and emphasises that the performance is directed to an audience. Usually the performers are all of one sex, preferably female, and often comprise all the students of a sex-segregated secondary school. During the *kātoanga* of 1962, *māʻuluʻulu* were performed by Queen Sālote College, Pilolevu College, Siuʻilikutapu College (all girls' schools), St. Andrew's College, the old women of Tongoleleka, and by the villages of Holonga, Teʻekiu, ʻUiha, and ʻOvaka.

As in *lakalaka* the poetry is basic and composed first with the specific performing genre in mind. The poetry is rendered rhythmically and melodically and visually enhanced by movements. Both the text and the movement incorporate the aesthetic principle *heliaki* by alluding to deeper meanings with formalised speech and movement motifs. Metaphorically each group delivers a speech in which poetry and movements point out and comment upon the occasion and the society.

Other *faiva* that have been performed as part of large-scale *kātoanga* were not entirely appropriate in their original forms, but were made appropriate by giving them a speechlike structure. Primarily this involves adding a *fakatapu* or altering a stanza of poetry to serve as one. During the 1962 *kātoanga* there were performances of two *sōkē*, two *meke*, and a *taufakaniua*. The latter is a performance local to one of the northern islands of the Tongan group and is considered their *faiva*. *Sōkē* and *meke* are considered to be non-Tongan, having come from Uvea and Fiji, but for various historical reasons were appropriate to the group that performed them.

During the 1967 *kātoanga*, a *meʻetuʻupaki* and a *tafi* were performed as specialities of the villages of Lapaha and Fuaʻamotu. These *faiva* were particularly appropriate on that occasion because they are associated with the two senior lines of chiefs and served the same metaphorical purpose as the second and third bowls of kava during the *taumafa kava*. Their performance demonstrated visually that these two chiefly lines were part of the genealogy of the king, that these lineages were still powerful forces in the society, and that the people and chiefs of these villages were proud of those affiliations. The performances also demonstrated that although higher in ceremonial prestige these lines acknowledged Tupou IV as head of government, and gave their allegiance to him as king of Tonga.

In short the performances of *lakalaka*, *māʻuluʻulu*, and other *faiva* at a *kātoanga* can be considered as an enlarged and extended kava cer-

Adrienne L. Kaeppler

emony in which the whole society takes part. Just as the *taumafa kava* demonstrates the allegiance of the individual titled men to the king and indicates their support of the sociopolitical system, so the performance of the *faiva* demonstrates similar sentiments village by village as well as those of every individual performer regardless of his place in society. Many villages have a special title by which they are called when it is time to perform – just like a man who is to drink kava is called by his title. These titles, like the titles of chief and *matāpule*, are based on history and tradition. For example, when the inhabitants of the village of Lapaha perform *lakalaka*, they are known as 'Lomipeau' – this refers to a large semimythical canoe associated with Lapaha and its chiefs; when the inhabitants of the village of Kolovai perform *lakalaka*, they are known as *Milolua* – even if performing a *lakalaka* that is not based on kava mixing. During kava mixing and its prelude of food presentation and enumeration, the use of structured movement makes information public. Group speeches with choreographed movements are also preceded by the giving of food and other gifts when they are presented in the receiving ground behind the palace before the actual day of the *kātoanga*. It is on this earlier occasion that the king and his *matāpule* note the support and allegiance of the village nonpublicly. This support is then presented publicly on the day of the *kātoanga* in a festive celebratory context. The social order is upheld poetically and visually in a nonpublic village-by-village treaty with the king and his government and then in a public presentation relevant to all other members of the society.

The structured movement dimensions of the activities associated with *kātoanga* (pig pulling, enumeration of foodstuffs, kava mixing, group speeches with choreographed movements) visually emphasise the importance of rank and social solidarity, which pervade the society. The underlying principles of hierarchical ranking and the mutual interdependence of the various societal dimensions are transformed into visual surface manifestations. To separate the movement dimensions of these activities into dance and nondance would mask the underlying concept communicated to the observer and participant that formalised movement imparts information about social relationships – sometimes objectively, sometimes abstractly.

Tauʻolunga – Tongan 'dance'

The movement dimension of the final activity to be dealt with here is known as *tauʻolunga*, which is separated by Tongans from the activity it accompanies known as *hiva kakala*, sweet songs. Informal in

110

style, *hiva kakala* are songs of a topical nature composed primarily to be sung. These songs appear to be an evolved form of *pō sipi*, short poems originally recited spontaneously by *matāpule* during informal kava gatherings. These poems consisted primarily of allusions to the female kava mixer on behalf of one of the young men in attendance. Allusions were phrased in terms of flowers, birds, and place names, which referred to the individual without naming her – a form of not-so-complex *heliaki*. During the nineteenth century, melodies usually in the form of Protestant hymn tunes in verse/chorus alternation were added. Movements, based on a Tongan prototype *ula*, were also added. These movements, now usually translated into English as 'dance', use many of the arm and hand movement motifs used in *lakalaka* and *mā'ulu'ulu* as well as motifs borrowed and adapted from Samoa. The main difference between Tongan and Samoan arm movements is that Tongan arm movements emphasise the rotation of the lower arm (while bending and flexing the wrists and curling and opening the fingers) whereas Samoan arm movements emphasise bending at the elbows (while bending the wrists and curling the fingers). The leg movements are also adapted from Samoa and include small rotations of the lower legs, which move the heels in and out, used mainly to keep time, and a quick lift of the foot by a bend of the knee upward. These movements are not characteristic of other Tongan performing genres. The *fakateki* head tilt may punctuate the performance, but it is not an important element calculated to capture the attention of the observers and encourage them to explore the *heliaki* of the movement for hidden allusions.

Like its Tongan prototype, *ula*, the movements of *tau'olunga* need not make reference to the poetry they accompany. Instead of alluding to poetry, the movements create beauty. In *ula* one or a few lines of text are repeated over and over and many movement motifs are used to accompany these verses. In *hiva kakala* the sentiment expressed verbally is often about an individual and specifically composed for one. *Tau'olunga* are often choreographed spontaneously, that is, not preset into a well-thought-out sequence. The movements are well-known motifs which in other performing genres are often used as fill-in motifs and need not attempt to go around (*heliaki*) the poetry. The *heliaki*, instead, alludes to the individual performing. The performer is judged on the execution of the motifs rather than on the interpretation of the poetry.

Hiva kakala with *tau'olunga* movement have a limited sphere of public or nonpublic appreciation, the movements being a showcase for the performer. For example, after the nonpublic presentation behind

111

the palace of the *lakalaka* of the village of Kanokupolu preceding the 1975 *kātoanga*, the composer and leader of the *lakalaka*, Ve'ehala (who is also a high-ranking chief, noble, and cabinet minister), gave a marvellous speech that moved the audience to both laugh and cry. Following that he performed an improvised *tau'olunga* in which the movements had little to do with the poetry that was being sung. Ve'ehala is one of the most respected choreographers in Tonga and it is likely that allusion to the text was superfluous for this occasion. The beautiful movements alluded instead to the accomplishments of the performer – another kind of social metaphor. Such a showcase for an individual is enhanced by the addition of one or more *tulaufale* (supporting dancers), who perform movements that would be considered inappropriate if performed on their own. These movements allude to the proper movements through contrast. The *tulaufale* may do virile movements in opposition to the main performers' graceful ones, strike the ground, or even throw himself on the ground. The cultural preference for allusion rather than statement can be conveyed by *heliaki* of beauty and nonbeauty as well as by *heliaki* of text.

Tau'olunga are only occasionally elevated to this semipublic venue. This *tau'olunga* was not part of the performance during the 1975 public *kātoanga* because choreographic and speech-making accomplishments of an individual were not relevant on that occasion. Instead it was the time to show publicly the support of Kanokupolu for the occasion, the king and his government, and the centennial celebration of the constitution. Kanokupolu's *lakalaka* was first to perform. The poetry concerned the aristocratic sport of snaring migrating pigeons. In addition to this historical allusion, the *heliaki* alluded to the high-ranking Samoan female who was 'snared' to Tonga as the female progenitor of the Tupou dynasty. The ranking female performer was Pilolevu, the king's eldest daughter – his descendant of highest rank, who, in time, would be snared to continue to elevate the dynasties of Tonga. The ranking male performer was Baron Vaea, and there was no immediately apparent reason why he should be performing with Kanokupolu. Vaea is the noble of the village of Houma and is of the highest personal or 'blood' rank although his title is not of the highest ranking. His performance as the central male performer of the village of Kanokupolu communicated visually, however, what it was not appropriate to state orally – that if other societal rules had been activated, he could have been king. By performing he also demonstrated that although he was of very high prestige, he was subservient politically – yet part of the power structure. Baron Vaea, noble and of elevated personal rank, also happens to be one of the best 'dancers' in the kingdom. Had he refused to perform, it would have been a personal affront to the king and his daughter. By performing, however, he demonstrated his support of the status quo and the socio-political system.

As a postlude on this public occasion a *tau'olunga* would have been appropriate if performed by the king's daughter. *Lakalaka* are occasionally followed with a *tau'olunga* performed by an important descendant of the village chief. This serves a similar function to the taking of the *fono* of a chief during a kava ceremony by an appropriate descendant of the title holder. Such a *tau'olunga* would be of relevance specifically to the village that was performing, and often occurs when the *lakalaka* is performed nonpublicly behind the palace before the day of the *kātoanga*. Usually *tau'olunga* are not permitted during the *kātoanga* itself, except for some publicly relevant reason. A *tau'olunga* performed by the king's daughter at this point would have served a similar function to the taking of the king's *fono* by Tu'i Soso – that is, demonstrating that the genealogy of the king is relevant to all.

Tau'olunga performed on public or semipublic occasions are different in character from the original spontaneous performances that accompanied evolved forms of spontaneous poetry. Carefully composed poetry is given a melodic and rhythmic setting (based on European prototypes) and string band accompaniment. Movements are choreographed to emphasise the beauty of the performer, to allude by *heliaki* to the text, and, in the best compositions, to have an overall *heliaki*. One such exceptional composition is '*Manu 'o Palataise*' (Bird of Paradise). It was composed by the late Queen Sālote and the overall *heliaki* was conceived by her. Performed by two females and a male, the latter, as a bird of paradise in the Tongan role of a *tulaufale*, challenges others to stay away from his two females, who move about preening themselves. Wearing costumes of *kakā* (parrot) feathers, the different sets of movements illustrate appropriate movements for men and women, and by *heliaki* point out the proper role of men in regard to women. Women are elevated in rank within the *kainga* (bilateral kindred) and while men have power, women have prestige. Women are to be pampered, elevated, and protected by specified kinsmen from threats to their dignity. A man will challenge anyone who might harm any of the women for whom he is responsible. *Tau'olunga* is the performing genre par excellence that can be used to instil attitudes and traditions dealing with the extended family and appropriate behaviour between individuals. Although superficially it might appear that the performance makes reference to male/female sexual relationships and advances, it does not. The *heliaki*, instead, alludes to non-

113

sexual relationships and the female/male traditions that deal with prestige and power. In addition, the whole performance infers that Tonga is a paradise and is the proper place for Tongans.

Tauʻolunga, thus, can vary from spontaneous 'dances' for nonprogrammed entertainment to elegant compositions on the most important occasions. Semiformal occasions such as a concert to raise money for a church or a floor show at the local hotel could be made up entirely of *tauʻolunga* or might have the addition of a *māʻuluʻulu* or other *faiva* with appropriate text. *Tauʻolunga* are intended primarily to be light in spirit and are entertaining, while other performing genres, although they too can be entertaining and are performed in a festive atmosphere, have an underlying social message. Group speeches with choreographed movements are visual manifestations of social structure through movement and express political and social reality in a supportive form. *Tauʻolunga*, when organised with an appropriate structure, can also express a social message, but that is really not their function.

Dance and nondance – the Tongan view

The distinction between *ʻaho meʻe* (day dance) and *pō meʻe* (night dance) illustrates the Tongan view. *Pō* (literally 'night') adds informality to the word with which it is associated. For example, *pō talanoa* refers to informal conversation regardless of what time of day it takes place. *ʻAho* (day), on the other hand, is when important things take place. Thus *ʻaho meʻe* and *pō meʻe* refer to occasions during which *meʻe* are performed and not what kind of *meʻe* are performed. *Meʻe* is a now obsolete inclusive term for various performing genres. *Meʻetuʻupaki* (*meʻe* standing with paddles) were separated from *meʻelaufola* (*meʻe* based on arm movements). The term *meʻe* (the Tongan version of the Fijian term *meke*) fell into disuse when Protestant missionaries attempted to eradicate heathen dances. Instead of eradicating these important sociocultural forms based on formalised movement, Tongans 'invented' new ones and gave them new names. The newness resided in new combinations of old pieces of movement. It is apparent, however, from the existence of the term *meʻe* that Tongans had a cultural conception of *meʻe* as distinct from other ritualised movement and one which could be further categorised. *ʻAho meʻe* and its successors are preeminently social metaphors that can be used to convey information – some of which is best not conveyed orally – or can be used as a visual extension of oral literature.

The cultural preference for alluding to deep meaning in an indirect manner gives both composers and audience aesthetic pleasure. Structured movement that has its own *heliaki* transcends ritual movement, which functions primarily to make public. Structured ritual movement is made ritual by a formal structure and often by the addition of *fakateki* head tilts. In the public rituals of pig pulling, food enumeration, and kava mixing the formalised movements are (in spite of elaboration) real. That is, they do not say one thing and mean another, they do not involve allusion and *heliaki*. In short, structured movement in Tonga functions to make information public and to convey certain kinds of information as movement itself. When movement is given the additional dimension of *heliaki* it becomes something else. *Heliaki* makes movement aesthetic, in addition to public, and functions primarily as social metaphor. Movement, like language, serves different forms of communication, as well as entertainment. *Pō me'e*, and its modern successor *pō faiva*, like conversation, is to be taken lightly. Public structured movement such as pig pulling, enumeration, and kava mixing communicates important information as movement. Group speeches with choreographed movements have the additional dimension of movement *heliaki*. By the addition of *heliaki*, structured movements are transformed into dance.

Tongans who speak English translate dance as *tau'olunga*. If pressed they might agree that *lakalaka* and other choreographed speeches can also be dance. But dance to a Tongan is entertainment and probably ephemeral and frivolous, while choreographed speeches are social metaphors to be remembered and passed on. The act of performing double *heliaki* and the information it conveys in poetry and movement is of primary importance, while the *product* dance is a form of entertainment that conveys joy. What choreographed speeches and *tau'olunga* have in common is that their products derive from performing double *heliaki*.

Various activity systems in Tonga have conspicuous structured movement dimensions, most importantly *pō faiva* (the successor of *pō me'e) and kātoanga* – the latter composed of several subactivities having formalised movement. A *tau'olunga*, dance in its narrow sense usually performed as *pō faiva*, can be elevated to a choreographed speech at a *kātoanga* by its inclusion as the end piece of a group's performance and the social metaphors that it reveals. It thereby becomes part of a group's speech, giving an additional *tau* (in the form of a *tau'olunga*, that is, an elevated *tau*) to the performance. Thus the Tongan cultural conception that might be translated as dance lies in the performance of a product made up of structured recognisable movement sequences in the form of double *heliaki*, that is, movement *heliaki* embedded in

115

Adrienne L. Kaeppler

either text or beauty, which enhances poetic *heliaki*. This cultural form based on double *heliaki* is but one of the formalised structured movement dimensions of various activity systems in Tonga that are social metaphors, expressing the underlying principles and cultural philosophy of hierarchical rank and prestige.

GLOSSARY

ʻaho meʻe – day dance, formal dance
ʻāvanga – sickness or infatuation believed to be caused by spirits
ʻeiki – chief
faiva – any kind of task, feat, craft, or performance requiring skill or ability, or anything at which an individual or group is clever
fakamuifonua – style of wringing kava
fakatapu – introductory section of a speech
fakateki – side head tilt
fau – fibre strainer used for mixing and straining kava
fono – relish of pig and yams to be eaten with kava, but ritually taken away
haka – to move the hands rhythmically, especially while singing
haka fakalongolongo – *haka* performed without accompanying poetry
heliaki – not going straight, to say one thing and mean another
hiva kakala – sweet songs
kai fono – person who ritually takes away the *fono* and eats it
kāinga – ego-based kindred
kakā – parrot
kātoanga – festival, public festivity or celebration
kava – an infusion of the root of the pepper plant, *Piper methysticum*
kotone – tree with fruit eaten by wild pigeons
lakalaka – to advance or make progress (literally 'to step out')
maile – a bush with small leaves (Alyria sp.)
matāpule – ceremonial attendant
māʻuluʻulu – choreographed group speech, performed while seated
meʻelaufola – *faiva* emphasising outstretched arms
meʻetuʻupaki – *faiva* performed standing with paddles (*paki*)
meke – Fijian performance with formalised movements
milolua – style of wringing kava
mokopuna ʻeiki – grandchild of high status
moʻonia – way of stringing flowers
ʻotu haka – seated *faiva*
pō faiva – informal *faiva*
pō meʻe – night dance, informal dance
pō sipi – spontaneous love poems
puaka toho – pig of the largest category
pulotu haka – choreographer
siale – flowering plant
sēkē – *faiva* using long sticks
tafi – *faiva* similar to *māʻuluʻulu* often performed first in a group of *faiva*
tatau – closing counterpart of the *fakatapu* or closing statement

116

tau – section of sung poetry which contains the essence of the poetry and during which the performers do their best

tauʿaʿalo – work songs

taumafa kava – kava drinking in which the king partakes

tauʿolunga – 'dance' or *faiva* which often emphasises the performer rather than the poetry

touʿa – persons whose duty it is to prepare kava for drinking, especially on ceremonial occasions

tulaufale – supporting dancers who accompany the primary dancers in a *tauʿolunga*

ʿufi – yams

ula – *faiva* or dance which often emphasises the performer rather than the poetry

NOTES

Research in Tonga was carried out for twenty months from 1964 to 1976 supported by Public Health Service Fellowship No. 5–F1–MH–25,984–02 from the National Institute of Mental Health and by the Wenner-Gren Foundation for Anthropological Research, to whom I wish to express my appreciation. I also wish to thank the Government of Tonga under their majesties the late Queen Sālote Tupou III and the present King Tāufaʿāhau Tupou IV, as well as the many Tongans who helped me in my work, especially Sister Tuʿifua, Tupou Posesi Fanua, the Honourable Veʿehala, Baron Vaea, Vaisima Hopoate, Ana Malia Hopoate, and Tuʿimala Maʿafu.

1 Hanna critically reviews various definitions, but there is still something lacking (1980:17–24).

2 I was present at the state *kātoanga* and *taumafa kava* during which the validation of the titles of King Tupou IV and the crown prince took place (1967 and 1975).

3 Food presentations are also given nonpublicly by bringing the gifts to the kitchen or private entrance of the receiver. This is often the case when the giver is of higher rank than the receiver. For such nonpublic presentations formalised movements or counting are not done.

4 Apparently because on the previous day the king had stopped the *lakalaka* performances before Kolovai had their turn to perform.

5 This is not a complete description of a kava ceremony. For more information see Collocott 1927.

6 As will be seen below, one function of the *fakateki* head movement is to draw and hold the attention of the observers.

7 For more defined *fakatapu* see Kaeppler 1967, 1976a, and 1976b.

8 I am indebted to V. Huluholo Moungaloa for the text and assistance in translation. Here, as in all Tongan texts, there are many possible interpretations, all of which add to the *heliaki*.

9 The composer of the poetry is known as *pulotu taʿanga*. The individual responsible for giving the poetry its melodic, polyphonic, and rhythmic setting is sometimes known as *pulotu hiva*; however, this is often a communal activity which can be accomplished almost spontaneously, owing to the distinctive stylistic characteristics which are well known. An indi-

117

Adrienne L. Kaeppler

vidual who can compose poetry, musical setting, and movement is known by the more elevated term *punake* – even if he was not responsible for all three elements of a specific composition.

10 For a description of a set of movements that accompanies a stanza of *lakalaka* poetry see Kaeppler 1972:212–13 and 1976a:209–10.

REFERENCES

Collocott, E.E.V. 1927. 'Kava ceremonial in Tonga'. *Journal of the Polynesian Society*, 36(141):21–47.
Hanna, Judith Lynne. 1980. *To Dance Is Human*. Austin: University of Texas Press.
Kaeppler, Adrienne L. 1967a. 'Folklore as expressed in the dance in Tonga'. *Journal of American Folklore*, 80(316):160–8.
1967b. 'Preservation and evolution of form and function in two types of Tongan dance'. In Genevieve A. Highland, et al. (eds.), *Polynesian Culture History: Essays in Honor of Kenneth P. Emory*. Bernice P. Bishop Museum Special Publication 56. Honolulu: Bishop Museum Press.
1971a. 'Aesthetics of Tongan dance'. *Ethnomusicology* 15(2):175–85.
1971b. 'Rank in Tonga'. *Ethnology* 10(2):174–93.
1972. 'Method and theory in analyzing dance structure with an analysis of Tongan dance'. *Ethnomusicology* 16(2):173–217.
1976a. Dance and interpretation of Pacific traditional literature. In Adrienne L. Kaeppler and H. Arlo Nimmo (eds.), *Directions in Pacific Traditional Literature: Essays in Honor of Katharine Luomala*. Bishop Museum Special Publication 62. Honolulu: Bishop Museum Press.
1976b. 'Dance in Tonga: the communication of social values through an artistic medium'. In Daniel Lerner and Jim Richstad (eds.), *Communication in the Pacific*. Honolulu: East–West Communication Institute.
1978. 'Melody, drone, and decoration: underlying structures and surface manifestations in Tongan art and society'. In Michael Greenhalgh and Vincent Megaw (eds.), *Art in Society: Studies in Styles, Culture and Aesthetics*. London: Duckworth.

4 'A line of boys': Melpa dance as a symbol of maturation

ANDREW STRATHERN

You, you have men,
Their arms linked in long rows together.
But we, we do not have men,
We are few, a line of boys dancing.

So sang the men of two allied clans in 1974, when they danced on the occasion of their gift of six hundred pigs, ten thousand Australian dollars, and many accessory items to a multitude of partners in the prestigious pair of clans living to their east. In truth they were out-numbered; but the song, with its delicate, almost pathetic message, in fact also conveyed an opposite meaning of strength. It was sung by many men, whose voices carried it far beyond the confined, rec-tangular ceremonial ground where their dancing line was drawn up; whose performance was watched by crowds of people from all the neighbouring groups; and whose material gifts would percolate into dozens of further networks of exchange as a result of the day's trans-actions. The song, apparently self-deprecating, is in fact the reverse of this: it points out how much its singers could do, even though they are fewer than their partners. To be men is to hold occasions like this, known as *moka* ceremonies. Hence the mere fact of holding the dance denies the song's overt message again: the singers are men, and the time also is 'mature' for their prestation.

These ceremonies were performed by men of the Melpa, who live in the Highlands of Papua New Guinea. In previous publications on the Melpa, Marilyn Strathern and I have discussed their exchange system, leadership, group structure, gender roles, and forms of self-decoration (M. Strathern 1972, 1979; A.J. Strathern 1971, 1972; A.J. and M. Strathern 1971). Yet in none of these have we concentrated specifically on dancing as an integral part of the social process. Our nearest approach to such an exposition was in the book on self-dec-oration, where we described the main dances and explained, in a descriptive manner, the way in which they form a part of exchange ceremonies and religious rituals (see index, s.v. Dances, in A.J. and

119

Andrew Strathern

M. Strathern 1971). The emphasis of the book was rather on decorations as forms of display and the apparent codes that underlie these. Here I attempt to examine the dances themselves in more detail, though I am without professional ability to analyse them in depth; in particular I consider exactly what part dance movements as such have to play in the activity complexes where they are found. The question is thus 'why dance?' or rather 'what is it that we are referring to in talking of Melpa dance'?

The key to this problem is located back in the decorations themselves, and in the obvious point that the chief, though by no means the only, stress in these is on the adornment of the head with plumes, primarily those of the birds of paradise that are found in the Highlands of Papua New Guinea. These birds not only possess such plumes, they also dance with them as part of their sexual displays; and although Melpa dances are not just sexual displays, the people themselves do consciously draw analogies between their actions and those of birds.[1] The overall analogue is that of maturity: the birds grow their full plumes only when mature, and after a period of dancing they lose them again in moulting. The process is a cyclical one of growth, display, decline, and new growth, exactly analogous to the cyclicity of *moka* exchange festivals. What dancing 'does' at these festivals is, then, to make the statement that 'the cycle is at its climax'.

Melpa dances and moka exchange

The Melpa have no general term corresponding to the word 'dance'. My delimitation of the set of activities for discussion here is therefore an observer's construct; but the construct is no more than a list of named categories which the Melpa do recognise: *mørl, kenan, werl, mørli, yap, kng kui, ware, amb kenan, kor kondi*. It is not vital for my argument to set out criteria in terms of which these form a unique set, sharing any single common element exclusive to the set itself. However, they all involve rhythmic, concerted movements; the first seven are performed always with large numbers of participants whose movements are coordinated by drumming and/or singing; the eighth (courting song) shares all the features of the preceding ones, except that it takes place between two partners at a time, and only the upper parts of their bodies move; and the ninth shares the same features again except that it is unaccompanied by song. All the major dances are also performed en masse by members of social groups such as clans or their in-marrying spouses, and those who dance together also cooperate in many other ways.

120

Mørl and *kenan* are the main, formal men's dances performed at *moka*; *werl* is the corresponding dance for adult women. *Mørli* (or *mølya*) and *yap* are dances for young girls and young men respectively, done at the same time as *werl*, *mørl* and *kenan*. *Kng kui* and *ware* are terms for special dances occasionally performed at pig-killing festivals. *Kng kui* properly belongs to the neighbouring Wahgi Valley culture. The term means 'cooked pork', and the dance is performed to celebrate pig sacrifices. *Ware* is a dance imported into the Hagen area in pre-colonial times from the Jimi Valley region to the north, and older informants in the Dei Council area were able early in 1983 to describe how this dance was first imported by their forefathers. In December 1983 men from the Mokei Komonke clan held a large *moka* dance, at which they performed *mørl*, other Mokei came dressed for both *kng kui* and *ware*. For the *ware* they held long painted sticks and sang words reminiscent of those used in the women's *werl*. *Amb kenan* is the term for a courting ceremony in which couples sway in time to accompanying songs sung by spectators. *Kor kondi*, 'to finish the spirit (cult)', is a term which refers to the highly distinctive dance movements that accompany the ending of the Female Spirit cult, in which the cultists stream out in pairs from an enclosure and describe a U-shaped course through the crowd of spectators, stamping the ground with great speed so that it shakes under their feet.

From these preliminary remarks it can be seen that the central categories for consideration here are *mørl*, *kenan*, and *werl*, with their counterpoints *mørli* and *yap*. Courting song and spirit dance are special cases in my argument, and I will return to them later.

The formal characteristics of the dances to which I am attributing (as I think the Melpa do) central significance are as follows. *Mørl* is performed by rows of men in full decorations, standing in a line and facing outwards to the ubiquitous crowds who come to witness the final days of a *moka* prestation (obligatory gift). The men stand in an almost statuesque pose, with full headdresses and wigs, their faces charcoaled and eyes picked out in white. They carry spears or bows and arrows as a reminder of their male warriorhood; or they hold drums, which they beat in unison, while they execute the dance itself. This consists simply of rising on their toes, then bending the knees in a downwards movement, so as to make the full front apron which is worn sweep gracefully outwards in time with the nodding of plumes on the head. Spectators comment particularly on the dancers' ability to keep in time with one another, to hold their shoulders and back straight while bending the knees (a difficult task, requiring concentration and bodily tension), and to make their plumes and aprons

121

move gracefully together. Failure in these regards, like other short-comings of decoration, are taken as omens of misfortune for the future, while success indicates ancestral favour and therefore future as well as present prosperity. *Mørl*, therefore, is a rather static dance, but is the ultimate in display: literally a tableau for the minute examination of detail in dress and movement. Spectators jostle each other to see the dancers clearly; men walk up and down in front of the line whacking the ground with sticks to clear a little space and enable the row to be seen; wives occasionally correct a part of a husband's attire and offer drinks. Sometimes a man decorates his eldest unmarried daughter as a man and she joins the line; or a girl, decorated in female style, will join her brother.

Kenan is more lively. It is often performed as a second stage of dancing, after an initial period of *mørl*. It is also less technically demanding. Before a *moka* there are usually several days on which men get together to practise *mørl*, organising their decorations, tuning their drums, and testing out the song that they will sing as an accompaniment to the dance itself. *Kenan* is not practised in this way. For it, the men line up in sets of four or more, and march round the whole ceremonial ground, stamping the ground with purposeful tread, beating their drums in exact time with their feet, and usually making a special ssh-ssh-ssh hissing noise which at a climax becomes 'ish-waa-ish, ish-waa-ish', giving a sense of surging movement. Aprons decorated with pigs' tails are sometimes worn if *kenan* is to be the main dance for a *moka*, and these fly flamboyantly from side to side as the men stamp forward. The dance executes a complete figure around the oblong shape of the ceremonial groups, especially encircling the raised tub of planted cordylines that is to be found at the front of a communal men's house, which heads the ground itself. In this tub, the *pokla mbo*, are planted magical substances to draw in wealth goods, and ancestral ghosts are thought to cluster around the cordyline plants. The full name for *kenan* is *nde mbo kenan*, 'the *kenan* [for] the tree shrubs', a term that indicates the significance of the action of marching around the cordylines. I see a structural parallel, as well as a contrast, here between the basic encircling movement in *kenan* and the movements in funeral sequences when mourners race around the ceremonial ground, then return to encircle the corpse of the dead person (usually a big-man or leader) raised on a trestle above them. (My inclusion of funeral behaviour here indicates an artificiality in the initial set of 'dances' that I listed: while the Melpa would certainly agree that *moka* dances are in a sense the opposite of funerals, the stylised movements of grief, done as a kind of parade, might reason-

ably be considered a form of dance. And I am arguing that understanding *kenan*, in particular, is enhanced by seeing it in a relationship
of contrast with funeral sequences.)

Werl is the most stately of the women's dances. Men are never
inducted into it as girls are into *mørl*, and it is dominated by married
women rather than by girls. Essentially, women decorate and perform
werl in celebration of their role as rearers of pig herds for their husbands and equally to display a profusion of female ornaments and
headdresses as well as their skill in the dance itself. The row of *werl*
dancers, however, is always shorter than that of the men doing *mørl*.
Usually the women gather in a knot at a spot removed from the men,
though on the same ceremonial ground. They turn inwards to one
another, singing and beating their drums rather slowly and carefully,
as though swift movements would disturb their elaborate decorations.
In the dance they bend their torsos forward to left, then right, at the
same time executing a rubbing movement with their knees. They
appear to be communicating primarily with one another, whereas the
men clearly throw their personae outwards to the crowd. The words
they sing parallel in sentiment those of the men, describing their
supposed inadequacy in facing the public gaze, because they are so
few, and are 'ashamed': in fact, of course, the dance is a unique
occasion of display for them.[2]

Mørl, succeeded by *kenan*, and *werl* are all often done at the same
time, and the noise that rises from the *moka* ground, mingled later
with the squeals of pigs brought out for transfer and the long drawn
out cries of orators, is an overpowering testimomy to the tumult of
human energy and communication suddenly concentrated in one place.
The dances stand for the convergence and control of that energy, and
the three chief dances that I have described are concerned with overt
political and public aims: the success of the gift, marking the success
of the husbands and wives of the group and the big-men who are
the driving force in the *moka*. But decorations and dancing are thought
to be sexually attractive also; and this concern with sexuality is shown
overtly in the two companion dances to the main ones, *mørli* and *yap*,
sometimes known simply as *mørli*. In the first, girls, other than those
in full decorations, link arms in a circle and sing, surrounding a
number of other girls, women, and children. As their song reaches
a crescendo they leap up and down vigorously until they are mo-
mentarily exhausted. More girls join them, until the circle grows un-
wieldy and splits. Boys and men form rival circles, which grow faster
than the girls', and they spin constantly round a mass of spectators,
male and female, watching from inside. Married women and men

123

Andrew Strathern

also join in these circles enthusiastically. Men can dance with anyone they wish, but their wives must choose unmarriageable relatives or else risk their husbands' anger. Wives sometimes attack their husbands also, when they are joined by unmarried girls who might represent a sexual threat. Altogether, *yap* and *mørli* dances are occasions both of boisterous enjoyment and high sexual tension, and the songs sung in them often reflect this very clearly, being quite explicit about the actions of sexual intercourse. The songs are sometimes connected with the *moka*, and occasionally in fact may convey a serious message (for example, a challenge to one of the groups involved in the *moka* or an expression of veiled joy at the death of a big-man in another group). But often they are simply sexually provocative. The main *mørl* dancers may even join in the *yap* once their other business is finished, and the whole ground is transformed into a swirling mass of men in dancing circles, a complete transformation from the thin, solemn line of *mørl* dancers, watched by a jostling but otherwise inactive mass of spectators. *Amb kenan*, or courting dances, often follow in the evenings from *mørl* and *yap*, and many a young man ends up bleary-eyed and exhausted for a week after two days and nights of continuous involvement.[3]

Amb kenan itself is highly formalised, and has to be learnt as a skill. Young men, unmarried and married, arrive at a girl's mother's house in the evening, and ask if the daughter will court with them. They have usually heard in advance that the girl will do so and that she has some companions with her who will also join in. They sit down and begin to sing, until the first girl emerges from a back room and kneels down. A boy sits cross-legged near her, waves his head in a sinuous invitation answered by her own, then they make contact with their noses and foreheads, in time with the singing, duck down together once, twice or more, and begin again. It is a definite art to perform this with correct timing, and if a boy makes a mistake the girl may hit him, and he is entitled to pass the blow on, so that it makes the rounds of everyone. Then they try again. Boys are supposed to put love magic into cigarettes, which they offer the girls, or to rub it on their skin with deft touches; girls to place similar magic in the paint they wear on their foreheads. *Amb kenan*, as may be gathered, is a cross between a dance, a kiss, and a conversation in our culture, but it is distinct from all these in its precise form. In the skill that it requires it interestingly resembles more the *mørl* and *werl* dances than the *mørli* and *yap*. Like these main dances, it is also a sign of seriousness. To 'turn head' with a partner on successive nights is likely to indicate a definite interest rather than a passing fancy.

124

(Numbers of examples of *amb kenan* songs are given, with text and translation, in A.J. Strathern 1974.)

The set of dances I am considering has opened with *mørl* and closed with *amb kenan*; but the overall place of the dance in the context of *moka* itself has now to be considered. In days preceding the final transfer of goods at a *moka* the speeches and promises of partners have gradually been transformed into actual wealth goods, and knots of men holding practise sessions. There are rival attempts at marking the final day, until the word of one big-man or another prevails. An important man expects to have to find feathers and shells with which to decorate his wife and perhaps a daughter as well as himself and any close male relatives who ask for his help. He has to borrow some plumes, repaying their owners with pork (from pigs killed in sacrifice just before the final day) or money. A tremendous amount of individual effort, worry, and expense is thus needed before the *mørl* dance can occur. Indeed the procurement of decorations is only a minor part of the whole process, the main purpose of which is to give away pigs and other wealth goods, and a big-man's prestige is shown most crucially in these goods, which he gives away, rather than in the decorations he wears or the part he plays in the dancing. At the same time there is no doubt that decorations and dancing are also important in their own right. A big-man may refer in speeches to the number of plumes he has, and younger big-men, who may still be keen to attract more wives to themselves, take meticulous care in making themselves up for dance occasions. On the day of the dance, although enduring prestige is gained from the numbers of pigs given away, in the shorter term many more people come to the ceremonial ground just to see and evaluate the appearance of the dancers themselves, both men and women.

It is for this reason, perhaps, that the day's proceedings always begin with the dance itself. Participants prepare themselves at home or in secluded spots nearby, then gradually assemble. Desultory and tentative drum beating and singing soon build up to a powerful crescendo that rises above the chatter of the crowd, like a canopy of sound capping the tremendous scene of colour and movement that fills the *moka* ground from end to end. The point I wish to stress here is that the dance develops to its full pitch of excitement just before the pigs, and other gifts, are actually given away; that is, while the group of men and women is still fully in possession and is about to show its power in the act of prestation. An appearance of transcendental unity is thus imprinted on an occasion which in practice is also marked by individual rivalries: neither the gifts nor the decorations of partici-

Andrew Strathern

pants are equal, yet equality and unity are suggested by the orderly fact of participation and by the customary meiosis employed in the songs.[4]

The sign of a switch to the next stage is given by doffing the head-dresses. This is done sometimes to avoid the spoiling effects of rain, which often falls in the early afternoon, and to make it easier for both sexes to race up and down the rows of pigs which their helpers – kinsfolk and recipients – have tied to the lines of stakes prepared for them. Or they may make the race in a more stately and restrained manner, the women especially beating on their drums as they do so; in this case the headdresses are retained. This race is called *el rangkek ongk poromen*, 'they seize their weapons and go', and it culminates in a heel-kicking dance around the *pokla mbo*, just before the transfer; after it the speeches follow.[5]

It is obvious from the use of weapons as decorations, and from the meaning of the dark charcoal disguises that men wear on their faces – in contrast with the women's brighter colours – that some of the intensity in these *moka* dances comes from their suggested reenact-ment of the hostilities of warfare. In almost every case, a *moka* pres-tation relates to a history of killings, either between the groups involved, or as a result of one group helping the other as an ally. While the exchanges are meant to bring peace, it is clear that the dance itself also contains a reminder of hostility, which can be ex-pressed more forcefully in that it is nonverbal and implicit. This theme of hostility to others is sometimes actually picked up verbally: in a song that Ongka, a prominent leader, composed for a *moka* in 1971, he referred to some mutual enemies of both his own group and that of the recipients. He thus threw hostility out beyond the circle of performers and spectators. Yet it is also true that hostilities exist closer to home. One of Ongka's own exchange partners, an in-law of his, previously tried to poison him when he visited to ask about a present of pearl shells (A.J. Strathern 1979a:92–5, 145–6).

The 'war rush', then, marks the end of the dance phase. It trans-mutes hostility into the claims of achievement, emphasised by the final leaping at the *pokla mbo*. Then an orator moves down each row of pigs, kicking them and intoning a formal phrase of presentation, 'Kill this little one and eat it'. (The pigs are usually full grown and are destined for more prestations before being finally consumed.) Then come the speeches, fully ritualised as *el-ik* (again, this means 'war talk' or 'arrow talk'), or as more lengthy, individualised state-ments. Each speaker voices sentiments on behalf of his group, while also making claims and seeking impact for himself. Women do not

126

speak at all, nor do they bother greatly to listen, though some do. They are more likely to busy themselves with sorting out the pigs, careful removal of their decorations, seeing to their families, or eating a snack. The men's seemingly untiring talk continues till rain or sundown force an end to the day.

The serious dancing dies just before the wealth is given away. It is a celebration of strength, the ability to give, to outshine others, which must be followed by an actual prestation, yet the prestation is almost a low-key affair by comparison. In effect, all major decisions have been taken long in advance. The act of handing over the goods is a public, legal gesture. Many of the speeches concentrate as much on future plans as on the occasion in hand, for each *moka* leads to another in the 'rope' or chain of partnerships. The dance itself makes the most emphatic of claims on behalf of the donors, and it does so by presenting them as a group, in one sense undifferentiated and at the height of their communal existence, although in other senses (quality and numbers of plumes, for example) they clearly are different to the discerning and interested eye. The dance thus presents an amalgam of counterposed unit and differentiation. Drums beat together, voices are raised in unison, 'suits' of decorations are worn by agreement: yet still one individual may look more attractive or may out-perform the others. And those who look and dance best are not necessarily those who hold the highest status in the *moka* transactions themselves. The same is true of dancers in the Female Spirit cult, where the dance emphatically shares the quality of climax, followed by prestation, that I have outlined for the *moka* dances. After the spirit dance, too, the men remove their plumes and distribute meat from high trestles to hundreds of spectators who jostle at them with upturned spears. The prestation phase is almost like a dismantling of the portmanteau of persons which the dance phase has temporarily put together, at the same instant achieving a timeless restatement of the group and its values. In prestations, people give of themselves, cut up their pigs, take off their plumes one by one and pack them away, show themselves from behind their disguises, talk to their partners instead of singing and dancing to the general public. They become partitioned and individualised again.

The themes of maturity and climax

In earlier analyses of Hagen decorations we have stressed two separate points: one the persistent contrast between effects seen as 'light' and 'dark'; the other, that decorations are seen not so much as en-

Andrew Strathern

hancements of the body but as indications of the inner state of the person. This inner state is evinced both in the overall quality of decorations worn and in their colour schemes, which project hostility or friendship towards exchange partners. But the dance itself, I am now arguing, also represents the values of maturity and climax, by which time itself is socially marked and structured.

This argument is not one that I have devised at random. It is my own analytical invention, but it stems from the reflections of Ongka, a big-man, in answer to questions put to him in the course of enquiries about birds of paradise and the use of their plumes for decorations. The enquiries were made in 1978, as a part of a project to film the birds and to explain their significance for the New Guinea Highlanders. Ongka went with the film-maker (Mr. David Parer) and me up to the forest places where birds of paradise display and began to tell us about their behaviour:

When the bird is young and its plumage has not yet grown, it just flies around feeding on fruits and drinking water, but when its crests grow long, it realises and says 'Ah, now my plumes have grown' and so it goes to a display spot and there it dances. When its plumes are not grown, it will not display like this. It is in the same way that we people wear these plumes only when we are making a *moka* festival, at ordinary times we just keep them carefully wrapped up and hidden away, this is like the times when the bird does not have its plumes. When we take them out and use them for a dance, this is like the time when the bird's plumes have grown. We measure the times when we wear them like this, we do not do this all of the time. When the bird moults also and its plumes fall off it stops dancing and calling out and it does not display itself. Later its plumes grow back and it says, 'Ah now let me dance and let the birds see me and people hear me and know I am here.' That is what the birds do, and we people do likewise [*to tendep etimon*] . . .

When the crest plumes of the *ketepa* [King of Saxony] bird rise up high it makes its call kit-kit-kit-kit, they are like the tail of a snake standing up. We see the dance of that bird, we shoot it and take the plumes home and we wear them for our *mørl* dance in imitation of the bird itself. We do everything as the bird does it. Now, as to the *mek* [Princess Stephanie] bird, when it dances it makes its long tail feathers sway about. The *rumba* [Sicklebill] comes to a branch and says mbra mbra mbra mbra and when its two tail feathers are showing clearly, it does its dance. We make our *mørl* dance as these birds make theirs, as the *rumba* dances so we dance, as the *mek* dances so we dance, as the *ketepa* dances so we dance. Our dances, *mørl, kenan, ware, kng kui*, these are all like the birds' dances. We do not do it only by our own wishes, we obey all these birds and do our dances.

In these two statements, both recorded in the same sequence of questions, Ongka sets up two models, one general and the other particularistic:

128

1 The cyclical nature of *moka* festivals, with their long period of latency followed by climax, depletion, latency, and climax again, is compared to the natural cycle of the growth of birds of paradise, their acquisition of plumage, dance, and moult, followed by regrowth of plumage and resumption of dance.

2 Particular movements in the *mørl* dance that involve the swishing and swaying of plumes are traced back to the movements made by the birds themselves in their courting displays. (It is important to add here that none of these movements are regularly described in these terms by people themselves. We are not dealing with any direct form of 'magical' thinking or of actions thought to represent those of birds. Instead, Ongka is drawing a conscious analogy, in which his particularistic second model is really there to back up the force of his general first model.)

Model one conflates the individual growth cycles of the birds from infancy to maturity with their regular moulting cycle in adulthood. I think that this is not fortuitous, because this conflation is 'required' by the complexity of the social analogue that Ongka is suggesting. In the *moka* dances those who dance claim maturity in the sense of their own adult status, their ability to acquit themselves well in a public performance by adults. They are mature in this sense, grown-up like the crests of the grown-up birds that they wear. Buried in this claim there is also an implicit idea, it appears, that such status is associated with male gender, just as only male birds grow plumes.[6] Yet if so the idea is muted, because women too wear these plumes and thus claim the values associated with them. Second, there is the sense of maturity and social climax. The birds display before mating. The people dance before giving away their wealth. Wealth grows 'on the skin of people' and is then disbursed. People dance when they have wealth to give away, and they wear the plumes both as forms of wealth in their own right and as signs that wealth goods such as pigs are now being given. Climax also means depletion, and the climax is brief compared to the long periods of building up resources. At these times, plumes are kept hidden away, while people get their hands dirty with work. Then they wash, put on their plumes, dance, give away their pigs.

Finally here, we may note that maturity as climax is brief but cyclical. Maturity in the life-cycle sense is enduring and leads to recurrent climaxes and depletions. In the same way an individual, once grown-up, enters the *moka* system and stays in it for a lifetime, building up and disbursing wealth cyclically.

If the conjunction of dance with bird of paradise plumes has now

Table 4.1. *Form and movement in Melpa dances*

	Dance steps	Orientation	Coverage of space
Mørl	Bending of knees, followed by rising to tiptoes and falling again. Body stiff, shoulders square, accompanied by drum beating and singing in unison. Eyes staring straight outwards at the spectators, but no communication takes place in conversation with these.	Facing outwards to the crowd in a long, single row at one side of the ceremonial ground, or around it, always facing the spectators. Donors and recipients in separate sections of the line, but still conceptually a part of it in contrast with the spectators.	Static. The line remains in place. Its rear side is not strictly part of the display until the line breaks up and the men do *kenan* instead of run up and down the row of pigs.
Kenan	Rhythmic stamping of the feet in time with drum beats, producing a sense of surging movement and slightly rolling gait. Weapons may be held stiffly in one hand. The front dancers may stamp on one spot for a while, then move forward.	The dancers make a pathway through the crowd. The single line of *mørl* is replaced by serried ranks. The dancers do not look directly at the crowd at all this time but at each other's backs.	An encircling movement, in which the dancers go round the top of the ceremonial ground and back again, once or several times, before ending the dance and beginning the actual transfer of wealth.
Kor kondi	Rhythmic stamping but very much faster than in *kenan*. Men lined up in pairs, body held stiff and arms support pearl shell or piece of fern. No singing or drumming.	Pathway movement, encircling. Orientation as in *kenan*.	Encircling movement, through the crowd, which leaves a narrow space only for the dancers. Spasmodic, with sudden stops and starts as dancers become tired.
Werl	Bending of knees, but accompanied by movements from side to side with knees pressed together. Drum beats follow	Dancers may be in a row, but tend to face inwards to one another, and then outwards again. They occupy a space in	Static, as in *mørl*. The women stay in a knot together in a particular part of the ground. They may move en masse to a better

	the movements of the body. Singing in time also, with very deliberate and slow emphasis.	the interior of the ceremonial ground also, rather than at its margins. In this sense, they are 'enclosed', whereas the men 'enclose' the ground.	position and re-form as before.
Mørli	Dancers link arms and sing, then at climax of song leap up and down vigorously. Rest, then repeat.	The dancers form a circle, and enclose in it women and girls as captive spectators. They thus create a body of spectators within the wider body, which remains encompassing.	Static in one spot, although the circle may grow.
Yap	Dancers link arms and sing, and continuously twirl round. No single climax.	Circle, with captive spectators as in *mørli*.	Expanding circle. *Yap* circles tend to grow and fill the whole space of the ceremonial ground.
Funeral sequences (1) Men	The mourners rush in, greeted by men already there. Together, they may run round the ceremonial ground before returning to encircle the raised corpse.	There is no separate set of spectators. The mourners incorporate one another into a total movement, revolving itself around the dead person.	Right round the ceremonial ground at first, then encircling the corpse, with tears, song and wringing of hands.
(2) Women	Rush in, after the men, and immediately begin encircling the corpse. They are dressed in wild leaves and carry paw-paw and cordyline branches. Skin caked with mud, as men. They also perform the shuffling, hopping movements known as *ka okli*.	As men.	Encircling the corpse.

been correctly explained for the Melpa as a condensed symbol of maturity and climax, we can see the force of those songs that deny this central theme by suggesting that the men are in fact boys or the women are just weak creatures, suffering from shame, with no strong men to support them. The facts of their decoration, their bearing, their production of wealth goods for prestation, all belie these words, so that their meaning becomes: although we are below par in our own terms, we are still strong enough to excel over our rivals. The technique of communication here is similar to that of the *amb mui pukl wal* ceremony, in which women, dressed in a kind of reversal of what would constitute good decorations, march silently around their men, who are performing *mørl* for a *moka*. The women's decorations are a way of saying to rivals, who have whispered that the dancing clansmen are 'rubbish-men', that they know these rumours and are ironically conforming to them. Yet it is all a pretence, for in reality they are strong and will make a fine *moka* to humiliate their rivals (A.J. and M. Strathern 1971:54).

Function and form in the dance

What do dance movements express? As with decorations themselves and their meaning, the problem is not easy. Ongka's exegesis, quoted in the previous section, gives us a clue to what *moka* dances in Melpa society basically represent, but it is equally clear that the dance movements as such are not a one-to-one recreation of the dance patterns of birds. The wearing of plumes is itself a metonymy that assimilates the qualities of birds of paradise into the figure of the dancer: the plumes are not just symbols of wealth, they are themselves directly a form of wealth and directly a source of attractiveness. It might seem as though all the emphasis is on the external accoutrements of the dancers, and not on the condition of their bodies or the actions they perform. But this also is inaccurate. Oil is used to make the skin light and shining, and the dancer has to be fit and well-balanced in order to perform properly. *Mørl* and the earth-shaking dance for the Female Spirit cult are exhausting activities, and this is why they have to be carried out in short bursts of a few minutes at a time with brief periods of rest. It is worth while to consider again the actual movements in these dances, and I shall do so in terms of (1) the dance 'steps' and associated aspects of body posture, (2) the orientations of the dancers in carrying out the steps, and (3) the space covered or moved over in the course of the dance.

Table 4.1 summarises some information under these headings. It can be seen that *mørl* is the most static and fixed of the dances, and gives the spectators the maximum opportunity to view its performers. Donors and recipients combine to present the tableau, which consists preeminently of the front of the person, the part that exchange partners show each other, the public self par excellence. It is this very fixedness of *mørl* that I suggest is connected with the idea of maturity and achievement. In one of Ongka's songs there are the lines

> I am a man who was pushed around
> By the strong groups here, and so
> I can only muster a line of boys
> To dance here before you.

(A.J. Strathern 1979a:145)

In these, the 'line of boys' theme is combined with that of being 'pushed' off one's land, of inability to hold one's place. It is exactly that, again, which the form of the *mørl* line denies, by representing strength and stability. The drum beats and song move up and down that stable line, like currents of electricity, giving a sense of pulsating communication within permanence.

With *kenan*, strength is activated into further movement. The static encompassing action or *mørl* is converted into an active encircling. In *mørl*, one might suggest, the ancestral ghosts who stay at the backs of people remain latent. In *kenan* they are invoked by the act of stamping round the *nde mbo*, the tub of planted cordylines at the head of the ceremonial ground, for this also is a site of ancestral power.[7] The dancers are in formation and do not look at the crowd, but they are still entirely exposed to inspection by them and are therefore on display as performers to spectators. The *kor* (Female Spirit) dance also falls into place here as a greatly heightened and intensified version of the *kenan* movement. Its atmosphere is appropriately that of a sacred drama, for one side of the dancers is said to represent the Spirit herself, while their partners on the other side are said to be her husbands, the men of the clan (A.J. Strathern 1979b:38). The transformation of men into spirits is marked also by the cessation of singing and drumming. The Spirit does not speak: she has no need to, for her power works directly. This point suggests that singing and drumming are human evocations of power, structurally contrasted with spirit power, although I would not wish to claim much certainty for this proposition. Finally, funerals can be seen as a kind of anti-*kenan* movement. The mourners run, rather than stamping; they twirl weapons, rather than holding them stiffly (twirling is a sign of hostility to enemies, a threat to kill); everyone who comes is incorporated into the movement rather than a clear performer/spectator distinction being maintained; and the encircling action returns the mourners to the corpse with their sense of grief and dissolution rather than to the cordyline tub, which presents the dead reconstituted as powerful guardian spirits, as is done in the *kenan*.

The women's major dance, the *werl*, is neither static nor encircling, unlike the men's *mørl* and *kenan*. The women form a separate group to dance, though their songs parallel those of the men. They orient themselves alternately inwards to one another, and outwards to the crowd; at each point they also move from side to side with their bodies, in an action that Ongka compared to the dodging of arrows in war:

Do you see the big dark plumes of the *rumba* bird [sicklebill]? The women are wearing those, obtained for them by their husbands, because they do hard work in caring for the pigs. They are doing their *werl* dance which marks the movements of dodging arrows in war, or the action of a divination stick pushed backwards and forwards into the floor of a house; or perhaps it is like using a piece from a corncob to scratch one's skin. (Interview of 26 August 1978)

Ongka repeats the theme of men decorating women as a return for their hard work in pig rearing: that is, they are repaid by access to the wearing of plumes, which men associate with their own world of publicity and prestige. Then he goes out of his way to describe women's dance movements in a *jeu d'esprit* that moves from the serious to the apparently absurd. In the same vein I have once heard the men's *mørl* dance described as involving the flicking up and down of the dancers' penises inside their aprons.[8] The sexual innuendo implied is, however, one that is almost entirely edited out of the meaning of those dances I describe as 'major' (the *mørl*, *kenan*, and *werl*). It appears more clearly both in song and movements when we consider the minor pair of *mørli* and *yap*. In *werl*, it is the structural movement of inwards/outwards turning and side-to-side orientation that appears most striking, and I relate it to women's overall role in exchanges as mediating, linking persons, who are seen from both front and back, who move between groups or 'lines' of men, who face more than one way, who must balance claims. In practice men must do these things as well, but in ideological representation they do not, whereas ideology directly represents women as doing so, because their interstitial role is both what makes them valuable and what reduces their own potential for solidarity and power. Thus they sing and dance to one another in the *werl*, but their movements express a balance between alternatives, whereas the men seemingly dance for the spectators, but the form of their dance represents their claim to internal group solidarity.

Mörli and *yap*, finally, are marked off clearly from the major dances by their creation of mini-groups of spectators encircled by the dancers. The public is thereby fractionated, and the dancers may explicitly sing of sexual themes as a separate show from the main business of the day, or when the main business is over. Here again, however, a male/ female contrast appears, in that the men continuously encircle their spectators, moving round and round them all the time, whereas the girls express the excitement of their own climax by leaping on the spot. There is no close or necessary correspondence here with patterns of sexual action as such (indeed, if one looked for such, one might be puzzled in that the girls' pattern could more plausibly have been the men's). Rather, I think, the message is still social and political. In *mørl* the men stand still in a row and spectators move inside their line; in *yap* the men still encompass, but they move while the spectators are supposed to be motionless and quiet. In *mørli* the girls' leap may be thought of perhaps as the climactic analogue of the dignified *werl* action, just as I have suggested that the spirit dance is a speeded up analogue of *kenan*.

Conclusion

In this chapter I have been concerned with very limited problems and sets of data. I have attempted to build on, rather than repeat, ethnographic materials on Melpa social organisations and self-decoration published previously; yet I have no technical expertise to describe the dance movements on which my discussion is based. The questions I have asked are: why does dancing form a part of *moka* and other festivals, that is, what is the specific role it plays? And what is the expressive force of the total set of dance movements? In answering the first question, I have taken my cue from an exegesis by a Melpa big-man, Ongka, and suggested that dancing represents a unique statement at maturity or climax, analogous to the growth and display cycles of birds of paradise. On the second question I have outlined what appear to me to be the main features of the three main *moka* dances, the spirit cult dance, and two minor *moka* dances, and have argued that *mørl* indicates static male maturity and solidarity, *kenan* the encirclement of the ceremonial ground and its ancestor spirits with male energy, *werl* the graceful balancing act of 'women in between' (M. Strathern 1972), and *mørli* and *yap* the insurgence of sexual

135

interests. Through these contrasts one can also see the continuing themes of the distinction between performers and spectators, and between the encompassing and the encompassed. In identifying such themes, I have moved away from the initial approach via Ongka's exegesis to an observer's approach based on acquaintance with the larger structures of Melpa society.

These methods of investigation and analysis have been largely improvised to meet the needs of the case study in hand. The conclusion, however, can be related to Anya Peterson Royce's distinction, in ideal terms, between mimetic, abstract, and metaphorical dance forms (Royce 1977:204). Ongka, in his account, makes what might be called an abstract model of Melpa dances in terms of the sequence growth/climax/depletion/regrowth, but he also uses the metaphor of the bird of paradise plumage as the vehicle of his analogy; furthermore, these are the actual plumes worn by dancers, and he says that people are in some sense imitating the birds in wearing them. So his explanation contains elements corresponding to all three of Royce's categories. My further examination of the structure of dances is also couched at an abstract level, for I attempt to see in them qualities of form and movement, regardless of whether the Melpa themselves identify these. Yet here also the distinctions are tricky, since implicit metaphors and mimetic actions are involved in my account too. One can only echo the observation made long ago by Murray Groves in an essay on Motu dancing. Arguing that statements about dance, political structure, and the like are overlapping abstractions that 'fundamentally lack precision', he adds: 'Society itself is an abstraction of this special, puzzling sort, and . . . we shall have to accept the special condition that applies to social abstractions: they merge one into the other, they sometimes conceal as much as they reveal, and therefore causal relations between them cannot be precisely stated' (Groves 1954:88). Royce similarly says 'dance phenomena are elusive and often difficult to assign to any one of the categories' (Royce 1977:205). Given these limitations, I have therefore attempted simply to situate Melpa dance within its own local context. At the same time it appears likely that Melpa dances in general have similar functions to those of other peoples with comparable social and political institutions. For example, what Hanna has to say about Ubakala dance plays is applicable also to the Melpa. She refers, for instance, to the 'vigorous movement of the pelvic girdle and upper torso by young people to highlight secondary sex characteristics and energy. . . . Women symbolize fertility stylistically with undulations and hip shifts to mark status advances with the birth of a child' (Hanna 1979:322). The distinction she makes between dances of young people and dances of adult women is reminiscent of the contrast I have made between *mørli* and *werl*. More generally, she writes: 'dance is metonymical to the motion of life and the Ubakala ethos of action. The processes of reproduction and re-creation in the human–supernatural cyclical pattern . . . merge. The ancestors continue their existence in the dancers' bodies' (ibid.). For the Melpa there are two sources of re-creation: one the ancestral spirits, as with the Ubakala; the other, birds of paradise and their plumes, which evince remarkable powers of regeneration and attraction particular to themselves.

NOTES

1 The Melpa are aware that it is the males of these birds of paradise that develop special plumes and perform dances of display with them. We see here a part of male ideology in choosing such plumes for symbolic emphasis. It is interesting to note that the Kalam, a people who live quite close to the Melpa, declare that it is women's souls who change into the long-tailed birds of paradise (Princess Stephanie; sicklebill). Yet here, too, male ideology is at work, for we read: 'Their plumes are . . . like women in that when they are new they are beautiful, but after a season or two they are faded and tattered, just as a young woman may look beautiful but after she has had one or two children her beauty has gone. But the feathers of the parrots into which men's souls turn stay good for several years' (Bulmer and Majnep 1977:57).

2 Bulmer and Majnep (1977:138) note that Kalam dance songs also often have 'an ironic or self-deprecating twist to them.' Another apsect of meaning which is conveyed in both men's and women's songs is regret for the dead. When they say that 'Only the boys are left, all the big-men are dead' they are paying their respects to the ghosts of those who have died and thereby enlisting the approval of the ghosts for current enterprises. At a festival held by the Kawelka group in 1971, for example, the *werl* dancers sang:

> The elder brother is no more,
> He is eaten by grass and trees at Reipa
> The younger brother is pushed around,
> His foot slips and he falls.

The 'elder brother' referred to was a noted big-man of the particular subgroup whose ceremonial ground was being used for the dance. He died more than a decade before the dance was held, yet his loss was still felt. (Mel, of the Kurupmbo clan section, at Maninge ceremonial ground.)

3 Kalam dancers explicitly make beauty magic when they decorate themselves. In their spells they call on the bright red and green parrots and lories, and on the trees where they feed and on cool green plants that grow by the sides of streams. There is also a Kalam myth that explains the origins of beauty magic in a manner similar to that of the famous Trobriand story of brother–sister incest and love magic. A miraculously born boy meets his

137

sister, and she falls in love with him, refusing to recognise that he is a sibling. She sees his image in a pool and drains the pool to find it, then chops down the tree above the water to see if he is in it. She chants a secret song of love, beauty, and attraction as she does so, which her brother hears, and since then men have appropriated the spell and use it secretly, away from the ears of women, when they decorate. In the myth the boy turns into a lory bird in order to escape from his sister's illicit attentions, and in response she changes into a schefflera shrub, saying, 'Wherever you wander, you will always have to come and eat of me.' This is why the schefflera blossom is the favourite food of this type of lory (Bulmer and Majnep 1977:50, 164–5). Attraction of girls is also one of the aims of male decorations and dances among the Maring, neighbours of the Kalam (Rappoport 1968:186–8).

4 There is competition at the individual level between men, both in terms of their ability to attract girls into the dancing line to join them and in terms of the numbers of pigs they will give away in the *moka* itself.

5 Usually some extra pigs are brought in at this point, with another special rush and accompanying *kenan*-style chant. The pigs are tied to a special stake set up near the cordyline tub at the head of the ground (or sometimes at the opposite end), and are expected to lie still without squealing while men make their speeches; otherwise there is a bad omen. Such omens are, not surprisingly, rather frequent, just as is actual dissension following a *moka*.

6 An association between birds and male initiation is found widely in the highlands, from the Kuma, eastern neighbours of the Melpa, through to the Fore of the eastern highlands. In all these cases boys are initiated by hearing and seeing bamboo flutes, whose cries are said to be those of the birds. The Melpa do not practise initiation for either males or females, and yet Ongka's text appears to suggest a unifying reason for the significance of birds in the societies where such initiation rites are found. Detailed research work among the Huli by Laurence Goldman and in the Wahgi Valley area by Michael O'Hanlon has uncovered numerous codifications centred on birds. For example, the Huli compare the emergence of young initiates from their retreat with the way in which the Six-wired Parotia bird of paradise comes to its display ground and shows its beauty. The common theme here is one of withdrawal, maturation and return, marked by a move from the secret to the revealed. For published references see, for example, Reay 1959:170; Read 1952; Berndt 1962:67–72.

7 The wearing of pig's-tail aprons, which is special to the *kenan*, may recall, at least indirectly, the sacrifice of pigs to the ancestral spirits. Indeed, whether this is consciously intended or not, that is what the killing of pigs must signify, for every such killing is by Melpa definition also a sacrifice.

8 Gell (1975:252–3) has made a discerning point regarding Highlands festivals that appears to support my argument here regarding 'climax'. He suggests that Highlanders have an economic theory of the body, in which the storage and expenditure of both semen and wealth are seen as requiring careful regulation. It would be in line with this, then, if *mørl* dances were subliminally seen as forms of representation of sexual climax, but strictly under control rather than orgiastic. If one returns to the analogy with birds of paradise, one can see that these birds, too, perform an elaborate and con-

trolled dance as a preliminary, and a means, to sexual activity. The idea of physical effort is expressed in the *mørl* dance also, for the knee bending and standing on tiptoe actions are like static versions of the actions required to climb up the steep mountain paths that are such a prominent part of the Melpa environment.

REFERENCES

Berndt, R.M. 1962. *Excess and Restraint*. Chicago: University of Chicago Press.
Bulmer, R.N.H. and I.S. Majnep. 1977. *Birds of My Kalam Country*. Auckland: Auckland University Press.
Gell, A. 1975. *Metamorphosis of the Cassowaries*. London: Athlone.
Hanna, J.L. 1979. 'Movements towards understanding humans through the anthropological study of dance'. *Current Anthropology* 20(2):313–40.
Rappaport, R. 1968. *Pigs for the Ancestors*. New Haven, Conn.: Yale University Press.
Read, K.E. 1952. 'Nama cult of the Central Highlands, New Guinea'. *Oceania*, 23(1).
Reay, M.O. 1959. *The Kuma*. Melbourne: Melbourne University Press on behalf of the Australian National University.
Royce, A.P. 1977. *The Anthropology of Dance*. Bloomington: Indiana University Press.
Strathern, A.J. 1971. *The Rope of Moka*. Cambridge: Cambridge University Press.
——— 1972. *One Father, One Blood*. Canberra: Australian National University Press.
——— 1974. *Melpa Amb Kenan*. Port Moresby: Institute of Papua New Guinea Studies.
——— 1979a. *Ongka*. London: Duckworth.
——— 1979b. 'Men's house, women's house: the efficacy of opposition, reversal and pairing in the Melpa *Amb kor* cult'. *Journal of the Polynesian Society*, 88(1):37–51.
Strathern, A.J., and M. Strathern. 1971. *Self-decoration in Mount Hagen*. London: Duckworth.
Strathern, M. 1972. *Women in Between*. London: Seminar Press.
——— 1979. 'The self in self-decoration'. *Oceania* 49(4):241–57.

5 Dance as antithesis in the Samburu discourse

PAUL SPENCER

The Samburu of northern Kenya live as pastoral nomads, principally in an area of desert scrub and thick bush with a low and unpredictable rainfall.[1] These are harsher conditions than those of their distant Maasai kinsmen further south, and their settlements are smaller and more mobile. In such conditions, any art form has to be transportable and it is dancing, combined with singing and body decoration, that provides the principal aesthetic idiom of their culture. The term 'play' (*enkiguran*) is often used as a metaphor for dancing or singing. This is consistent with the apparent triviality and sometimes nonsense of the words of the songs, and the readiness with which a half-muttered song merges into an informal dance movement wherever young people are collected together for no purpose other than their own company. However, there is within these dances, and especially on more formal occasions, a variety of implicit signals that are as relevant to the discourse of social existence as any gossip. Those who stand opposed to the dancers as older age groups or as the other sex may not understand the precise content of the songs and may seem to ignore the performance, but they cannot afford to ignore the concealed message. There is a concentration of interest and a sense of power expressed in the compulsive throb of the rhythm generated by the wordless choruses, clapping, and stamping characteristic of each dance. It is more than mere play or gossip: it expresses the concerted force of a suppressed sector of Samburu society that has a relevance for all.

The circumcision dance and the aspirations of boyhood

As a vivid example of this evocative quality of their singing and dancing, one may consider the boys' circumcision dance, *lebarta*. Regardless of the abolition earlier this century of widespread intertribal warfare, the warrior tradition has been sustained and was regenerated for a further generation by the total breakdown of administration in

140

the area in the 1960s. For the boys, therefore, their initiation into warriorhood is more than an outmoded practice: it is a coveted ambition, and the circumcision dance is an expression of this desire. As mere herdboys their education focuses entirely on acquiring basic cattle skills. They may be on cordial terms with their older warrior brothers, but on the whole they are despised by other warriors for their juvenile gaucherie, and are forbidden any association with girls of their own age. The warriorhood to which they aspire on the other hand has a unique charm for all Samburu, and to emphasise this special status I adopt the local term for warriors: *moran* (s. *lmurani*, pl. *lmuran*). During the earliest years of childhood, both parents may play with their sons on their laps, crooning moran songs, dancing them through the motions of the chorus, and fondly addressing them as 'moran'. Their fathers as elders look back with affection to their own period of moranhood during their twenties. Women and girls dote on the notion of moranhood. The existing moran jealously guard against any attempt by boys to usurp the privileges of moranhood: their close association with girls, their postures, their songs, their hairstyles and adornments. Eventually, as one age-set of moran reach the age when they must shortly retire to elderhood, marry, and settle down, boys who form the next age-set, on average fourteen years younger, are beginning to flex their muscles in anticipation of moranhood. At first, there is a certain restlessness among the older boys. There would be no question at this stage of openly defying the moran or of assuming privileges of moranhood and risking a beating. However, a number of boys may muster to dance at night in settlements where they are well represented in number, and the spirit of restlessness spreads. They process in a dance around the countryside, singing their circumcision song and vowing to endure the agony of circumcision without batting an eyelid. It is a song that anticipates the critical test of the ceremony itself. Each boy's readiness to show his mettle and sing this song just before the operation adds to his ordeal: he displays a confidence that will bring him great credit if he maintains his composure throughout, but it will magnify his dishonour if he then flinches at the critical moment (Spencer 1970:134–5). It is the song itself rather than dancing as such that might seem more pertinent to the occasion, yet the words draw particular attention to his bodily composure. At the supreme moment there is a dancelike resemblance as the initiate sits motionless with complete control over his body, on display before spectators, his composure loaded with meaning. One might almost say that his complete motionlessness is to the circumcision dance what silence can sometimes

141

Paul Spencer

be to music: the decisive antithesis that plays an essential part in shaping the occasion.

The song may first be heard a full three to five years before the new circumcisions, although the Samburu themselves do not expect so long an interval. During this period, the developing timbre of their singing is a measure of the mounting strength of feeling and unity among the boys, and an indication of the passing of time. Initially, it is sung hesitatingly with a few deep voices mixed with some not so deep; the tune and rhythm, only half remembered from an earlier period of boyhood when there were previous circumcisions, will be uncertain and variable; and they are self-conscious about displaying themselves and broadcasting their immaturity. But it is a beginning, and as their voices, confidence, and style develop, so they take heart and use this song and processional dance to recruit other boys to join them, with an implied element of coercion: if a father withholds his eligible son from joining them then this song is thought to have the force of a curse.

For the moran of the previous age-set, the gathering assertiveness of this dance is a signal of their own impending elderhood, a future that many of them, notably the younger ones, wish to delay; they therefore assiduously keep the boys in their place and discourage them from any thoughts of an early circumcision. Ultimately, as the pressure increases, there are incidents of defiance from the oldest boys. Some leave their homes and wander in pairs or small groups in the bush, impatient and footloose, even pilfering food. Surreptitiously, boys may begin to practise the songs and dances of moranhood and to flirt with the younger girls. The words of the circumcision song hardly change, but there is a hint of mounting tension in its delivery, an irrepressible demand addressed to the elders to recognise that a new set of future moran are proving their worth and that to deny them circumcision much longer could provoke widespread lawlessness. The retiring moran for their part recognise this sense of impending change and resign themselves to a less colourful future as the limelight passes to a new age-set.

Of the various signs that indicate the trend of this development, it is this dance and song in particular that serve as a dominant symbol, a barometer of the pressures that are building up towards the new set of circumcisions; and the atmosphere becomes filled with an expectation of change within the system. It is a motif that has rich associations. For the boys' parents, there is pride that their status will be enhanced and the family honour put to the test. For the elders, it anticipates the time when there will be a redistribution of power

142

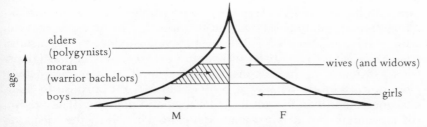

Figure 5.1 Distribution of Samburu roles by age and sex

between the various age-sets and requires careful handling. The moran, who previously as boys loudly sported this song and processed in gathering strength, now complain that the sound provokes a nausea, their 'stomachs hate it', and the more elated the boys' singing, the more despondent the moran. One of the most impressionable groups in this process are those boys who are still too young for circumcision even though they may join in at the periphery of the dancing. A feature that they learn is not just the circumcision song itself (which they may half forget), but also the notion that it is a song and dance of assertiveness against their seniors by age, and that in due course circumcision will only be theirs by uniting to demand it. With the change-over to a new age-set of moran, the mounting pressures and rivalries between age-sets are eased, but through the dance the seed has also been sown for perpetuating the underlying aspirations of a future, as yet embryonic, age-set of younger boys whose time is not yet ripe.

The dances of the moran *and their girls*

The principal dances among the Samburu by universal acclaim are those of the moran and these can only be fully appreciated by reference to the anomalous position of the moran in the wider society. This is related to the flexible nomadic existence of the Samburu, which encourages widespread polygyny, since a monogamous family is normally too small to be economically viable as an independent household unit. Polygyny on such a scale inevitably creates a shortage of marriageable women and correspondingly a surplus of unmarried men. This is a widespread problem throughout rural Africa and is resolved most often by delaying the age of marriage for men substantially as compared with women (Figure 5.1).

The Samburu moran form this sector of unmarried men, biding

143

their time until about the age of thirty when they marry for the first time and become elders. There is a sense in which the moran are in a limbo; more than mere boys, but not accepted by elders as mature adults and not permitted full domestic responsibility. In the distant past, they would have been warriors in a very real and prestigious sense, shouldering the responsibility for defending their land. However, since then they have been given no general purpose to their existence other than to wait for elderhood and marriage. They relish their position, but it is a vacuous situation in which the ideals of warriorhood are offered no ready outlet. It is in this context that the incipient rivalry between Samburu clans erupts in a form of sporadic gang warfare, and tends to centre on their possession of the girls within each clan as sexual playthings. Any moran can have one mistress from among these girls, but because she is a clan 'sister', he may not marry her, even when he becomes an elder. He is bound to lose her eventually, but so long as she remains unmarried, his standing among other moran and girls hinges on their relationship. He would be expected to attack any other moran who makes advances towards her or molests her, and if this moran is of some other clan, then feeling may mount, and the incident may develop into an interclan affray. The significance of their dancing is that dances form the arena in which girls and moran of rival clans may meet in peace. One has, in fact, a situation very similar to the musical drama *West Side Story*, in which two ethnic gangs of youths keep jealous possession of their girls, but they all meet on 'neutral territory' at dances, where they agree to avoid fighting.

The moran are thrust into the foreground as the most spectacular and controversial sector of the society, an army in reserve who retain at least some of the glamour of their traditional role, colourfully adorned, generally free of economic commitments, capable of impressive physical feats, unpredictable in their behaviour, and (with good cause) suspected by the elders of adultery with their wives. This is the price the elders have to pay for their monopoly of formal power and nubile women. There is little doubt that the elders retain command over the situation. What constitutes reality for the moran, holding so much glamour and absorbing their energies, is treated by the elders as a mere game among 'children'.

The principal weapon of the elders is their control over the marriages of their daughters, which override the more transient claims of the moran over these girls. It is the elders who decide when each bond between lovers should terminate by marrying the girl off to some other clan, where she will start a new life in a position of complete subservience. Thus each wedding is a sharp reminder for all moran and girls of the elders' power to interfere in their affairs, and significantly this is the principal occasion at which moran are popularly expected to express their protest in a display of anger through dancing. Their ultimate impotence brought to a head, they take the centre of the arena, while the elders look on from a discreet distance. More prominent among the spectators are the girls, also adorned for the occasion. It is the presence of the girls that makes the moran especially sensitive in the dance to any slight or insinuation. They are in an assertive mood with less than total control over themselves, and this adds an undercurrent of apprehensiveness. Their feelings are brittle and no-one can predict exactly how the dance will develop. Events are beyond the immediate control of the elders.

Preparing for the dance, the moran take great care over their appearance, with clean cloths neatly wound round their trunks, over-hung with strings of beads. Glistening red ochre forms a clearly defined pattern around their faces and shoulders, and highlights their long braided hair which hangs loosely behind them. The polished, leaflike blades of their spears point skywards. Self-consciously they gather at a short distance from the wedding settlement, snorting in moran fashion, tossing their heads to shake their hair into position, and glancing down at their own appearances. Then as a body they march to the settlement, watched keenly by everyone, and their dance begins.

This dancing entails a succession of phases, each associated with a characteristic mood. I refer to the first phase, which may last up to one hour or more, as *dances of display*. In it, one of the more assertive moran takes the role of soloist, boasting in narrative form of his own or his group's prowess and achievements in stock thieving, while the others join in a wordless chorus and occasionally wrest the solo lead. As one worldly moran explained to me: 'It's like an auction, each man tries to bid higher than the last.' Claim and counterclaim build up, while the girls look on. This altercation between *laingok* ('bulls' – brave assertive moran) is a dominant feature of the first phase, structuring it up to a point.

Each dance of this phase has its own musical form and pattern of movement. The first dance is invariably *nbarinkoi* in which the moran form a tight chanting group, and then move forward as a body with a rhythmic movement, twice raising their heels, bending their knees, thrusting their heads forwards and exhaling audibly – in fact not unlike bulls – and then straightening themselves and lifting their spears on the third beat. At certain points individual moran on impulse hop to the front of the dance and away from it. Increasingly

145

others follow suit, and together may leap upwards with rigid bodies. The whole sequence is then repeated several times. One might almost describe *nbarinkoi* as the keynote of the whole occasion. If there is a serious lull during the later dances or some interruption, the dancers will normally return to this dance in an attempt to start anew. It appears to be quite invariable throughout the Samburu district so that any moran visitor from another clan or region will have no difficulty in participating fully. It sets the tone for the subsequent dancing, displaying the moran as a body of dancers. There is at this stage some competition for the lead, but the soloists' words are generally stereotyped, indistinct and drowned by the chorus.

Another very popular dance of this phase is *nkokorri*, which gives greater scope for elaboration of the song and competition for the solo part. The loud assertions of the leader are more distinct, and the notion of a multi-sided auction becomes especially apt. A few girls and some rather small boys (too young to be out herding) may join the fringes of this dance, following its movements; but the moran, now facing inwards, take no notice of them. At certain points several moran may spring together in a succession of high jumps.

It is in this dance that one may sense a gathering power and momentum as the rhythm quickens, and sometimes, if guided by a skilful and assertive soloist, its rhythm may be elaborated. While it is hard to pin down any precise jealousies aroused by the boasting and counter-boasting, the moran claim that it is at this point that their rivalry and anger come to a head. If a fight breaks out during the dancing, it is likely to be at this stage. Inadvertently one moran may jostle another whose nerves are on edge, and he will react violently. If they happen to be of one clan and surrounded by their kinsmen, then others may attempt to seize them to prevent a more serious incident. However, if the incident is misconstrued, or there is a score to settle, or they happen to be of different clans, then almost in an instant the dance can be transformed into a general affray.

The possibility of fighting is very real and adds to the tenseness of the occasion, but it is no more than an outside chance. More usually the climax is reached when a number of moran with taut expressions begin to shiver. This is described by the Samburu as a symptom of their anger, a desire to lash out at almost anything, although knowing that they must restrain themselves. In battle, a moran is said sometimes to shiver beforehand until he can release his aggression in the actual fighting, and then he stops shivering. In the dance, his shivering displays his urge to fight and his manliness, but to give way to this urge would show a lack of self-control. It is in this ambiguous and tense situation that one or two moran can be expected to break down in an insensible fit of convulsive shaking, held firmly by their fellows to prevent them from hurting themselves or others. The larger and more successful the dance, the more likely it is that as many as five or more moran will break down in this way, following one another in relatively quick succession; and then after the shaking subsides and they regain their composure, they return to the dance apparently cured of their bout of anger as they merge almost passively into the main body of dancers. The climax of shaking does not necessarily end this display phase of the dance, but it takes away the sense of melodrama, and the moran more obviously enjoy sporting themselves with less compulsion to compete and a greater chance to concentrate on the actual dancing.

Although the Samburu do not elaborate on this phase of the dance in clear analytical terms, they are aware of an acute anger generated in this climax by two opposed forces: constraint and assertiveness. The element of constraint is symptomatic of their whole moranhood and of the regime under which they are placed. This is a society in which loyalty to age-set and clan and conformity to the mores of Samburu society as a whole are supreme virtues. A man is expected to suppress private desires that conflict with public expectations, to show an aloof respect, and to stand on his dignity. This self-restraint is a social grace that the moran in particular cultivate and carry through to elderhood. In the dance, the moran have a uniform appearance, a compactness in their grouping, stereotyped movements, and a synchronisation to a collectively induced rhythm. One is reminded of Radcliffe-Brown's analysis of the constraining effects of rhythm in the Andamanese dance, which subordinates the dancer to the wider society (Radcliffe-Brown 1922:249).

This constraint extends to the expectations that they should comply with the peace of the dance and master any desire to fight. They associate their shivering and fits of shaking with the angry struggle within themselves to overcome the urge to attack some adversary. As their anger is aroused, they shiver and experience a tightness gripping their chests, inducing a sense of breathless suffocation as they sink into unconsciousness and shaking. They do not elaborate in greater detail, but when moran assert themselves aggressively at each rhythmic climax of the dance with boasting and loud exhalations from deep down in their chests, it is as if their anger is induced by the conflict between their own assertiveness and some external force pressing relentlessly inwards. In the grip of this extreme contradiction between assertiveness and constraint, they lose consciousness and achieve relaxation. They have no theory of possession by some spirit, yet at a metaphoric level a somewhat similar explanation suggests itself. In a society such as this, the collectivist slant of Durkheim's sociology is particularly apt, and at times when moran shiver and shake one is led to suggest that this sense of suffocation is none other than their experience of society itself as a constraining force bearing down on them and taking possession as their anger and urge to break free mounts. This is to imply that Samburu society as a moral force is assimilated as a physiological response over the extended period that youths prime themselves for moranhood. It is in their dances during this phase and at other times when they should control their desires to fight that shaking is actually expected of them. Shaking is a sign of their assertiveness and of their self-mastery, in other words a proof of their worthiness as warriors. When they become elders and are no longer expected to assert themselves, they cease to shake altogether.

When the dances of display seem to have run their course, moran turn for the first time towards the girls and start to perform dances of the second phase. The girls as a compact group now join in the dance, facing towards the group of moran, and they perform a similar rhythmic thrusting action towards one another. I refer to the dances of this phase as *clan dances*; the moran and girls of each clan build up a repertoire of songs for those dances (*sesiei*), generally relating to cattle rustling as in the previous phase, but with a new and more gentle note of competition. They indulge in a game in which the moran tease the girls for their unworldliness with riddles: 'What is iron that writes?' [Answer – a *taipiraita*]; 'Who are descended from monkeys?' [Answer – Europeans because they are hairy all over]. The girls respond, taunting the affectations of the moran. It is the skill of individual singers on behalf of their peer group that is now more important than the individualistic assertiveness of 'bulls' noted in the preceding phase.

The tone and topic of this musical repartee is significant. The boundary between the sexes (as illustrated in Figure 5.1) is firm and uncompromising; and there is in addition the vast difference between the worldliness and wanderlust of moran in their twenties and the domestic horizons of girls barely in their teens. In their sparring based on moranish ideals and sexual attraction, they have little in common outside the idiom of their songs and dances. There is, however, their shared misgiving concerning their subordination to the control of the elders, which expresses itself as a scorn for domesticated elderhood tinged with fear of the elders. So long as the moran are footloose and causing trouble through stock thieving they are indirectly provoking the elders, while the girls' encouragement is also an expression of defiance. Just as each wedding is a symbol for each group of their ultimate powerlessness against the elders, so stock theft has become a symbol of their unwillingness to submit completely. It provides a central topic for the songs of their clan dances. The moran are amused when the girls with their limited experience sing of exploits in a world they have hardly seen and garble their descriptions; but there can be little doubt of the effect on the moran of the girls' taunting. Thus a girl may sing: 'If you're a coward who goes out to steal stock and returns with nothing, then you may as well go and dance from settlement to settlement [do not return for the girls will not be impressed]'. Describing the effect of such goading, one moran claimed: 'You are standing there in the dance, and a girl starts to sing. She raises her chin high and you see her throat. And then you want to steal some cattle for yourself. You start to shiver. You leave the dance and stride into the night, afraid of nothing and only conscious of the fact that you are going to steal a cow.' One should not however underestimate the fear and respect that the moran also have of the elders. Stock theft is a serious problem in the area, but a considerable proportion of moran are thought to go from settlement to settlement, goaded by the girls, perhaps even joining in some half-hearted sorties outside the district, but deferring ultimately to the elders. It should also be emphasised that shivering is not common during this phase, and (in my experience) never serious enough to lead to shaking.

After a while during this phase, a moran may on impulse detach himself from his group, go up to one of the girls, and toss his head so as to flirt his long hair over her face, or he may just place a hand on her head, and then as the girl shies away from his advances he returns to the body of moran. Other moran follow suit. These sorties gradually become more frequent and dancers on both sides begin to relax. One or two moran may draw some of the girls aside from the dance in conversation. Each sex maintains a certain reserve, remaining as small groups, some silent while others converse by innuendo, adopting the stilted idiom of the singing, teasing, and taunting with well-worn clichés. Yet despite this reserve, one senses a progressive warming of the atmosphere from the earlier period when the moran ignored the presence of the girls altogether.

This leads to the third phase, which the Samburu term 'boys' dances'. These are not the circumcision dance, but a wide selection of dances the moran performed as boys, and which have remained in their repertoire since they became moran. They are altogether more tuneful

149

than the earlier dances and with a lively rhythm. The words have a lilt rather than any meaning. The dancers stand in a circle, bounce, bend their knees, and clap, and then holding hands jump in time. The sexes are mixed to a considerable extent, and beyond the circle of dancers small groups, even pairs, chat and laugh. There is a growing excitement and hilarity as the process of thawing out continues. Someone starts to chant to a rhythm that appeals to them all. As one of the dancers once said of this phase: 'When someone beats out the right tune, you find yourself jumping higher and higher and you can't stop.' It is during this phase that moran may make surreptitious advances towards the girls, arranging to meet them at some less public venue, and, if they are not careful, sowing the seed for some future confrontation between rivals.

The transition from one phase to the next appears to depend on the judgement of any skilful singer. At an appropriate point, he may start to sing the first measures of the next phase, and the success of his initiative will depend on the response he gets from others. If they do not share his confidence then the initiative will quickly lapse and the earlier phase will continue. This succession of phases is well illustrated with several examples.

Example 1. The wedding of Leparit's sister coincided with another wedding nearby that attracted many of the moran from Leparit's clan and left only about ten to attend the wedding dance at his settlement. They were hopelessly outnumbered by visiting moran, including an impressive contingent from the bridegroom's clan who, with expert singers and dancers, dominated the first phase of the dance and out-displayed their hosts in front of the girls of the hosts' clan. Leparit and his close friends had been apprehensive of this prospect beforehand, and during the dance itself they were demoralised. At the height of the dance, in quick succession, four of the host moran including Leparit himself broke down and shook, held by their remaining clansmen. The visitors continued to dominate the occasion and none of them shook. Eventually the hosts rejoined the dance, and it proceeded smoothly to the second phase. Although this entailed clan dances, it no longer provoked serious rivalry between the various clans, and the hosts clearly recovered their nerve. The girls only knew the songs of their own (Leparit's) clan, and in singing verses from them they were indirectly lending moral support to their kinsmen. For the visitors, the dance had moved on, and any rivalry between the versions became an aspect of the rivalry between the sexes. This second phase was prolonged, and by the time it gave way to the 'boys' dances' of the third phase many of the visitors had left to return to their own homes, and this became more of a local event and shortly stopped.

Example 2. Moipa discarded his mistress in disgust after she had been seduced by a moran of another clan. Later, during the display phase of a wedding dance, an affray broke out between the two clans, and Moipa was later accused of having precipitated it by jostling and attacking a close clansman of the seducer. The affray was quickly quelled as the local elders asserted their authority and the dance was abandoned. Subsequently the girl in question was married off to avoid further trouble, and the elders of the two clans met and agreed to order their respective moran to avoid each other by not attending the same dances until the issue between them had been resolved.

Example 3. At the wedding of Legilan's daughter, several attempts were made by the assembled moran to generate a dance; but for some unexplained reason they lacked the necessary spirit and the dance was unable to develop. Some of the moran started to leave, attracted by the prospect of another dance elsewhere. Those remaining, somewhat dispirited, made a further half-hearted attempt to start the dance, but with even less success. At this point a new contingent of moran, splendidly embellished, arrived and immediately began their own dance in another part of the settlement. The girl spectators immediately flocked towards this new dance, and the earlier attempt faded out. All the moran now joined the second dance, which proceeded smoothly through each of the phases. Some of the moran shook, but no clear-cut pattern underlay their shaking as had occurred in the first example.

Example 4. At another wedding, a dance had proceeded smoothly through the display dances to the clan dances of the second phase. There was then a lull, and unaccountably the momentum was lost and the dance stalled. Several attempts to renew this phase found no response among the dancers. The dance then reverted to the display phase, beginning again with *nbarinkoi*, and on this second occasion proceeding more smoothly through the subsequent phases. (I cannot say whether the initial transition to the phase of clan dances had been premature, but this reversion to the first phase following some interruption is not uncommon.)

Example 5. Following the circumcision of a new age-set in 1960, two sets of moran dances took place at weddings simultaneously for a

Paul Spencer

time: that of the senior moran due to retire and that of the new age-
set of juniors. The junior moran had no established repertoire beyond
their 'boys' dances' and they lacked the panache and spectacle of their
seniors. Yet time was on their side, and many of the younger girls
who had previously been drawn towards the dancing of the senior
moran now deserted them and switched their attention to the juniors,
whose lack of accomplishment was offset by new hope, high spirits
and the remoteness of their own elderhood. With this switching of
the limelight away from them, the senior moran began to reconcile
themselves to elderhood and lost the incentive to compete or to dance.
There was now a radical shift in the type of dancing and singing to
be seen at weddings: a fresh unruly spirit mixed in with the various
dances that could be expected to lead to a spate of trouble as rivalries
built up. But there was also a shift in their language in song. The
junior moran sought to establish a new set of songs that they could
identify as their own, and up to a point a new slang and double
entendre in these songs, a secret language of their own to tease and
ultimately share with the girls and to keep hidden from their seniors.
Yet for all their efforts to be different, the past experiences of successive age-sets indicated that they would unwittingly continue to
follow the basic pattern of dances and of phases as their predecessors.

Example 6. Evening dances begin more spontaneously than wedding
dances which always take place during the afternoon. With only
moonlight to see by, there are no display dances, and the occasion
is marked by informality. In a typical evening dance, a group of moran
gather together and call to the girls of the settlement to come and
join them. The idiom of this invitation (*ntemerr*) is very similar to the
clan dances which shortly follow, and thus the dancing may be said
to begin with the second phase. This is generally a very local clan
affair and the clan dances may last for some time, before the 'boys'
dances' of the third phase are attempted. There is in these dances a
certain hilarity normally missing from the afternoon sessions. Gradually a fourth phase may emerge, which I would describe as 'play'.
The 'boys' dances' begin to lose their form and become mixed with
an element of horseplay, which merges into the general babble. Bois-
terousness increases further and some of the less skilled singers,
having lost their earlier inhibitions, may try to take the lead for the
first time. The result does little to dampen the high spirits of the
dancers. Small groups, or even individuals, begin to jump and dance
and clap without establishing a rhythm. There is general mirth, and
playful skirmishes between moran and girls. Nothing, it seems, can

152

spoil their enjoyment, and the general atmosphere of intoxication may last until the small hours.

As 'play', this phase is comparable with the attempts of smaller children who earlier in the evening may have mimicked dances they do not really know, mixing them in with their play. Thus the evening dance starts at a later phase than the wedding dance, but progresses in the same direction and, under the discreet cover of darkness, unwinds further.

As the dancing progresses in these examples, one may note a shift of emphasis from the provocative thrusting movement with assertive bull-like grunting that tends to predominate at first, to the leaping movement later on as the rigid bodies of the dancers rise and fall, keeping absolutely together. This is a trend within the first phase and also within the dance as a whole. The horizontal thrusting expresses and even precipitates individualistic competition, whereas the vertical leaping in concert appears to reflect their unity. Increasingly, there is greater emphasis on dances that have more vertical movement, more compulsive rhythms, less grunting, and less competitiveness in their singing.

This development suggests a rather obvious sexual symbolism, even if the Samburu themselves do not emphasise this aspect. 'Bulls' vie assertively in the first phase before an audience of females. They approach these females in the second phase, and the two sexes thrust (their faces) rhythmically towards one another. In the third phase, hand in hand, they spring up and down together as the rhythm gets hold of them, rising to a climax. And then, relaxation. This process may be summarised as thrusting→springing→unstructured behaviour: competition→unity→informality.

At a less obvious level, the development of the dance can be taken further. Figure 5.2 depicts the evolution of a moran dance, illustrating this as the reverse of the process of social development of the individual. The dance evolves from the dances of display, in which the moran are disunited and engage in a choral brawl that at any point *could* degenerate into a fight; the girls are not directly involved at this stage, except as spectators. With the clan dances, the moran are now united and the girls are brought into a game in which brawling gives way to repartee. The two sexes confront each other, at first as peer groups, but progressively as individuals, detaching themselves from the dance, teasing and flirting, while awkwardly maintaining a certain reserve. With the 'boys' dances', this process of merging is taken a stage further. One is still conscious of small groups of girls clinging

153

Paul Spencer

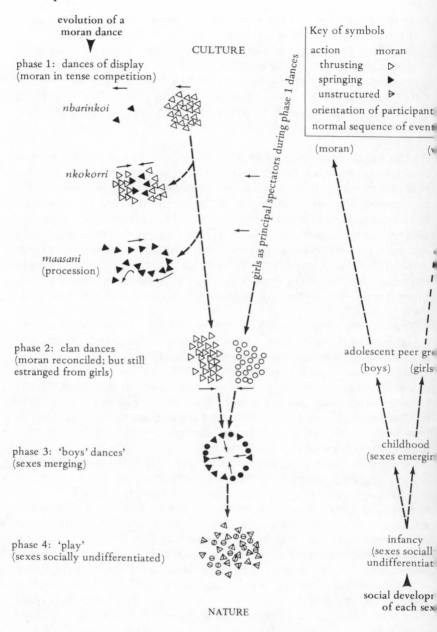

evolution of a
moran dance
▼

CULTURE

phase 1: dances of display
(moran in tense competition)

nbarinkoi

nkokorri

maasani
(procession)

girls as principal spectators during phase 1 dances

Key of symbols

action   moran

thrusting   ▷

springing   ▶

unstructured   ▷

orientation of participant

normal sequence of event

(moran)   (v

phase 2: clan dances
(moran reconciled; but still
estranged from girls)

adolescent peer gr
(boys)   (girls

phase 3: 'boys' dances'
(sexes merging)

childhood
(sexes emergir

phase 4: 'play'
(sexes socially undifferentiated)

infancy
(sexes sociall
undifferentiat

▲

social developr
of each sex

NATURE

Figure 5.2 The moran dance as a process of reversion

154

together and of moran holding themselves slightly aloof, but the peer grouping of the clan dances is broken up and the verbal play on the periphery rises to a general babble. Finally the last vestige of inhibition appears to evaporate in play and their consciousness of the social barrier that separates them lapses. Perhaps by this stage one should no longer think in terms of the evolution of the dance, but rather of its degeneration.

The process of social development proceeds in the opposite direction. In infancy, the sexes are at first undifferentiated, but with childhood, sharp distinctions are made: girls should be decently covered and taught to show an early respect for the elders, and boys are involved with a caring concern for stock as soon as possible. The two sexes emerge and long before puberty form themselves into self-conscious peer groups. This process is taken a stage further with their initiation following puberty. At this point the girls are married off individually to elders, and the boys become moran, separated from girls of their own age, forced to bide their time, and frequently at odds among themselves.

This process of social development may be regarded as the progressive imposition of a boundary that separates the sexes and comes between their natural attraction for one another, and then for the men creates further boundaries that divide them among themselves. The moran dance, on the other hand, is a process whereby these boundaries are successively broken down and the shackles of upbringing are progressively shaken off. From this point of view, the dance is not even a degeneration, but rather a retrogression.

Of the various types of explanation that might be put forward for the dance, the evidence here seems to point convincingly towards a temporary release of the tension that is built up among young people associated with their restricted position. This might be expressed in Freudian terms as a reversion to infancy; or in Lévi-Straussian terms as a transformation from culture to nature; or following Victor Turner as a transition from structure to antistructure, with the progression towards play seen as the development of *communitas* (Turner 1969; and see above, p. 27). The moran and girls do not merely release tension, but they also develop a camaraderie, united through the dance in a token protest against the regime under which they are placed. Bringing together these various ways of interpreting the moran dance is revealing. Freud's theory of the development of the personality, conscience, and acculturation focuses especially on the Oedipal relationship between children and parents – between inner nature and outer culture. It is a theory that has less to offer on the exposure

155

Paul Spencer

of the child to other children in natural play, which extends their experience beyond the formal structure of the family and has relevance to the development of relations of equality between peers. When conditions allow the development of a dance between moran and girls to approach the natural play of childhood, this does not appear as a regression to an earlier stage *within* the family situation, but beyond it. This is not quite 'communitas' in Turner's sense of embracing humanity at large regardless of all differences of status – older people are not drawn into the revelry; but perhaps this widest concept of communitas is seldom if ever achieved on a universal scale. This is to suggest that the roots of communitas, in ritual as much as in dance, lie perhaps in the natural play of childhood, beyond the authoritarian structure of the family and of the culture it represents. In this way one can reconcile the apparent contradiction that the Samburu regard dance as play and yet give it pride of place in so many of their rituals and endow it with the sanctity of a collective representation. It is not the irrelevant luxury of idle moments, but a by-product of the contradictory forces that permeate Samburu society and cannot be wholly contained by the force of law and order dictated by the elders.

Viewed within the wider context, the dancing of the moran appears as a stabilising factor. Their delinquencies stem from the anomaly of their position as physically mature men who are denied marriage, the odd men out. They remain in a situation of suspended adolescence – more than mere children, but not yet fully accepted as adults. Ostensibly the element of protest in their dances proclaims their autonomy and a breakdown of the regime of the elders. Yet in a sense it reintegrates them into society, since it reduces them to the innocuous status of childhood, and as dependent children they have a place. In this way a major source of disorder in Samburu society, the threat from dispossessed warriors in their prime, is removed through dance, and order is reestablished. Perhaps this is why a lively moran dance at a wedding is regarded as an auspicious event.

Dancing and elderhood

When the senior moran have settled down as elders, there is no new set of songs and dances to replace those of their moranhood. The elders are the only sector of Samburu society who do not in practice perform dances (although I was assured that they could and perhaps would), and they can never again wholly recapture the undomesticated charm of their past moranhood. The rift between moran and

156

elders is emphasised, echoing the earlier rift between moran and boys. Reverting to the model of Figure 5.1, one might say that each of the dividing lines in this diagram indicates a social boundary (by age or by sex) in the distribution of power, but also entails a certain polarity between complementary opposites. A Samburu definition of an elder would tend to emphasise that an elder does what a moran does not do, and vice versa (Spencer 1965:133–4; 1976:166). If moran dance, shake, and attract popular attention, then it is not appropriate for the elders to attempt these activities. Similarly, because the elders make important decisions in debate, the moran are not encouraged to cultivate debating skills. The debating elder is as popular a stereotype as the dancing moran.

Yet among elders, their rivalries are played out in debate in a way reminiscent of the dance, and one might also discern a certain dance-like quality in their oratory. In a moran dance, a skilful singer in competition with others can convert an otherwise flat occasion into a memorable one and stimulate others to respond. Similarly, a skilled orator among the elders, gathered in the shade of an acacia tree, can convert a meandering discussion into a lively debate. Wielding his stick deftly to make his points, he asserts himself as master of the space around him and of the time he takes to hold his audience in his spell. In making his points, he provokes other elders to respond and to exercise their skills to the limit, wresting the initiative as in an auction. Precisely as a successful moran dance is expected to proceed through the earlier phases of competition before unity is achieved, so the elders should debate, airing all points of view 'like the branches of an acacia tree' before they arrive at a unanimous decision, 'the trunk'. An inadequately attended debate, like an inadequately attended dance, does not fulfil its end.

One could argue that this is more than a mere parallel between moranhood and elderhood: it is a transformation from dancing to debating, and an aspect of the transformation from protest to power. On becoming elders, moran enter a new realm, which consciously contrasts with their past in a number of ways. But inevitably there is a basic continuity, and at a very basic level one might argue that the moran dancers are learning to debate just as the debating elders continue to dance.

The dances of married women

The subservient position of married women to their husbands places them in an oddly similar situation to the moran. They too slip uncomfortably from the direct control of the elders at times, and the ambiguity of their position is again reflected in their dancing.[2]

Throughout the year, the most common venue for women's dancing also is a local wedding ceremony. This is a highlight of a generally confined existence in which for the most part they are dispersed and tied down by domestic responsibilities under the heavy-handed control of their husbands, who may be typically between fifteen and forty years their seniors. On the morning of a wedding, women of the locality process to the wedding settlement in small groups, chanting their *ntorosi* song, in which they pray to God for children with gleefully obscene allusions to their own sexuality coupled with allegations against elders in general. As they dance their way, the song creates a minor ripple of attention and is an inviting call for other women, promising a measure of temporary freedom from domestic drudgery. It sets the tone for the dances that follow once they are gathered together, marking out an inviolable domain from which males, as the principal butt of their jokes, are firmly excluded. Rather as the *nbarinkoi* dance is the keynote for the dancing of the moran, which quite eclipses that of the women later in the day, so *ntorosi* is the keynote of women's dancing. As a fertility dance, *ntorosi* has an affinity with the boys' initiation dance. Both women and boys in relation to their dance have a ritually privileged position with powers to coerce their peers as they dance from village to village, the boys as potential moran and the women as potential mothers.

During the brief period of an unusually good wet season, the women's *ntorosi* dancing may become an everyday event, and then it can acquire a new significance. During such a season, a vague rumour may spread among the women of some malignant presence affecting their fertility. In such circumstances the pressure may build up to marshal their numbers in any locality and perform their *ntorosi*. They may process for a few days or even (it is claimed) weeks, dancing from settlement to settlement, coercing elders for food and gifts, blessing them and their wives when they comply, but with the power to curse any man who refuses them or prevents his wife from joining them. Away from the village, no man would want to cross their path; if they catch one in the bush, they will mob, manhandle, and even rape him in the belief that this could cure their barrenness. The term *ntorosi* generally conjures up an image of militancy. It is primarily associated among Maasai-speaking peoples with a defiant vow among warriors to die rather than yield ground in a cattle raid. In borrowing the term, the women are proclaiming that it is they who are prepared to defy anyone standing in their way. It is *their* legitimate domain:

ust as the *ntorosi* moran went on sorties to snatch cattle from their enemies, so metaphorically the women are out to fight the malignant force, and to snatch the babies that are equally necessary for the survival of Samburu society:

moran:cattle :: women:babies

This idiom of assertiveness against an adversary provides a superficial parallel with the dances of the moran. Once again it suggests a certain reversion to an earlier period of their lives when as girls they danced with moran and proclaimed the virtues of warriorhood and cattle snatching, while at the same time undermining the authority of the elders. As with the moran, the effervescent overtones of their behaviour in dance are referred to as 'play' and they are 'children'.[3]

Their concern with fertility, however, is absolutely serious and in order to fathom an underlying logic in this metaphor of moranhood, it is useful to compare explanations put forward for similar dances among the Gogo by Rigby (1968) and among the Zulu by Gluckman (1963:112–18). Ostensibly the Samburu women's *ntorosi* is closer to the Gogo, where the element of violence and obscenity appears to have been more pronounced than among the Zulu, and where also there is a fear among the women of an impending misfortune, a ritual contamination that can be 'danced away' (Rigby 1968:159). On the other hand, while Rigby insisted that the status of Gogo women is equivalent to that of men, among the Samburu they are clearly subordinate and in this respect they are similar to the Zulu as described by Gluckman. The question therefore arises: should the *ntorosi* dance be more aptly regarded as a 'ritual of rebellion' (following Gluckman) in which the frustrations of male domination are acted out, or should it be regarded as a 'ritual of purification' (following Rigby) in which their reversal of behaviour is an attempt to reverse misfortune, to dance it away? Here I would question Rigby's argument that the two explanations are incompatible, and suggest that among the Samburu at least they have a close bearing on one another.

The intriguing feature is not so much the conditions under which misfortune spreads, but the conditions under which a *rumour* of such misfortune spreads, threatening the one affliction that all Samburu women dread. This is the height of the wet season, which brings a whole range of disturbances after months of drought and hunger (cf. Gluckman 1963:131–2). The expected reaction is one of relief; but there is also a surplus of nervous energy as people turn their attention from the rigours and anxieties of economic survival to broader issues. Generally people are expected to dance, and elders are freer to debate clan affairs and as individuals to go visiting, staying away from home,

159

calling in cattle debts, broking marriages, and so on. This is a time when outbursts of raiding and counter-raiding between tribes for cattle may be expected, and the moran too have a role to fulfil as the traditional defenders of their herds. The Samburu also recognise that the rains can bring a certain irritability and an unsettling feeling that despite the good times all is not quite well. My own personal impression was of a spate of requests for medicine for headaches and vaguely defined disorders, especially from women. It was as if people were disoriented by the sudden change of fortune, and they did not immediately adjust to this (cf. Durkheim 1897:247–50, and Middleton in this volume, p. 179). Unlike the dry season, which builds up slowly and relentlessly, giving Samburu time to adjust themselves mentally and physically, the onset of the wet season has an immediate impact. Milk is not at first plentiful, but it is assured; the long trek for water involving both men (for the cattle) and women (for domestic use) is ended; options for migration suddenly open out.

For the women, however, there are no new options, and they remain subservient. They are in no way consulted by their husbands during their flurry of consultation, which may concern the marriages of *their* daughters, the introduction of a new cowife and potential rival into *their* homes, or giving away cattle previously allocated to *them*. The gulf of inequality that divides the sexes seems to widen. At least during the dry season, with the survival of the family and herd at stake, there is a spirit of cooperation; but this spirit does not appear to carry over to the easier times of the wet season.

The rumour of a threat to women's reproductive powers at this time, even among those who already have children, threatens their whole future, which hinges on bearing children for their husbands. If it is to be explained at a symbolic level, the credibility of this rumour seems to indicate a loss of confidence among women in their domestic status. Within each household this loss of confidence may appear at first as an idiosyncratic domestic issue. Repeated over a whole region at this time, and a sense of crisis gathers momentum suggesting a breakdown of normal communication between the sexes and a widening of the gulf. The rumour appears as an apt expression of this crisis, raising the whole issue to a supernatural plane and challenging the women to recover from their inertia and to assert their rightful role as the reproducers of Samburu society, rather as moran have a rightful role in asserting themselves against any threat to Samburu cattle.

As the rumour gains credibility, it builds up to a force that legitimises the women's response. From their situation of semi-isolation and domestic discord, the *ntorosi* dance brings large numbers of women together, where in militant mood they act in concord. Their consciousness awakened beyond their domestic subservience, their notion of a direct contact with God himself, and the widespread respect they acquire from the elders, seem to revive their spirits and give them renewed confidence to reestablish themselves with greater self-respect in their own households.

Seen from this point of view, this dance is more than a mere safety valve for domestic claustrophobia, and the women are more than passive invalids needing to pamper one another. They are mobilised as a social class, fully conscious of their position and temporarily asserting their right to an independent domain from which even the elders cower. Ritual reversal and a notion of impending ill-fortune (Rigby) may thus be linked to ritual rebellion in a system of oppression (Gluckman). Through a ritualised expostulation, a slump in morale among women is reversed; moreover it is not just the women who are purified, as Rigby suggests, but the whole atmosphere in this reassertion of the importance of womanhood. Their *ntorosi* dance has a brief reality of its own, which readjusts the balance of power between the sexes, and is felt to bring with it a diffuse blessing on their fertility and on the birth of future generations.

Conclusion

Samburu elders measure success through the acquisition of wives and steadfastly deny that many of their problems concerning these wives and virile young bachelors stem indirectly from this pursuit of polygyny. The various dances reflect their areas of concern: the boys, whose pressure for initiation anticipates a general changeover of power within the developmental cycle of the age system; the moran, whose delinquent tendencies have to be contained; and the wives, whose total subservience can never be taken quite for granted. The performance of these dances and the tone of their associated songs might almost be regarded as a gauge of the changing pressures facing the elders' regime. Obviously they rely also on other evidence to make their critical decisions, but the dances are a particularly pointed reminder, coming to a head in the wet season when generally there is trouble abroad, and at full moon when there is a flurry of ritual activity and protest. It is at full moon that initiations take place leading to moranhood for the boys and weddings for the girls. Ostensibly these ceremonies may be regarded as expressions of the gerontocratic power of the elders, who arrange them down to the last detail and control

161

the destinies of the young. But the weddings in particular bring with them dances with pointedly embarrassing themes for the elders, referring on the one hand to their own hypocrisies regarding adultery and on the other to their inability to control the adulterous and stock-thieving activities of the moran. The moonlight also brings ideal conditions for night dancing between moran and girls – and for stock theft. At full moon, as with the onset of the rainy season, there is a general awareness of the interplay of powerful social forces expressed through religious beliefs and associated activity that elders cannot wholly control.

While the elders deplore the topics of the songs, which dent the credibility of their regime, they accept and up to a point encourage the dancing that these songs accompany. There is a general notion that these dances are a propitious part of Samburu life. The women's *ntorosi* is a prayer to God and brings children; boys during the period of their initiation have a ritually protected status and are the future defenders of the society; and the spectacle of moran dances is the central feature of display at a wedding and its omission would be regarded as a bad omen. Just as the elders show little insight into the source of their problem, so they do not suggest in so many words that these dances serve to clear the atmosphere in any way. However, their explicit stamp of approval and acknowledgement that these dances hold a central place in Samburu ritual seem to reflect an intuitive wisdom, based partly on their own earlier experience as moran. The elders may try to limit the worst excesses of some of the dances (as in the second example above), but they cannot and do not wish to eliminate the dances themselves.[4] They bow to forces that they know lie beyond their control, and accept them as God's will.

When protest periodically comes to a head, this may express itself in individual incidents, but collectively, it is expressed in dancing. Following Victor Turner, one might say that this dancing exhibits the antistructure that complements the elders' regime; the elders' passive connivance is the extent to which they too share in its spirit of communitas. The Samburu dance is a coordinated response in a discourse that takes place beyond the confines of the formal political structure, beyond the family, and beyond the realm of normal speech. It provides a transcendental reality that has its roots in play, and yet is greater than the individualistic babble of high spirits. It stretches beyond the dancers themselves and their cultivated skills to reveal an inner vitality that opposes vaguely felt threats. These threats, I suggest, are not from malignant outsiders but from within. They are the excesses of the rule of the elders. Play is pitted against the abuse

of power. Dancing among the Samburu is a display of the irrepressible
antithesis to the shaky premiss of gerontocracy.

NOTES

1 In this account, the ethnographic present refers to the Samburu as they
  were in 1960. More recent visits suggest no fundamental change in the
  model presented here. For a fuller account of the social organisation of the
  Samburu and acknowledgements to those who helped and participated in
  this study, see Spencer 1965.
2 More recent fieldwork among the Matapaato Maasai (1976–7) suggested a
  close similarity between their women's fertility dances and those of the
  Samburu, and my understanding of these dances gained considerably from
  further clues offered by the Maasai. This combined insight did not extend
  to other dances, although clearly there was a broad correspondence in
  dancing as well as in other respects between the two peoples.
3 The Maasai term 'to play' (*a-iguran*) is often used when referring to light-
  hearted dances, and this would be especially appropriate for the women's
  dancing once they have assembled for a wedding and the sombre overtones
  of their *ntorosi* give way to a variety of more jocular dances. The term
  'children' (*inkera*) tends to be extended to all dependants and younger
  persons. Thus from the point of a view of an elder, it is as appropriate for
  women to dance as it is for children to play.
4 This statement is less obviously applicable to the dances of the moran than
  to those of the women. However, an attempt by the British administration
  to curb stock theft by prohibiting moran dances in the 1930s and holding
  the elders responsible failed, demonstrating their lack of control over this
  dancing (Spencer 1973:163).

REFERENCES

Durkheim, E. 1897. *Suicide*. Trans J.A. Spalding and G. Simpson, 1951. New
  York: Free Press.
Gluckman, M. 1963. *Order and Rebellion in Tribal Africa*. London: Cohen &
  West.
Radcliffe-Brown, A.R. 1922. *The Andaman Islanders*. New York: Free Press.
Rigby, P. 1968. "Some Gogo rituals of "purification": an essay on social and
  moral categories'. In E.R. Leach (ed.), *Dialectic in Practical Religion*. Cam-
  bridge: Cambridge University Press.
Spencer, P. 1965. *The Samburu: A Study of Gerontocracy in a Nomadic Tribe*.
  London: Routledge & Kegan Paul.
  1970. 'The function of ritual in the socialization of the Samburu moran'. in
  P. Mayer (ed.), *Socialization: The Approach from Social Anthropology*. ASA
  monograph no. 8. London: Tavistock.
  1973. *Nomads in Alliance: Symbiosis and Growth among the Rendille and Samburu
  of Kenya*. London: Oxford University Press.

Paul Spencer

1976. 'Opposing streams and the gerontocratic ladder: two models of age organization in East Africa'. *Man* (N.S.), 11:153–75.
Turner, V.W. 1969. *The Ritual Process: Structure and Antistructure*. London: Routledge & Kegan Paul.

6 The dance among the Lugbara of Uganda

JOHN MIDDLETON

In this chapter I discuss certain aspects of dances that are performed by the Lugbara people of northwestern Uganda. There are several ways in which one may consider dance: as an aesthetic form of expression in which the key factor is movement, as an outlet for or expression of certain psychological states, as a form of drama for a watching audience, as a means of entering into communication with spirits by becoming possessed, as enjoying the sense of one's own physical movements irrespective of whether one is being watched or not; and there are others. Here I wish to see dance as part of a totality of social behaviour, and to avoid any suggestion that the question 'what is dance?' can simply be answered by stripping dance of its social aspects and functions so as to leave an irreducible basis of human activity. My aim is not to understand what dance is in itself, partly because I am uncertain whether it is a separate and meaningful category, but also because it is its social context that gives it meaning. So I first ask what is that context and its significance for the people who are involved in it. I am concerned to study the Lugbara dance as a way of understanding Lugbara thought and the ways in which they order their experience. I am not primarily concerned with choreography, which is outside my professional competence.

One of the best-known statements about the dance is that reported of Isadora Duncan: 'If I could tell you what it meant, there would be no point in dancing it.' She was referring to inner psychological states and emotions that together made up the 'it' of her remark; they were beyond expression in words and could only be expressed by non-verbal means. Yet these states 'existed' in her own experience and were meaningful both to herself and presumably to those to whom she communicated them by movement and gesture. Bateson notes that her statement 'is a message about the interface between conscious and unconscious' (1973:110). In this chapter I try to show that by their dancing the Lugbara are communicating messages about the structure of their society. These messages are that although they wish their

165

John Middleton

society to be stable, in fact it is never so; that although they desire continuity, certainty, and knowledge about the social relations in which they are involved, in fact these relations are always uncertain and beyond their comprehension; that each lineage group regards its constellation of lineage ties that is part of the total social structure as unique and different from others, as a network that is centred upon itself; and that they can never directly admit to or state these paradoxes in words. Like Isadora Duncan's 'it', Lugbara social structure 'exists' in their experience as constraining it, but it is always ambiguous and conflict-ridden and its continuity is beyond their control. The interface here is not that between conscious and unconscious, at a psychological level, but is at a sociological level, between the idea of structure and the experience of its working and constraint. The Lugbara can express their knowledge about this interface in several ways: by fighting, by sacrificing to the dead and spirits, by verbal arguments about the proper behaviour associated with social roles, by playing games, by notions of pollution, and by dancing. They are all means – and there are others – of trying to comprehend and so control or resolve situations of structural ambiguity: here I consider only the last of them.

The Lugbara and their view of the world

The Lugbara are an agricultural people of some quarter of a million, living on the high open plateau between the headwaters of the Nile and Congo rivers (see Middleton 1965). They lack traditional chiefs, although there have been administrative officials known as chiefs and headmen for the past eighty years. The population density is high, with more than two hundred persons to the square mile in much of the country. The basic social organisation is one of dispersed patrilineal clans; the largest jural communities are the sixty or so subtribes, each based upon a subclan. These are segmented into several levels of territorial sections, each based on a lineage. The smallest is the family cluster formed around a three- or four-generation lineage of which the genealogically senior man is the Elder or Head. Other than these many Elders, each with domestic authority based on his control of the lineage ancestral cult, the only other traditional holders of authority are the rainmakers, one in each subclan, occasional prophets, and 'men whose names are known' whose authority is temporary and based on personal wealth and influence. Thus there are few holders of formal authority outside those at the level of the family cluster. This is a very egalitarian society and one in which due largely

166

to land pressure there is much competition for available resources and perennial intergroup hostility.

The Lugbara believe that the Creator Divinity, *Adroa* or *Adronga*, dwells in the sky and remote from men. *Adroa* has an immanent aspect, *Adro*, which is said to be visible and to dwell in the bushland outside the settlements. There are also many kinds of spirits or divinities, generically known as *adro*, that can harm and possess the living. The nature and powers of all these forces are beyond the understanding and control of ordinary people.

These live in their compounds, the centre for every family cluster of order, authority, certainty, and stability. Beyond are various kinds of fields and beyond them the bushland, some of it open and some of it forested. The dead are buried in graves, some within the compounds and others in various places outside them; most are in liminal areas between the compounds and the surrounding bushland. Lugbara notions about death are complex, but in the context of this chapter it is enough to mention that the process of change from living to dead is marked by the most important rites of transition in Lugbara culture. At death the constituent elements of the person separate and move from the social sphere to those beyond it. The soul goes to Divinity in the sky, the spirit to the wilderness with *Adro*; the soul is later redomesticated by diviners and the spirit remains in the bushland. During this process the social status of the deceased is uncertain, beyond contact by the living, who cannot enter into any direct relationship with him or her: after the establishment of a shrine they may do so again (see Middleton 1960, 1982).

The Lugbara hold certain views about time. It is thought generally to unroll season after season and generation after generation in an ordered and foreseeable manner. However, there are occasions when this process is disrupted and there are then disorder and confusion in social relations: these occasions include the end of an over-long dry season when people are waiting in desperation to plant crops; the end of an unusually wet growing season when too much rain will prevent ripening and harvesting of crops; and the period between a death and the redomestication of the soul as an ancestral ghost. The former two occasions are dealt with by rainmakers, who have the power to 'control' time, the last by diviners; both are persons of ambiguous status who can mediate between men and Divinity.

Death dances

All these factors are relevant to an understanding of the functions and meanings of the dance for the Lugbara. There are several kinds

167

John Middleton

of dance. A dance is generally known as *ongo*, a word that also means 'song'. The verb 'to dance' is *ongo tozu*, 'to tread or step a dance or song'. Although there are songs without dance there are no dances without song. More specifically the word *ongo* refers to those dances danced as integral parts of mortuary rites. There are also courtship dances known as *walangaa*, a word that has the connotation of 'to move sideways so as to form a circle'. There are also women's dances, harvest dances, and prophetic dances. I wish first to consider the death and courtship dances.

Properly speaking the dances called *ongo* are those dances after a death by groups of men and women related to the deceased by patrilineal lineage ties. Other *ongo* dances are specifically known as *abi*: these are danced by groups of affines at various periods up to a year after the death. The *ongo* proper are also referred to as *auwu-ongo*, 'wailing dances', and the *abi* as *avico-ongo*, 'playing dances'. Both include some half-dozen distinct dances, each with different names and slightly different musical patterns; but details are not significant here.

The wailing dances are begun as soon after the death as possible, in some cases even before the actual burial. They are held mainly during the daytime, but may continue at night if the deceased was an old and senior man. The dancers are his lineage kin: the more senior he was the wider the span of lineage concerned and the longer the total period of the dancing. The *abi* dances are danced later, properly a year after the death. The dancers come from their own lineage homes to that of the deceased, where they dance and are given arrows as a sign that the affinal link is reaffirmed, even though the person who originally linked the two groups is dead. They come either as 'sisters' sons', or as 'sisters' husbands'. The lineage members of the deceased come to dance and wail; the affines come to 'play' and to create and show joy, *aiiko*. This word is used in many situations and refers essentially to the sense of joy and satisfaction that disrupted lineage and kinship ties have been reaffirmed. One wails for the deceased but is joyful that the disruption caused by his death has been repaired.

If the *ongo* is not performed, then the deceased is believed to have been insulted by the lack of respect shown to him, and may then send sickness or nightmares to his living kin or appear to them as a spectre. In this case great care will be taken to have *abi* dances performed about a year after his death. Of course, a man who leaves no daughters or who has only one or two sisters will have no affines or only a handful of scattered ones who would not dance an *abi* dance

168

for him in any case. The dances for a young person, especially a young woman, or a child are small and may last for only a few hours. On the other hand, those for a chief or a very old and respected man may last for days on end, and the *abi* dances may be spread over a year or even longer as various groups of affines come from far away to pay their respects to him. Death dances are not performed for infants, lepers, or those struck by lightning, all of whom are exposed in the bushland. Nor is the *ongo* danced for a rainmaker: his powers come to him directly from Divinity, and he is regarded as having 'died' symbolically at his initiation as rainmaker.

Both *ongo* and *abi* dances are performed in the open as a convenient flat piece of grassy land not far from the compound of the deceased. The site is chosen in relation both to the grave and to the shrines that will later be placed for the deceased. Most adult people are buried in a space in the homefields between the compound and the bushland; the grave is marked by stones but is soon hoed over and may be forgotten. The heads of minimal lineages are buried farther away and a fig tree is planted at the head of the grave, which stands there for many years and marks its site. Thus the dances are held in various places according to the status of the deceased, the higher the status the farther the arena being from the compound. Although to the casual observer the differences may not appear very noticeable, they are in fact symbolically highly significant.

Ongo and *abi* dances are at first sight similar, but there are significant differences between them, especially as regards personnel and the nature of the songs sung by the dancers. Both are danced by men in groups and by women as individuals, the men in the centre of the arena and the women at its periphery. As I have mentioned, the *ongo* proper are danced by members of lineages that are related patrilineally to that of the deceased. As the dancers dance they sing songs that praise the prowess of their own lineage segments and insultingly attack that of others whose members are present. They also praise the personal qualities of the deceased: they 'bewail his name'. Most of the dancers are youngish men, both married and unmarried, those known as *karule wara*, 'big youths'. The dancers have shaven their heads, often leaving small tufts of hair in which they put feathers, and the occasion is one of competition and hostility, both among themselves and more especially between the dance groups that succeed each other in the dance arena. Often there are fierce arguments, which will be calmed by the elders present or which may lead to fist fights in which teeth are knocked out. A group will usually dance for about half an hour, to be followed by another group, which tries to oust its predecessors from the arena: there is frequent quarrelling between waiting groups as to which will dance first. The point here is that the order of dancing expresses the actual constellation of lineage ties which has been disrupted by the death and which must now be restructured and reaffirmed. It is similar in this regard to the pattern of seating for sharing meat at sacrifices to the dead. Women who are close patrilineal kin of the deceased shave their heads and cover their faces with white clay or white ashes, to show their close personal relationship to the deceased. But the aggressive and competitive elements in the men's behaviour are lacking in that of women, who do not enter the lines of dancers but stand outside it.

The group – perhaps two dozen men of a single lineage – dances as a single team, divided into two lines facing each other. The women dance outside, not in lines but in pairs or small groups and without the precision of the men. Every now and again a man will run out of the line or from the group of spectators and do a short individual dance, but one of the same movement as those in the lines are doing. He will also call his *cere* in honour of the deceased. The *cere* is a falsetto whooping cry which is 'owned' by every adult, both male and female. The Lugbara language is tonal and the 'melody' of the call refers to a sentence associated with its 'owner'. To utter the *cere* of another person is a deep insult, tantamount to trying to take over or possess their personality. A man calls his *cere* in warfare and at death dances, and when drunk men often call them when lurching homewards as a sign that they are not enemies to be attacked. Now and again at a death dance a man will run out of the arena hand in hand with a related women (at wailing dances a lineage sister, and at *abi* a sister-in-law), and at the edge of the bushland, facing it, he whoops his *cere* call and shoots arrows into the bush (or he may imitate doing so). The woman also gives her own *cere* call and imitates shooting an arrow. The pair then returns to the arena. This is an integral part of the dance and is done to show that the dancers wish both to avenge the deceased and also show the powers of the bushland, which are divine and dangerous, that they have no fear and will protect their homesteads from the terrors of the wilderness, which they are thus driving back to their proper domain – at death the powers of the bushland are thought to close in on a village. This also shows the *adro* or spirit of the deceased that it has no future place within the settlement.

A death dance for an important old man may be attended by well over a hundred people. Most of them are drinking, many are drunk and often hostile and aggressive. Most will dance now and again individually and in small groups even if not taking part in the main dance. All join in singing when they can although the main words are sung only by the dancers themselves. These dances are said to be times of confusion. People say that they are then 'like children', not because they are behaving in a childlike way but because order and the recognition of legitimate authority have been destroyed by death. It is said that subclan and lineage siblings, normally separated by a rigidly observed incest taboo, may have intercourse in the bushland during the height of the dances, especially when these continue after darkness. A marked feature of these dances is the trancelike condition of the dancers after a long period of dancing and drinking, and usually with little food also; they also stagger about shouting incoherently and have often to be physically restrained by onlookers, who take their arms and hold them on the ground until the seizure wears off.

These dances attract onlookers from wide areas, especially younger men and women: *ongo* are considered to be public spectacles to a greater extent than are *abi*, which are rather the affairs of the respective groups of affines. The onlookers stand at the edge of the arena, often breaking into dance steps. This is not considered as 'dancing', *tozu*, but as a sign of sympathy with the mourners. Their presence helps to define the arena: all are looking inwards to where the dancers and drummers are and their backs are turned towards the surrounding fields and bushland. They break ranks to allow through those who run out to call their *cere* and to shoot arrows, then close ranks again once these have returned.

Abi dances are essentially similar in that they are held in the daytime and are performed by members of lineages dancing in lines; in this case the lineages are affinally related to that of the deceased. However, their songs are not expressions of hostility but rather only of self-pride, and there is no running out of the arena to shoot arrows and call *cere*. The *abi* marks the closing of the full period of mourning and is complementary to the *ongo* proper in that together they make the restatement of proper lineage and affinal ties that is begun at the *ongo* and ended by the joy of the *abi*.

Dances of courtship

The dance known as *walangaa* is different. This is a dance of younger men and women, held in the evenings when there is a moon, usually in a marketplace after the end of market day. The generally accepted purpose of the *walangaa* is to enable people from a wide area to meet

John Middleton

and to make sexual assignations, as well as simply to have the pleasure of dancing in a crowd. It is not attended by married women or older widows, but by unmarried women and younger men; old men rarely attend. Children take part on the edges of the arena in the early part of the evening. There is not really an audience of onlookers but only of dancers who are taking a temporary break from the hurly-burly of the dance itself. Instead of watching and being clustered around the central arena, as in the *ongo*, the onlookers are themselves mainly engaged in flirting, talking, and taking and sending messages between lovers: couples are continually leaving the arena and newcomers entering it. Finally, in some places the licensee of the marketplace itself may take a small fee from those wishing to dance, which would be unthinkable in the case of death dances.

The pattern of the dance is very different from that of the death dances. Whereas in the latter men enter the dance by lineage segment and the women stand at the edge of the arena, also more or less according to their lineage affiliation, in the *walangaa* men and women form dance lines that dance a foot or so opposite the other in a wide circle. Usually a group of brothers dances opposite a group of sisters, which is the pattern of visiting the girls' sleeping houses at nighttime. But often a single boy dances opposite a single girl, both in the main ring and also on the edges, where they dance surrounded by a few friends who admire their skill. There is great display of originality and agility in the dance movements, and pairs of dancers may give impromptu dance exhibitions while their neighbours in the ring stand back and applaud them. A man and girl dance opposite each other, their hands usually resting on each other's shoulders; if they are very skilful they may rest their foreheads together and leave their arms free for balance. In any case there is usually direct physical contact between them.

The dances compared

I wish here to make a brief comparison between the dances. Their various characteristics may be arranged in certain obvious categories: those to do with personnel, time, and place; gesture, music, and song; associated forms of individual and group behaviour; and the social relationships involved.

As regards personnel, the death dances are performed essentially by men. Women play a less important part as onlookers and they may run out to shoot arrows into the bushland; but these women are not otherwise dancing although they may join in some of the singing.

172

In the *walangaa* the personnel comprise younger men and unmarried women, that is, the socially less important members of the community. They do not dance or attend the dance as members of lineage groups as such, although they may dance as groups of siblings. And nonkin and even passers-by may attend if they are known generally to the local people, whereas at death dances, although neighbours may stand nearby and watch, they stay on the edge of the arena, and passing strangers would be beaten if they tried to attend at all.

As for the occasion, the time and the place, *ongo* are mortuary dances, *walangaa* are for courtship: the former are for 'wailing' and for 'joy', the latter for *o'buzu*, 'cajoling' or 'seduction'. *Ongo* are generally danced in the daytime, *walangaa* in the late evening and night, although both may spill over into other times on occasion. *Walangaa* are danced throughout the year, whereas death dances are not danced during the height of the planting or harvesting seasons but mainly in the dry season (November to March) and the time after the first harvest (May to September) when there is fresh grain available for beer making. As regards place, the *ongo* are performed in the liminal area between the safe and social centre of the homestead and the asocial and dangerous wilderness of spiritual power, where there are no social boundaries at all. *Walangaa* are danced mostly in marketplaces: these are in a sense liminal, because if near the centre of a settlement they are not used for housing, and often they are set between settlements on a road. They are places where passing strangers may bring in foreign 'medicines' to harm people, and they are not attached to nor associated with any particular local descent group. Both dances are danced in liminal areas but these are of different kinds.

Death dances are characterised by permitted, indeed by almost obligatory, near-trance and drunkenness (on beer); *walangaa* are characterised by lack of trance or similar behaviour and the disapproval of drunkenness (and if a man is drunk it is typically on nontraditional local gin made from sugar). Death dances are expected to be competitive and aggressive: an individual nudge may lead to a fist fight and even to one with weapons, and there is often fighting between groups to decide which will enter the arena first. Violence at *walangaa* is strongly disapproved and I have seen a dance stopped completely by the drummers in protest against loud and physical quarrelling between sets of brothers over the same girls.

The form of the dance itself is important. The male dancers in the death dances form two lines set within a circle of onlookers (who should really be regarded as participants in the sense that a theatre audience is composed of participants with the actors). This circle is set very close to the line of dancers and the whole forms a rigid pattern. On the other hand the *walangaa* is a circular dance without any straight or clearly defined linear pattern, and the edges of the dance are not clearly marked, people standing watching, resting, and talking, haphazardly without any pattern.

These dances are also occasions for music and singing. In death dances the music is played on various instruments: drums, horns, trumpets, rattles, and bells. There are three double-ended drums (the membranes being of skin from the ears of elephants), known as the daughter (treble), mother, and grandmother (bass). They play together, the mother supplying the main beat, the grandmother the steady bass supporting beat, and the daughter the high chattering that the Lugbara say makes the music exciting. They are accompanied by horns (cattle horns), by the small trumpets of wood with a finially attached gourd in which is the mouthpiece, and by the six-foot-long wooden trumpets made of hollowed-out tree trunks, often shaped like a man and sounding a slow and majestic deep note that can be heard for many miles. In a dance there are always many false starts (often because a drum needs further tightening over a fire), but once the dance becomes 'sweet', when the exciting and pervasive rhythm takes hold, then the drums may only rarely stop; new drummers take over from tired ones without breaking the rhythm and the music can continue for several hours without a break. There is also singing. Only the dancers sing, there being a soloist accompanied by the remainder chanting. Women join in often and punctuate the men's singing with ululations.

In *walangaa* the same three drums are used, but not horns, trumpets, or rattles. The rhythms are different from those used in death dances, and innovation in movement and beat is approved, whereas this is not so for the death dances. The songs, sung by women's and men's voices antiphonally, are topical and come and go in and out of fashion after a few months, whereas those for death dances remain year in and year out without change (although of course the details of lineage names change on every occasion). *Walangaa* songs are not sexually obscene, whereas those for *ongo* may often contain obscene insults directed at lineages other than those of the singers. In the *walangaa* a burst of singing and drumming may last for twenty or thirty minutes, followed by a break of a few minutes before the next dance as people catch their breath, think of new songs, or change drummers; *ongo* may continue for many hours without stop. Whereas in death dances there is a pattern or structure of dances and songs that fit into a programme, associated with the rivalry between dance groups that succeed one another, in the *walangaa* there is no programme of this kind: the dances and songs are similar throughout the evening, and although individuals come and go the general body of participants and observers does not change its identity or form itself into distinct groups.

There are also differences in the dance movements. The movements in both *ongo* and *abi* death dances are similar. Those of the men consist of leaping up and down. This is not the spectacular leaping of peoples such as the Maasai and Samburu but it has something of the same quality. It is a physically separate activity, with little variation in movement, with immense expenditure of energy that leads often (or indeed usually) to a condition of trance. Lugbara often refer to this condition as being *azazaa*, a word used also for prophets and for sexually promiscuous and 'wandering' women. The dance appears as an essentially inward-directed dance, in the sense that the dancer is intensely serious, unsmiling, intent on leaping up and down although also being conscious of fellow-dancers, because to nudge one of them while dancing in line can lead to quarrels and even wounding.

Men and women in the death dances make different movements, a distinction related by the Lugbara to their notions of the social characteristics and positions of men and women. In the *ongo* men dance from the feet, the legs being straight and together; the arms are either stretched out above their heads or holding weapons – spears, quivers, bows and arrows – or flywhisks made of cows' tails: all these objects represent masculinity and men's place in society. Women, in contrast, hop loosely, merely bending their knees, and the arms are held out in front of them at shoulder level and usually bent at the elbow; they hold their arms in a supple waving manner. In the *walangaa* there is no difference in the gestures of men and women. Whereas in the death dances the closest link between individual dancers is between those dancing side by side and of the same sex, in the *walangaa* it is between individual dancers of opposite sex who dance directly opposite one another and form a single unit. The gestures of both are identical and very free: if a man decides to lift his arms above his head in order to balance his body his partner will do the same. Much emphasis is placed on the agility of foot movements, and in the dancing of children on the edge of the crowd all their effort is put into using their feet gracefully and agilely so that they appear to be dancing several inches off the ground altogether. When I asked about these differences, I was told that men are heavier than women, with slower-moving limbs; they added that the real difference is that

175

in death dances men dance in groups whereas women dance individually or as groups of sisters only: men are said always to act in groups and 'therefore' to dance more rigidly than women who, being more individualistic, dance more freely as individuals. Women are also more liable to trance and so to act idiosyncratically: they are 'evil' and in touch more easily with spiritual power in the bushland rather than with the ancestors, who keep closer contact with men.

I turn now to what are in terms of symbolic meaning more basic differences. Death dances are elements in an important and elaborate rite of transition, virtually the only one among the Lugbara, who have no important rites at puberty. The funerary rites have certain main characteristics. One is the process from the physical death of a man, through the flight of his soul to the sky to be purified and strengthened by Divinity and that of his other spiritual elements to the bushland, and to the redomestication of the soul and its transformation into an ancestor or ghost with its own shrine. The other aspect is the process from the dissolution of the constellation of lineage, kin and neighbourhood ties centred on the status of the deceased to a new constellation of ties centred on the new status of ancestor and ghost. This is done by the distribution of arrows and the dancing of the *ongo* and *abi* dances. These have obvious characteristics of reversal and liminality (or marginality), both in space and time and in the behaviour of participants. Here the behaviour expected towards strangers – violence and sexuality – is reversed and carried out towards kin. They are associated with trance, the significance of which in this context is, I suggest, that the dancers become closely linked to the soul and other elements of the deceased in sky and wilderness. The wilderness is the seat of divine power and as such dangerous, and its forces are repulsed by the shooting of arrows and the demonstrations of personal identity in the face of otherwise overwhelming spiritual power by the calling of *cere*. Also by being in a state of trance the dancers forsake their customary relations with others within the lineage group and retreat into a form of total individuality, linked with Divinity and the dead.

The death dances are central elements in the most important rite of transition among the Lugbara and their characteristics represent that fact. The *walangaa* are quite different in this respect. There are fewer symbols of liminality and ambiguity attached to them. True, the space, that of the market, is outside ordinary social use and is associated with trade and nonkin, which represent the nonsocial. The night-time is a period of liminality, when the bushland is said to close in on the settlements. But the entire sense of ambiguity is much less clear than is the case with the death dances, mainly because the basic lineage organisation – ever-changing in fact although ideally unchanging – is not involved, nor the great and irremediable change of status from living to dead.

We may summarise the relationships between death and courtship dances by saying that they both make statements about the proper or ordered relations between men and women and between lineages. But there are differences that are complementary and that together add up to a single complex. Death dances take place in daytime, refer to situations of broken and then restored granting and control of women's fertility (by exchanges of arrows), and to relations of affinity. Wives take part, and dancers and movements are different, the difference representing their complementarity. Courtship dances take place at night, wives do not attend but only unmarried girls ('clan sisters' and 'lovers'), the emphasis is on sexuality and not on fertility, and the similarity of movement of men and women marks the lack of complementarity between men and women, whose roles only later become complementary with marriage.

Other dances

These are not the only dances found among the Lugbara, and I wish here to consider three others. The first two are known as *nyambi* and are performed by women. The *nyambi* that is performed very frequently is a small dance by the women of a minimal or minor lineage group only, the sisters of a woman who has died or of a girl who is leaving her natal home to get married and who is thereby lost to her sisters, who mourn for her. The music is played on a special board of wood carved with charcoal and laid across a hole in the ground; on it are grated or rubbed two sticks that produce a harsh percussive sound, which is accompanied by gourd rattles (as are used by diviners to send themselves into trance). The songs refer to the occasion and are usually sexual in reference: men say that they are so obscene that they are shocked by them and cannot bring themselves to repeat them. The attendant women dance in a rather shuffling circle. It lasts a few hours only and is not of great importance even though frequently performed. It draws few spectators.

The other dance called *nyambi* is very much larger, the dancers properly being all the women of an entire subtribe. It is performed on two occasions, neither of which occur every year. The first is either immediately after an exceptionally good harvest or after a harvest that is very late due to too much rainfall during the ripening season; the

John Middleton

second is at the very end of an exceptionally long dry season. These are both times when the orderly passing of everyday time is considered to have stopped, when there is likely to be much intergroup quarrelling and even fighting over scarce resources. The women come together in the bushland near the subclan raingrove and dance through the settlements, clapping their hands and shaking gourds and rattles, singing sexually obscene songs and abusing any man who may be rash enough to meet them. They may be led by a man wearing the antlers of a waterbuck or the horns of a buffalo, and sometimes women's pubic leaves worn over his male apparel. They dance finally up to the raingrove, where the rainmaker is waiting for them; he then enters to perform his rites. People say that this dance is a sign that the world has gone wrong and confused, that ordinary social hierarchies and relations are 'lost' or 'forgotten', and that the rainmaker must now 'start' the new year and the orderly passing of time again. He reorders temporal and social categories, and thereby orders interlineage relations that have been threatened, weakened or even destroyed by quarrelling over resources whose scarcity and allocation have become all-important at these times (see Middleton 1978). Thus they have certain resemblances to death dances, in the sense that they are performed in times of categorical confusion and uncertainty and of temporal liminality. In this *nyambi* dance some features of the death dances are reversed and as it were parodied. I have been told by old men that although a dance it is really the opposite of a dance, a kind of mirror reflection. Instead of men dancing in lines composed of patrilineal kin, it is danced by women of the subclan irrespective of their lineage and affinal affiliations; they have no organisation in the sense of dancing in groups but appear rather as a mob (I was told by men that they run like ants, in a fast-moving stream); and there are no dance steps or gestures, the women merely running and leaping while singing and shouting. The death dances resolve confusion and disorder in lineages and neighbourhood relations, the *nyambi* do the same in cosmic relations; the former are based, in Lugbara thought, on men, the latter on women. The distinctions between the dances are obvious and are hinged on the opposition between home and wilderness, marked especially by the *nyambi* being performed by women who come into the settlements from the outside, led by a transvestite hunter bearing the horns of the animals that he has killed in the bushland.

Both death and *nyambi* dances are concerned with the structuring of social and cosmological categories. There is a last case that is relevant here, although of course I have not witnessed it and details of

178

the dance are sparse. This was a dance performed by the adherents of the great prophet Rembe in 1915 and 1916. Rembe was a Kakwa prophet who led the Yakan cult, which was based on the drinking of water in which was thought to be divine power. The aim of the cult was to remove a series of associated disasters that came to Lugbaraland at the time: meningitis, smallpox, rinderpest, Arab slavers, and Europeans. Rembe attempted to build a new form of society in which men and women, and old and young, were to be equal, and, by the encouragement of clan incest, ties of descent were to be ignored: he was trying to abandon the principles of sex, age, and descent on which traditional Lugbara society was based. He went into trance and spoke divine messages with glossolalia. The adherents marched up and down under a flagpole (to represent the new government) and then, after drinking the water, danced all day and night until totally exhausted. Songs were sung about the powers of Rembe and Divinity. I was told by old people who had taken part that they expected to awake later in the new Utopia. So here again we have a rite of transition, on a societywide scale, and the restructuring of categories as part of the dance (see Middleton 1963).

Dance and the resolution of ambiguity

I wish now to argue back from these cases to my discussion of death dances. All are closely linked to notions of time, of external divine power, and of divine secrecy and truth. They are all elements of the processes of the cyclical development of lineage, neighbourhood, and the entire society.

Death dances, the *nyambi* dances, and the prophetic dance (the first mainly by men, the second by women, and the last by both men and women) are all associated with rites of transition and/or the changing of seasonal temporal rhythm; the *walangaa* is not so associated. The factor of ritual or formality is important. All the various features of behaviour, liminality, and reversal that mark the *ongo*, *nyambi*, and prophetic dances are formal and expected: they are items of ritualised behaviour. Whereas the *walangaa* is characterised by individual, free activity that lacks any content of authority, the other dances are characterised by formal activity and relations that contain and express authority (even when reversed, as in the *nyambi*). They contain movements that are clearly defined and proper, and behaviour by the participants is also defined and proper, even if sometimes absent (as with trance and drunkenness); movement is controlled and never free; and the occasions for them are all strictly defined – they are never

179

performed ad hoc. They are all ritual performances, at times of social or cosmic uncertainty and confusion. All are associated with ambiguity in social relations, liminality in time and space, and the merging of the realms of the social and the Divine and so with the redefining and restructuring of social categories.

Other Lugbara institutions are (or have been traditionally) associated with such times and with the restructuring of relations (see Middleton 1977). The most obvious is interlineage feud: this was also a formalised activity in which the participants were men grouped by lineage segment; it occurred mainly in the 'timeless' dry season; it was accompanied by the calling of *cere*; it took place in spatially liminal areas between lineage territories; the actual force was strictly controlled, and should men actually be killed or severely injured it was regarded as in a sense improper (even though both these did occur); it was an aspect of the working of a segmentary lineage system in which competition between segments lay at the heart of the activity whose aim was 'structurally' to remove uncertainty as to the proper relationship between lineages and to restore an affirmed constellation of these relations; like the death dances it resembled an organised game or sport.

The similarities between the feud and the dance should perhaps not be pressed too far. But consideration of them both brings us back to the original point of this paper: if Lugbara ritual dances are performed largely to mark, and thereby perhaps to effect, processes of restructuring social ties, why do they dance? Why their dances are performed in liminal places and liminal periods, and marked often by reversal behaviour, is understandable and makes sense, but why not use other means? Sometimes they do, as in the feud and warfare, and these are in a sense reasonably final in deciding the new and effective constellations of lineage ties and authority relations. Let us return to the notion of 'joy', *aiiko*, which is a central part of the *abi* dances. This notion is also an ambiguous one: the affinally related groups come to dance, to mourn, and to rejoice. I was told by a friend watching affines coming to dance the *abi* for his elder brother: 'Yes, it is good that they rejoice. Now we know that they did not cause my brother's death and that they respect us and are happy that we are still affines. Let them rejoice: you see, later they will die and then it will be our turn to go and rejoice there' (on the next occasion they will perhaps be sons-in-law themselves). I suggest that the death dances are performed as dance precisely because the situation is one of uncertainty and also of delicacy: verbal statements alone would – or might – be too crude. There is no single motive for dancing: it can be to rejoice in a Western sense (as in the *walangaa*), or to be glad that a difficult or ill-defined period is over, or even to insult in a subtle way. A similar ambivalence can be seen in the use of *cere* calls: it can be aggressive, protective, or insulting. In an ambiguous situation every participant can play as he pleases, and may if he wishes even retire altogether from his fellows by becoming in a state of trance and thereby being linked to the ancestors and Divinity; and also his actions and nonverbal statements may be interpreted by the onlookers as they please in their turn.

This notion of ambiguity needs more consideration than I can give to it here. Essentially it refers to the paradox that occurs in all Lugbara social relations. They hold that there is an ideally unchanging structure to their society, yet in actuality the constellation of relations that compose that structure is always changing in both form (the genealogical links between groups and persons) and in content (the distribution of legitimate authority among groups and persons). This paradox of disequilibrium comes about as a consequence of the structural and cosmic processes that have been mentioned earlier. In all these situations the Lugbara include dances as part of the rites that they perform in response to them. The dances are formalised ritual events in which the local groups and communities involved make certain statements, both to their own members and to the wider society and the ancestors. The central questions that I have asked in this chapter have been those of the content of these statements and the means used to make them. They contain two parts, details of which vary from one kind of dance situation to another. The first is that the group concerned shows that it has been thrown into temporary uncertainty and disarray by the confusion of social and cosmic categories, and they express this in terms of reversal and liminality. The second is that the group ends the dance, or sets of dances, by showing the re-formed and reordered social and cosmic categories, the means used being rejoicing, giving the rainmaker or prophet authority to perform their secret rites, and so on. In brief, they first demonstrate the existence of confusion or ambiguity in social relations, and thereby show that they comprehend it (as far as Divinity allows them to do so) and so intend to bring it under control. Then they act out this control and thereby bring about order and stability in society once again. We come here to a consideration not only of dance but of drama and ritual, which lie outside the scope of this chapter. What I do wish to suggest is that at least in the case of Lugbara the dance is hardly a natural or haphazard pattern of movements performed by people because they find it agreeable to do so –

John Middleton

although in the case of the *walangaa* this is to some extent true. To understand the Lugbara dance we must see it in its total context, as an expression of underlying structural contradictions and conflicts that cannot be expressed otherwise except by dogmatic or destructive statements.

NOTE

The field research on which this paper is based was carried out between 1949 and 1953 with assistance from the Worshipful Company of Goldsmiths and the Colonial Social Science Research Council, London. Initial writing up of the material was aided by a grant from the Wenner-Gren Foundation for Anthropological Research, New York.

REFERENCES

Bateson, Gregory. 1973. *Steps to an Ecology of Mind*. St. Albans, Herts.: Paladin.
Middleton, John. 1960. *Lugbara Religion*. London: Oxford University Press for International African Institute.
    1963. 'The Yakan or Allah water cult among the Lugbara of Uganda'. *Journal of the Royal Anthropological Institute*, 93(1):80–108.
    1965. *The Lugbara of Uganda*. New York: Holt, Rinehart & Winston.
    1977. 'Ritual and ambiguity in Lugbara society'. In S. F. Moore and B. Myerhoff (eds.), *Secular Ritual*. Assen: Van Gorcum.
    1978. 'The rainmaker among the Lugbara of Uganda'. In M. Cartry et al., *Systèmes de signes: textes réunis en hommage à Germaine Dieterlen*. Paris: Hermann.
    1982. 'Lugbara death'. In Maurice Bloch and Jonathan Parry (eds.), *Death and the Regeneration of Life*. Cambridge: Cambridge University Press.

7 Style and meaning in Umeda dance

ALFRED GELL

The objective of this chapter is the application of structural analysis to the dance, in particular to a sequence of ritual dances performed in the Waina-Sowanda district of the West Sepik Province, Papua New Guinea.[1] I made a study of this ritual, which is known as *ida*, in Umeda village in 1969–70, and the results of this study were published in a monograph (*Metamorphosis of the Cassowaries*, Gell 1975), which readers of the present essay may consult for more background information than can be provided here, both concerning the ritual itself, and the sociological setting. More recently, I revisited the area in the company of a film maker (Mr. Chris Owen of the Institute of Papua New Guinea Studies, Boroko, Papua New Guinea), who made a film of the *ida* ritual. This was subsequently put at my disposal, making the analysis reported on here possible (Owen 1977, 1979).

The *ida* ceremony occupies two nights and two days, and consists of the appearance of a sequence of masked dancers, who dance in the ritual arena before an audience of villagers and visitors from elsewhere. Music is provided by a band of wooden trumpets and women also dance, though without wearing masks or adopting named ritual roles, like the men. In the above mentioned book I provide an analysis of *ida*, which takes as its starting point the idea that each of the successive roles danced in the arena is a transformation of preceding ones, and an approximation towards the final apotheosis of man in the guise of a red bowman, the *ipele*. The initial dancers to appear are 'cassowaries' – black-painted men wearing bushy masks of treelike aspect. They stand for nature, the wild, the uncontrolled, the primordial. This role confers the greatest individual prestige, but is at the same time negatively evaluated. In Umeda the cassowaries are accompanied by two junior dancers (*motnatamwa*), whose repressed style of dance and red body paint underline the symbolic significance of the black paint and wild cavortings of the senior cassowaries. As the ritual progresses, the dancers enact roles that depart, ever more radically, from this initial stereotype. The cassowaries are followed

Alfred Gell

by 'sago' dancers, still wearing treelike masks, but lacking the warlike black paint, and then by the 'firewood' dancers with masks constructed on similar lines, but with a tall decorative shaft. Then during the daytime come the 'fish' dancers, emblematic of masculinity, erotically attractive, but also evoking cultural themes, particularly through their masks, which are constructed of the 'cultural' coconut palm (as opposed to the 'natural' sago/arecoid constituents of the cassowary mask) and are painted with clan designs.

During the second day, the fish are joined by more dancers, who diverge even more sharply from the cassowary. The 'termite' dancers lack the enlarged, weighted penis gourd which previous dancers wear (and exploit in their dancing in a manner to be described below), and have only the smaller penis gourds of everyday attire (cf. Gell 1971 for illustrations and discussion). Their masks are highly simplified versions of the cassowary mask. The termites represent domesticity and the care of children (they may be given babies to carry). On this day there are throwbacks to the uncivilised state represented by the cassowary, in the form of ogres of various sorts who make brief appearances to frighten and amuse the spectators. One is a transvestite man parodying the female dance style, another is the hateful creeping *kwod*, whose distinctive dance will be described below.

Finally the ritual culminates in the appearance of the *ipele* bowmen, who differ from all previous dancers in being identified as men, rather than natural species (sago, fish, etc.). They are accompanied by preceptors, because although they are hunters, they are 'new men' who have not yet learned how to shoot their arrows. They perform the final ritual of loosing off the *ipele* arrows, and with this the ritual is concluded.

The dancing at *ida* is very striking and varied. Most notable, perhaps, is the orgiastic style adopted by the cassowary, sago, and to a lesser extent the fish dancers. All these (male) dancers wear a weighted penis gourd, and a belt strung with hard seeds around the abdomen. They dance in a leaping, undulatory fashion, which causes the penis gourd to fly up, striking the abdominal belt with every step, so that it emits a sharp clicking sound. This dance is very overtly sexual, and I have discussed the symbolism involved elsewhere (Gell 1975:232–4). But this dance is only one of many different styles seen at *ida* and in this account I want to concentrate more on Umeda dances as a *system*, rather than on the symbolic meaning of individual dances. In my previous account, I was only able to indicate very gross contrasts between wild unrestrained dancing, associated with the ritual roles that fall at the cassowary end of the wild/civilised continuum, versus restrained

184

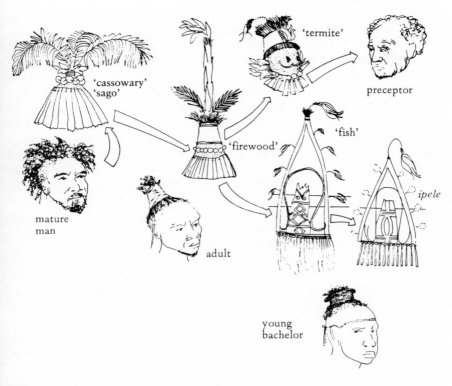

'termite'

'cassowary'
'sago'

preceptor

'fish'

'firewood'

ipele

mature
man

adult

young
bachelor

Figure 7.1 Transformation of mask styles in the *ida* ceremony

dances appropriate to such figures as the *ipele* bowmen, whose relatively cramped style of dancing expresses the repression of spontaneity that culture imposes (Gell 1975:289–90). With the aid of filmed
material, I think I can now go a bit further than this and construct a
model of Umeda dance as a set of variations on a basic armature. This
model that I propose is an 'observer's model' utilising behavioural data,
not an indigenous model provided by the Umeda themselves. A model
is a codified, simplified description, within which relationships between variables (here, patterns of movement) can be made explicit. It
may be helpful to the reader to indicate the application of structural
analysis of the kind I have in mind, by means of an example. Figure
7.1 is a flow chart showing the transformations of mask styles worn by
various ritual actors in *ida*. It will be seen that there are obvious generic
resemblances between the styles of mask worn by the cassowaries, the
sago dancers, the firewood dancers, and finally the termite dancers;

Alfred Gell

and there is also an obvious relation between the fish mask and the *ipele* mask. One can also see that the firewood mask is a kind of bridging example between the cassowary/sago mask and the fish/*ipele* masks. In other words, the masks worn at *ida* form a *set*, and each mask can be transformed into the others by means of simple operations (for example, the *ipele* mask is a miniaturised fish mask, the firewood mask is an elongated cassowary mask, and so on). It is through the patterning of these contrasts and continuities that the masks, as a set, encode meanings; that is, as mask A is to mask B, so ritual role A is to ritual role B, and so on. The masks are visible and tangible exponents of implicit dimensions of symbolic significance. Moreover, the mask set is not an isolated domain, but incorporates many references to the world outside the ritual – which is also the world to which the ritual ultimately refers. It will be seen in Figure 7.1 that there is a parallel between the bushy hairstyle of the senior married man and the bushy top of the cassowary mask, versus the controlled bachelor hairstyle and the neatly constructed *ipele* mask, while the mask set taken as a whole obviously makes references to, and is based on, the everyday traditional hairstyle whereby the hair is drawn up into a decorative open cylinder of woven rattan. Thus the mask set (as a group of transformations on an armature, the basic mask) draws upon elements of mundane life in elaborating its specific ritual meanings; in particular it recapitulates the sociological oppositions between various classes of men at differing stages of the life cycle via references to the variety of hairstyles these classes of males adopt. This, in effect, is the strategy of the ritual as a whole, since the purpose that lies behind it is precisely the acting out, through a ritual drama, of the general processes of biosocial regeneration, a task that culminates in the appearance of the *ipele* bowmen, who are new men, produced during the course of the ritual itself. The masks, through a variety of references too complex to be pursued further here, encode this regenerative cycle, but the point that I wish to stress here is the way in which in order to grasp their meaning it is necessary to consider them as a transformation set, rather than simply as a set of individual masks. The objective now in view is to provide an analogous analysis where the dance proper, rather than the accoutrements of the dancers, is concerned. This raises a number of rather special problems.

Graphic analysis

One of the difficulties that has prevented progress in the field of the anthropology of dance being as rapid as that in, say, the anthropology

186

of visual art, has been the need for a notation of dance movements that combines accuracy with some degree of readability for the non-dance expert. Art objects, such as the masks mentioned in the previous section, can be simply *reproduced*, but this simple graphic reduction is not feasible where dance movements are concerned. Labanotation and Benesh notation both have their advocates, but are equally incomprehensible to the rest of the anthropological profession, who are unlikely to undertake the task of learning complicated systems of hieroglyphics lightly. It seems to me that this problem can only be attacked piecemeal, in terms of particular analyses with specific ends in view. For present purposes I have devised a system, for whose crudity I make no apologies, that reduces Umeda dance movements simply to movements of the leg, seen sideways on. Of course, when dancing Umedas move the whole body in extremely complex ways, but the leg movements are sufficiently crucial to serve as discriminators between Umeda dance styles for the purposes of the model. Umeda dances can all be construed as different forms of gait, and can be analysed using techniques derived from the kinesiological study of human walking and running (Carlsöö 1972:94–120; Hoenkamp 1978). Gait can be described, among other ways, by measuring the angles formed by the upper leg (thigh) and the lower leg (from the knee down) to the vertical at successive points during the step cycle. As the limb swings and bends at the knee during walking or running – or dancing, for that matter – these angles vary continuously and can be plotted as functions on a graph.

Working from film, which is the most feasible way of measuring angles, we can produce functions for (a) the upper leg and (b) the lower leg. We only need to consider one leg, not both, because each leg goes through the same sequence of movements, only in counterphase. But the leg is an indivisible entity, and we need to combine the lower- and upper-leg functions, so that we can see how lower- and upper-leg angles correlate with one another. This is easily done by making use of a two-dimensional graph (which represents a two-dimensional phase space) in which one axis (north–south) corresponds to upper-leg angles, and the other axis (east–west) corresponds to lower-leg angles. Two parabolic waves plotted against one another in this manner yield an ellipse. However, the functions for leg movements are not parabolic, especially not the lower-leg function, which is quite irregular, so the graph for 'normal' Western walking looks more like a leg-of-mutton shape.

This kind of graph was developed by Hoenkamp (1978) for use in conjunction with computer registration of data, but its original form

187

is both too sensitive and too abstract for the analytical purposes I have here in mind. I measured angles off the film in five-degree steps, and subsequently rounded off even these figures when plotting them on my diagrams, which are calibrated in terms of ten-degree steps. This dramatic, but necessary, shedding of information at each stage of the model-making process should alert readers to the fact that this apparently 'mathematical' approach to dance analysis is not aimed at numerical accuracy, but simply at uncovering certain gross features of the shapes produced by plotting Umeda dance movements on to graphs. This raises the second problem of such graphs, which is the difficulty of mentally translating them back into concrete movements. I have tried to overcome this problem by constructing a master figure, which consists of an array of cells, inside each of which is depicted a little leg, which corresponds to the combination of upper and lower leg angles (calibrated in ten-degree steps) located at that point on the overall two-dimensional graph (Figure 7.2). The shape of this figure is that of a right-angle triangle, because many combinations of upper leg/lower leg angles are ruled out by the fact that the knee only bends one way (these are all the ones on the top right-hand side). I should stress that this depiction is valid only for specific purposes: many more possibilities exist but these are the ones relevant to the analysis.

The graphs can therefore be read as follows. On Figure 7.2 I have outlined two sets of cells. Sequence A→B read in the direction of the arrow shows a leg kicking forwards (kicking a football, say) while sequence C↔D shows a leg performing a series of knee bends – here the arrows go in both directions. One can imagine each cell as a separate frame in a cine film. It may be helpful to bear in mind, when reading the remainder of the graphs I will present, that the southeast–northwest axis always corresponds to sequences in which the upper and lower parts of the leg are both moving in the same direction with respect to the vertical, while the southwest–northeast axis corresponds to movements in which the upper and lower parts of the leg are moving in opposite directions with respect to the vertical (i.e. the knee joint is being flexed or extended). The north–south axis, meanwhile, corresponds to movements where the angle of the lower leg remains constant while the upper leg moves with respect to the vertical, and the east–west axis corresponds to movements during which the lower leg swings from the knee while the upper leg remains at a constant angle.

In Figure 7.3a I have projected a normal Western walking step cycle on to the master graph, and (dotted) a deviant version of walking. This version would be more characteristic of the Umeda standard

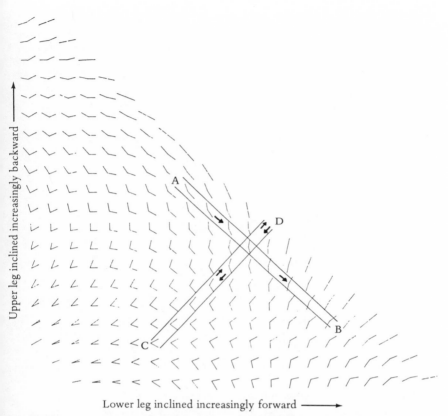

Figure 7.2 Graphic representation of upper and lower leg angles (after Hoen-kamp 1978)

walking pattern, which is not quite the same as the Western one (for explanation, see below). This latter shape is the basic armature of Umeda dance.

The advantage of this method of representation is that it permits instant visual comparisons between different versions of the step cycle seen as wholes, with the possibility of easy identification of the distinctive features wherein they differ. Moreover, it becomes possible, in this way, to see the different styles of movement adopted by participants in *ida* as a set of transformations of a single form (the cycle of Figure 7.3a), which is expanded, contracted, stretched this way and that, transposed bodily, etc., while maintaining its essential unity. Edmund Leach once advised his anthropological colleagues to ap-

189

Alfred Gell

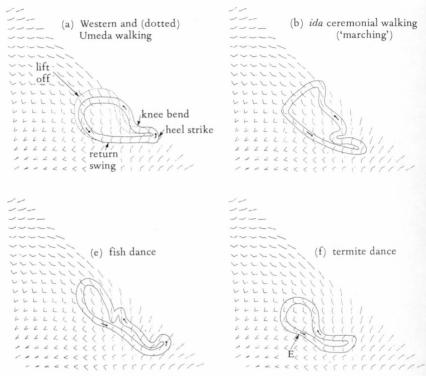

Figure 7.3 Graphic representations of *ida* step cycles

proach the analysis of anthropological data as a problem akin to the topological analysis of figures drawn on rubber sheeting (1961:7). The transformational approach to the analysis of mask styles presented earlier was intended to exemplify Leach's approach in the analysis of visual forms and meanings. We are now in a position to do the same for dance.

Dance and nondance

There is not, in Umeda or perhaps anywhere, a clear boundary between dance and nondance; we always find the self-consciously graceful walk that seems continually to refer to the dance without quite becoming it, and the half-hearted dance that lapses back into the security of mere locomotion. Yet it also remains true that there is a gap, a threshold however impalpable, that is crossed when the body

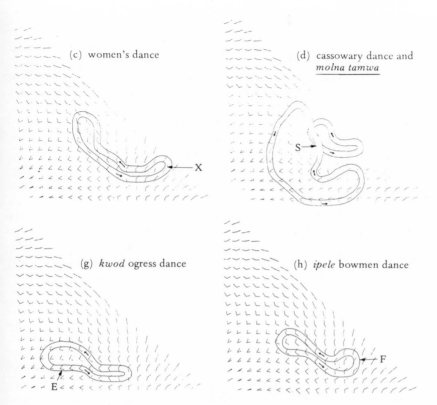

(c) women's dance

(d) cassowary dance and
molna tamwa

(g) *kwod* ogress dance

(h) *ipele* bowmen dance

begins to dance, rather than simply move. This gap is less a matter of movement per se than of meaning, for what distinguishes dance movements from nondance movements is the fact that they have dance meanings attached to them. But here is a paradox, fundamental to the whole question of dance, because what source can these dance meanings possibly have except the patterned contrasts, the intentional clues, embodied in everyday, nondance movement? Dance seems to separate itself from nondance by its atypicality, its nonnormal, nonmundane character, but dance acquires its meaning by referring us back always to the world of mundane actions, to what these performers would be doing, were they doing anything but dance. Even the most delicate ballroom dances seem to present us with innumerable scenarios of provocation, pursuit, flight, capture, rape; and what would one make of Umeda dance, the endless cycles of tumescence that fill two days and leave the dancers wearied to exhaustion? Dance escapes from nondance only to return to it in the

Alfred Gell

course of symbolically transforming it, and dance analysis can only succeed by following this double movement, back and forth.

Dance meanings originate through a process whereby elements, or components, of nondance motor patterns are seized upon, stereotyped (usually with some degree of formalisation and exaggeration), and are set within a particular context. The logic of dance is, in this respect, highly akin to the logic of play; the message 'this is dance' (like the message 'this is play': cf. Bateson 1972:151) is a metamessage, one that sets the subsequent communicative transaction in its correct logical context (. . . I am going to pretend to stab you with this knife, but only in play, really we are the best of friends . . .). The function of style in dance, the immediately recognisable but usually very impalpable mannerism that colours the complete gamut of dance forms in a specific culture, is to mark this logical boundary between dance and nondance, ambiguous though it may become in particular instances. We may profitably begin our analysis of Umeda dance, therefore, by seeking out the motor stereotype that conveys this context shift, that establishes the category of dance as one with ground rules that are distinctively different from those that govern the interpretation of behaviour in the nondance context.

Yet even here we do not escape from the nondance world, because the most notable mannerism that separates dance from nondance in Umeda proves to be no more than a caricature of a feature basic to Umeda motor style in *all* contexts, not just dance. Let me refer to Figure 7.3a, where I have indicated a certain deviation from the norm of Western walking that seems to me characteristic of Umeda. Umedas, especially when they are walking in a deliberate, careful way, seem to me to manifest a step cycle that differs significantly from the Western one at one point in particular, the commencement of the so-called support phase, following the moment when the heel of the leading foot lands on the ground. At heel strike the leg is quite straight in the Western walk, and the heel is brought sharply down. Subsequently there is a brief bending of the knee, which serves to bring the whole foot into contact with the earth, and then, almost at once, the leg straightens again so that before it has reached the vertical the knee joint is locked straight and remains so for the latter part of the support phase until the heel lifts off again. In the Umeda walk on the other hand, the front leg may already be bending at the knee before the heel hits the ground, and the knee bend following heel strike is more pronounced and prolonged, the knee straightening and locking only after the upper leg has passed the vertical.

It is interesting to pause for a moment to consider the source of

192

this apparent anomaly. The whole subject of the cultural ecology of walking is, so far as I know, unsurveyed at present, though copious materials which would shed light on the matter must be available in the film archives of the world. It would appear to me, at any rate, that the way Umedas walk is related to their environment (dense jungle, no roads, many obstructions in the form of exposed roots, thorns, rocks, and so on) and their technology (lack of shoes of any kind). Like all anthropologists, no doubt, who have worked in similar circumstances, I have spent time attending to the wounded feet of my hosts, and have had occasion to marvel at the wonderful callosities that the unshod develop; nevertheless foot injuries are common, painful, and pose a distinct threat to production and social viability. It must be reasonable to suppose that the gait pattern of the unshod reflects constraints not only of locomotor efficiency per se, but also constraints imposed by the need to minimise the chances of foot injury – constraints that impinge very much less heavily on ourselves. Examination of a worn pair of shoes is suggestive in this respect; the heaviest wear is always at the heel with another patch of heavy wear under the ball of the big toe, yet the feet of the unshod do not seem to show markedly thicker callosities in these regions, nor in my experience were injuries concentrated there. It might be the case, therefore, that the unshod walk in such a way as to minimise the possibility of damage (which is proportional to the local pressure on the part of the foot in contact with the ground at any one time) by maximising the area of weight-bearing surface of the sole of the foot at all stages of the step cycle. The exaggerated knee bend during the support phase has this effect (a) because the foot lands on the ground relatively flat, with no sharp impact of the heel, (b) because when the knee bends, weight is only gradually transferred from back foot to front foot (that is, the time during which both feet are on the ground and sharing the weight of the body is maximised) and (c) because the knee bend dampens the angular momentum of the body weight as it changes direction (moving down when the legs are widely separated and up as the support leg swings underneath the body). Although the knee bend increases the amplitude of this up-and-down motion of the body, it smooths out the wave-form so that there are no sharp shocks that would cause increased local pressure to be communicated to the foot–ground contact area. This is the same principle as the suspension of a car.

As I remarked earlier, the knee bend in normal Umeda walking becomes most pronounced when the individual is walking in a deliberate, intent fashion: there seems to be a clear carry over between

193

Alfred Gell

this and what I call 'ceremonial walking', which is a borderline form of dancing seen particularly in the case of the musicians – men playing wooden trumpets – who parade round the arena throughout *ida*. Figure 7.3b (taken from film) shows the step cycle of a man marching vigorously with the band of trumpet players. It is clear that this form of walking emphasises and exaggerates elements that are already present in normal walking; the ceremonial walk in Umeda, if I may be permitted the expression, is an hypostatisation of the normal walk, and as such is already a dance. We have an analogous case in our own culture that may help to clarify the point: military marching. What is most notable, comparing the Umeda 'march' with the Western one, is the way in which each selects, for formalisation and emphasis, quite different elements in the step cycle, which is only at a very abstract level a true human universal. I feel it quite appropriate to describe the Umeda ceremonial walk as a march, because that, functionally speaking, is what it is; but I am sure that any British soldier whose parade-ground style approximated to the Umeda one would spend most of his military career in the guardroom, peeling potatoes. Marching is a cultural, not a natural category, and as such is constrained by technology and environment. It would not be possible to perform the Western military march with bare feet, since it achieves its effect mainly in the simultaneous crashing down of rank upon rank of iron-shod boot heels (heavy boots have a natural tendency to swing out at the beginning of each stride). The Prussian goose step is the apotheosis of this 'shod' approach to ceremonial walking, (indeed the prominence that it gives to the boot as an item of military technology is not misplaced) but it stands at the opposite end of the spectrum from the Umeda ceremonial walk. The features to note in the Umeda ceremonial walk are (a) the increased stride length – this is the only feature that is in common with the European military march, (b) the exaggerated knee bend and the sharp upward rise during the latter part of the support phase, and (c) the tendency to exaggerated follow-through during the swing phase, the knee becoming quite sharply bent during the return travel of the nonsupport leg. The Umeda ceremonial walk is not just a means of locomotion, but is at the same time an expression, mediated through cultural categories, of the *idea* of walking. We have crossed the threshold of the dance.

The examples of dancing proper, which I will now go on to consider, all share with the ceremonial walk the features of stylisation of knee bend, follow-through, and (in some instances) abnormal stride length. These deviations from the norm, which at the same time seem to

194

caricature or exaggerate the norm, reflect the Umedas' own perception of the structure of their motor repertoire, and the meaningful articulation of different modes of motor performance. It is these perceptions that lie at the heart of their dance system.

Female dance

Figure 7.3c (taken from film) shows a woman dancing in an unusually vigorous manner: the graph diverges sharply from normal walking and is clearly a dance step. This gait is characterised by greatly extended stride length, deep and prolonged knee bending during the support phase, but lacks the upward spring characteristic of masculine leaping dances (see below). The dance as a whole might best be described as a stretched walk; particularly the exaggerated forwards extension of the leading leg (marked x on the graph).

What the graph cannot convey, useful as it is for comparative purposes, is the way in which female dancing exploits female dress in a sexually suggestive way. The purpose of the outstretched front foot (the ankle is maximally extended and the toes angled down) is to bring the body weight on to the front foot early on in the stride. As the foot lands it is angled sharply in, so that the dancer seems pigeon-toed. As the leg continues to move back during the support phase, the body rotates so as to align itself with the angle of the supporting foot, with the result that the hips swing sideways, causing the dancer's long grass skirt-tails to fly out in that direction. This pigeon-toed step and swaying skirt are also visible in the gait of women in nondance contexts. Some degree of hip rotation is present in any normal gait, but the curious angling in of the foot may, I think, be related, once again, to cultural adaptation of the gait pattern to specific circumstances. Umeda women are used to walking through bad terrain with heavy loads, carried in net bags, which they suspend from their foreheads and which rest on their backs. This obliges them to keep the weight on the front foot, which does not strike the ground heel first, but toe first. The reader may care to experiment for him/ herself, but my observations lead me to believe that toe-first walking gait requires a pigeon-toed approach, while walking on tiptoes with the feet angled out feels extremely unnatural. If pigeon-toed walking is indeed related to load carrying in net bags, then it would be true to say that the female dance is an exaggerated version of a normal but specifically *female* gait, since men do not carry loads on their backs, nor do they dance in this pigeon-toed way. It is certainly notable that

Alfred Gell

women always dance with net bags hung over their backs, and lean their bodies forwards as if they were carrying loads.

The female dancers at *ida* are not performers in the full sense, but rather active spectators. The ritual is an occasion for self-display by both sexes, and the female dance is intended to be, and indeed is, provocative. The point to note, however, is that female dancing is not a separate sphere of motor behaviour, but the occasion for realising, to the fullest extent, certain potentialities that are already present in female gait. Skirts sway whenever and wherever women move, only the amount of thigh on view is not usually so extensive. Only during *ida* are the distinctive characteristics of female gait permitted full expression: women become truly themselves only when they are permitted to behave abnormally – but this is true of most ritual behaviour.

Male dance

I do not have any film of the dance of the cassowaries, which occupies the first night of *ida*, and which is performed in darkness, so the next graph, Figure 7.3d, is a reconstruction, making use of the film, which shows roughly similar forms of dancing that take place during the daytime. Four masked dancers appear in Umeda during this night: the two cassowaries, who, I mentioned before, represent the wild, primordial state, and two *molna tamwa* (neophyte fish) played by newly initiated youths wearing the penis gourd (the small one in everyday use, not the weighted one like the cassowaries). The *molna tamwa* are insignificant, ritually, but are interesting because they are so completely contrasted in every respect with the cassowaries (their paint is red, not black, their status junior rather than senior, their masks of coconut fibre, not sago, and so forth). I have discussed the cassowary/*molna tamwa* relation at length elsewhere; they stand for opposite ends of the male life cycle, whose trajectory leads in the direction of asocial autonomy (represented by the cassowary) and a progressive casting off of the social constraints that impinge on youth (supposedly devoted to the ascetic pursuit of hunting) – represented here by the *molna tamwa*, and more fully, later on, by the *ipele* bowmen (for more detail cf. Gell 1975:243–4).

As one would expect, the dance of the cassowaries and that of the *molna tamwa* are highly contrasted, and in ways that clearly reflect their opposed symbolic roles. The *molna tamwa* dance is, in fact, a highly reduced version of the ceremonial walk: stride length is radically curtailed, and only the springy knee bend marks this out as a

196

dance at all. This suffices, however, to impart that sinuous, up-and-down bobbing that is the hallmark of Umeda male dance and causes the feathers on masks to wave (a feature of ritual display to which Umedas attach great aesthetic significance).

The cassowary dance is a very different affair and represents the most extreme departure from normal gait that the Umeda dance repertoire contains. The objective of the cassowary dance is to impart maximum momentum to the bushy mask (whose arms wave dramatically in the air) and to the dancer's penis gourd, which must strike resoundingly against his abdominal belt all night through. The phallic character of the cassowary is strongly emphasised and indeed his penis is believed to grow to enormous length during the performance. In the graph we can study the leaping movement whereby this effect is achieved. The leg movements approximate to those of a hurdler negotiating a series of closely spaced hurdles (much closer together than they would be at an athletics track of course). A deep knee bend precedes each leap, which is produced by the simultaneous straightening of the upper leg/trunk angle and flexion of the non-support leg, which adds upwards momentum to the leap (Figure 7.3d). The cassowary graph reflects this in its strong north–south emphasis, which is the hypostatisation of the episode of leg straightening (marked S on Figure 7.3d) visible even in the normal Umeda walk. Here this episode is grossly exaggerated and becomes the basis of the cassowary dance style.

It is interesting to contrast the graphs showing female dancing with the graph for the cassowary dance. Both are very divergent from the norm of standard walking gait, but in contrasted ways. The female dance is a normal walk pulled out lengthways, while the cassowary dance is a normal walk pulled out in the vertical axis, so that it becomes a series of leaps. Different aspects of the common armature of standard gait are used to encode the formal opposition of the sexes in ritual terms. The wildly swinging weighted penis of the dancer only makes this more explicit: but just as women's skirts sway even in normal walking, so the penis gourd of everyday male attire is subject, though to a much lesser degree, to up-and-down motions, especially if the man is running. The seemingly bizarre penis-gourd dance is only a caricature of normality, if a rather remarkable one.

In general, the cassowary dance is designed to convey the idea of uncontrolled, wild, primordial energy: the cassowaries, Lords of Misrule, represent the socially autonomous role of senior men in an acephalous society, a society where to marry, to control female labour and reproductivity, to live sufficient unto oneself, is to achieve all that

197

Alfred Gell

is open to a man to do. Such men are, like cassowaries, independent of society, while also being those responsible for reproducing it. Around this paradox *ida* has grown. The subsequent dances show the gradual process of incorporating the primordial autonomous man into the restraining fabric of society. With this, there also ensues a gradual transformation of dance style, a curtailing of motor exuberance, whose course we may follow in the ensuing graphs.

Figure 7.3e shows the more restrained type of fish dancing style, which is most typical, though fish, especially the brightly painted *tetagwana tamwa* played by young men, do occasionally engage in bouts of more vigorous dancing. Fish dancing is always more orderly and controlled than cassowary dancing – the fish maintain single-file formation and go round a regular path, while the cassowaries may gyrate all over the arena in a quite random way.

Structurally, the fish dance is a reduced version of the cassowary dance: the upward spring which gives momentum to the weighted penis gourd is present, but much moderated, and the athletic leaps become smooth and sinuous. There is one nondance parallel to the fish dance that is worth mentioning. During the fish dance the support leg is kept relatively straight, and the dancer gets his spring by extending the ankle joint rather than the knee (this cannot be shown on our graphs). In other words, fish dancers tension the leg much more stiffly than the other dancers, and dance on their toes rather than on the flat of their feet. This is very reminiscent of the typical stride pattern of Umeda bowmen making a rush in battle, which was demonstrated to me while I was in the field (there were no actual battles). Rather than creep up on their enemies, Umeda warriors preferred to look as tall as possible as they ran forwards to fire their arrows at an adversary (they were, moreover, protected by their woven cane body-armour). The springy tiptoe run of the advancing warrior seems to be incorporated into the fish dance style, which is very suitable because the fish dancers represent the male strength of the village, and moreover they carry bows and arrows, which they use to threaten spectators and one another. The fish dance, in Umeda terms, is therefore a warrior style of dancing.

The stiff-legged, vertical emphasis of the fish dance is progressively reduced as the ritual proceeds, though there are fish in the arena until the very conclusion of the ritual, usually between five and ten at any one time. The fish represent the aggressive and phallic aspects of Umeda masculinity, while later figures represent more domesticated and sexually repressed aspects. In dance terms this is reflected in a reduction in spring height, and a more creeping or loping style of movement.

Figure 7.3f is the graph for a termite dancer. Termites represent domesticity (because of their seemingly inexhaustible reproductivity) and the termite dancers, who appear on the afternoon of the second day of *ida*, are followed around by the children of the village, and are given babies to carry. They herald the successful culmination of the ritual, the taking over, by society, of the processes of natural regeneration. But they are, at the same time, figures of fun, lacking the autonomous, untrammelled freedom of the cassowary, or the erotic and military prestige of the fish. Their dance is a slow, undulating, loping step, designed to show off the glossy cassowary plumes on their headdresses to best advantage. They wear only the ordinary penis gourd, their sexuality having been neutralised by domestic responsibilities.

Looking at the termite graph, we can see the deep knee bend, which is the signature of Umeda dance, but what is lacking, compared to the cassowary, for instance, is the powerful spring at the end of the support phase, or the tense warrior stride of the fish. The whole termite graph is bodily displaced, relative to the fish graph, or indeed the ceremonial walk, towards the southwest corner of our master graph, Figure 7.2. This is indicative of the fact that during the termite dance the knee remains more sharply bent than heretofore, never becoming straight at all. This gives the impression of invisible fetters restraining the freedom of the dancers, epitomized by the gaggle of yelling children by whom they are followed. Another detail of the termite dance reinforces this impression. This is the feature of 'exaggerated follow-through', marked *E* on the graph; it takes the form of a little backwards kick at the beginning of each return swing, as if the termite was scraping the dust with his feet, like a restive horse. This exaggerated follow-through is partly necessitated by the sharp bending of the knee at that point in the stride by the other (supporting) leg but seems to be emphasised for its own sake. It seems to express the idea of excess energy, which the rather cramped termite dance style cannot quite accommodate. As we will see it is even more marked in the *kwod* dance, which I will discuss next.

In general, then, the termite dance, although still reflecting the generic up-and-down bobbing of Umeda male ceremonial display, does so in a muted and restricted form. Structurally this is achieved by a dimensional reduction of the general pattern of male dancing combined with a transposition of the whole cycle into a different and

Alfred Gell

darker key (the key of bent knees, so to speak). But the exaggerated follow-through still refers obliquely to the exuberant style of the cassowary, just as, in a rather similar way, the termite mask reflects the cassowary mask (cf. Figure 7.1).

Figure 7.3g shows the dance style of a *kwod* (ogress). It will be seen that this dance resembles the termite dance but is an extreme form of it. The southwest transposition is carried even further, and the exaggerated follow-through is even more marked. This is interesting because the dance analysis here allows me to go a little further in my overall analysis of this figure than I was able to do in my original account, where, by ignoring the dance, I failed to see the very close relation between the *kwod* and the termite, and so failed to pick up some important clues.

Kwod is a kinship term that means 'father's sister/father's sister's husband' – that is, it is an *intersexual* term for people who, in ego's kinship universe, are interstitial between (patri-) kin and (matri-) allies. *Kwod* also is the name of a mythological ogress with a *vagina dentata*, that is, who has both female and male (aggressive) characteristics. In the ritual, the figure of the *kwod* represents a strongly negative idea, the confusion of male and female traits. His/her red paint is associated with female sexuality (or else the half-formed sexuality of children and neophytes) and the dancer's penis is bound (sexuality negated); at the same time the *kwod* carried a spray of leaves with which, like a prudish female, he attempts to cover the genital area (men are often and shamelessly naked). He/she carries a bow, and creeps about on the periphery of the arena, threatening people until chased away.

The termites show domesticity and reproductivity taking its normal course, with a comic but inevitable reduction in phallic exuberance consequent upon reproductivity (copulation and nurture of children being regarded as mutually exclusive, complementary activities in the Umeda scheme of things); the *kwod* is a sardonic representation of this reduction in phallicism carried to its logical conclusion. Figure 7.4 shows the triple relation cassowary/termite/*kwod* as a sequence of reductions: just as the *kwod* dance is a reduction of the termite dance, so also is the *kwod* mask, the *kwod* genital ornament, and the *kwod* body paint. I have also included in this figure a drawing of another intersexual ogre, *sogwa naina*, who obviously forms a pair with *kwod*. Both these (admittedly minor) ritual figures represent witty variations on the basic theme of the ritual, hinting at the ultimate identity of the role of the separate sexes in relation to common reproductive tasks. But this subversive neutralisation of sexual stereotypes is introduced into the ritual only to be crushingly rejected, as the inter-

200

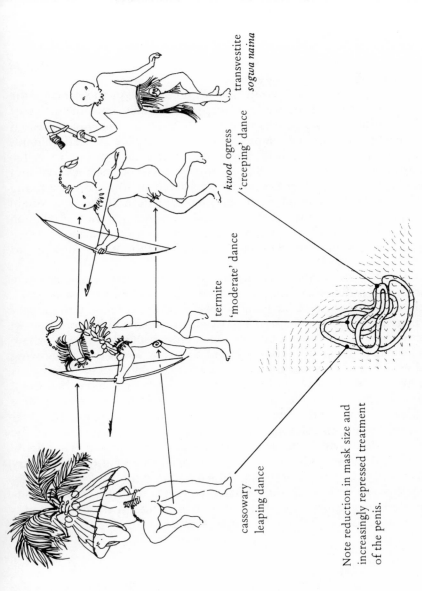

cassowary
leaping dance

termite
'moderate' dance

kwod ogress
'creeping' dance

transvestite
sogwa naina

Note reduction in mask size and
increasingly repressed treatment
of the penis.

Figure 7.4 *Ida* step cycles as a sequence of reductions

sexual ogres/ogresses are chased off. The creeping *kwod* is a figure from a collective nightmare.

To return to Figure 7.3, our final graph represents the dance of the *ipele* bowmen. This dance is relatively restrained, but not furtive or ignoble, like the *kwod*. It is true that the *ipele* are sexually repressed (bound penis) but here elements of masculinity are again dominant, though under strict control. The exaggerated follow-through has disappeared, and instead we find an emphasis not on the back foot, but on the front foot, which is sharply extended forwards at the beginning of each stride (marked *F* on the graph). This trait bears a certain similarity to the dance of the fish at the analogous point in the step cycle, and in general the *ipele* dance can be seen as a highly compressed version of the fish dance, though without the same upward spring.

The *ipele* are hunters, and in their dance one recognises more than a hint of ordinary hunting technique. They advance forwards stealthily, bent forwards, keeping a low profile, avoiding unnecessary movement. This gait is like a hunter stalking game in the forest. Most notable is the absence of display elements in the *ipele* dance; where the fish or even the termites seem to be self-consciously showing themselves off before the female audience, the brief *ipele* dance is unwitnessed by women (who turn their backs and hide their eyes) and has more the character of an instrumental act than an expressive display. Here, at the culmination of the ritual, it ceases to be a pretence; the imaginary frame of reference of the ritual drama and the real world in which the actors' vital interests are embedded suddenly fuse and intermingle, metaphors and reality become one. The very simplicity and understatement of the *ipele* dance contribute powerfully to this categorical sleight of hand whereby the ritual achieves its profoundest effects; the dance that is no longer a dance concludes the ritual that is perhaps no longer a ritual.

Conclusion

I would like to return briefly, in these concluding remarks, to the question of the relation between dance and nondance. In the preceding sections I have tried to show two things: (a) that all Umeda dances can be seen as variants on a common pattern; and (b) that the significant differences that distinguish them can often be seen as stemming from the incorporation into the dance of elements drawn from nondance motor programmes. My overall argument would be, therefore, that Umeda dance has two sides to it, style, which is the aspect of the dance that separates it from the nondance world, and meaning, which is the aspect of the dance that refers back to the nondance world. What I want to focus on now is the problem of style. It would be easy to suppose, but I think misleading, that each culture has a set of motor performances that, in and of themselves, communicate the message 'this is dance'. It would be difficult to imagine the elaborate features of Polynesian dance (Kaeppler 1972) or the stereotyped calisthenics of Melpa dance (Chapter 4 above) being produced outside the dance context; but none the less they all might be, and moreover it would be difficult to specify anything about these movements that made them purely and totally dances, as opposed to movements of some other kind. What gives dance movements style – and hence what separates them from nondance movements – is not their individual form, as movements, but the relationship in which they stand to (a) related nondance motor programmes, and (b) to other dance movements in the same system. It is here, I think, that the idea I have developed in the preceding analysis (i.e., that dances can be viewed as members of a transformation set) can be particularly useful. If dance style is essentially a product of the deformation or modulation of embedded motor patterns, then it can only be described by setting the dance movement against the template of the underlying nondance schema. The situation, in fact, is not very different in poetry. The meaning of a poem is its paraphrase (what it says about the world, just as the meaning of a dance is what the dancer would be doing in the world were he not dancing), but what dignifies a poem is the difference between the paraphrase and the poem itself, and it is with this that the translator will have problems. With dance – at least with rather transparent kinds of dance, such as that seen at *ida* – we can perhaps make better progress, because the variables are simpler and fewer in number, and can be analysed in physical, concrete terms. Let me recapitulate the essence of what I have been saying by making use of a classic method that dates from the archaeology of structuralism, D'Arcy Thompson's method of coordinates. Figure 7.5 shows the normal Umeda step cycle inscribed in a rectangular grid, like the rectangular grid D'Arcy Thompson used in his well-known comparison of the skulls of man, chimpanzee, and baboon (Thompson 1969:318). Next to this I have drawn the deformed grids that correspond to generalised versions of (a) the cassowary dance, (b) the fish dance. The transformational relation that exists between the coordinates in each case are stylistic relations in the sense defined above, whereas the mappings of the actual movements on to the master graph of Figure 7.2 and thence onto nondance motor pro-

Alfred Gell

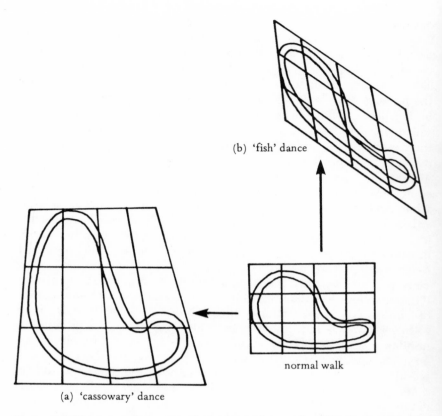

(b) 'fish' dance

normal walk

(a) 'cassowary' dance

Figure 7.5 *Ida* step cycles as transformations of normal walking (after Thompson 1969)

grammes correspond to meaning relations. Dance is thus finally interpretable as a stylised deformation of nondance mobility, just as poetry is a deformation or modulation of language, a deviation from the norm of expression that enhances expressiveness.

We understand dances, as communicative displays, by working back from the surface manifestation of motor behaviour, to the underlying motor schema: that is to say, we read a dance by undoing the process of stylisation that makes a dance a dance; in effect, by reversing the transformations. But what we value in the dance is not the surface motor behaviour, nor the underlying schema that gives it its meaning, but the gap that separates the two.

Style and meaning in Umeda dance

NOTE

1 My title and much else in my approach to the anthropological study of nonverbal communication is a borrowing from Anthony Forge (cf. Forge 1973). The group referred to herein as Umeda also includes the population of the neighbouring village of Punda, where, in fact, the *ida* ritual was filmed. The style of dancing I will describe is also found elsewhere in the Amanat-Imonda region of the West Sepik Province, and doubtless also across the border in adjoining parts of West Irian. Its distribution is co-terminous with the distribution of the kind of globular penis gourd characteristic of this cultural region (cf. Gell 1971), which plays such an important part in the dance.

REFERENCES

Bateson, G. 1972. *Steps to an Ecology of Mind*. New York: Chandler.
Carlsöö, S. 1972. *How Man Moves: Kinesiological Studies and Methods*. Trans. B. Michael. London: Heinemann.
Forge, A. 1973. 'Style and meaning in Sepik art.' In Forge, A. (ed.), *Primitive Art and Society*. London: Oxford University Press.
Gell, A. 1971. 'Penis sheathing and ritual status in a West Sepik Village'. *Man* (NS), 6:165–81.
1975. *Metamorphosis of the Cassowaries*. London: Athlone.
Hoenkamp, E. 1978. 'Perceptual cues that determine the labeling of human gait'. *Journal of Human Movement Studies*, 4:59–69.
Kaeppler, A.L. 1972. 'Method and theory in analysing dance structure with an analysis of Tongan dance'. *Ethnomusicology*, 16:173–217.
Leach, E.R. 1961. *Rethinking Anthropology*. London: Athlone.
Owen, C. 1977. *The Red Bowman*. Film. Abridged 1979. Boroko: Institute of Papua New Guinea.
Thompson, D.A.W. 1969. *On Growth and Form*. Cambridge: Cambridge University Press.

Epilogue: Anthropology and the study of dance

PETER BRINSON

The last two decades have seen a remarkable development of dance practice in most Western industrial societies and, for different reasons to do with rising national consciousness, also in the societies of many developing nations. With this spread of dance interest has gone a demand for the study of dance, theoretical as well as practical. Almost everywhere, however, theoretical dance study has lagged behind dance practice.

Major problems face dance scholars, from the establishment of dance study as a discipline in its own right to the difficulty of defining dance and its nonverbal language, to the influence of nature and nurture upon dance in different parts of the world, to problems of description and notation, history, aesthetics, and criticism. In approaching such problems dance scholars now have an ally of increasing importance, albeit not yet widely recognised among dancers: the anthropologists. This volume has indicated the nature of their contribution as well as the range of their future tasks. Any epilogue to such a survey therefore needs to assess the place of an anthropology of dance within the context of dance scholarship as a whole.

Even the most cursory glance through the studies here will show how social anthropology can help to correct the balance between excessive attention to stage dance, so noticeable in Western dance studies, and the broader issues that need consideration for any full understanding of dance in present-day society. Although none of the contributors, except Sue Jennings, claim to know dance from the inside, they show there is plenty an anthropologist can say. Paul Spencer especially, by identifying in his Introduction a range of issues drawn from the anthropological literature, points dance studies in directions considerably beyond the style of dance history and aesthetics current within most contemporary dance courses and their supporting literature. His notion that 'the dance reflects powerful social forces that demand some explanation' indicates that the issues it raises touch on the most profound problems of political control and organisation, social psychology, social morality, and so on.

None of these issues, apparently far removed from the daily experience of professional dancers in, say, classical ballet, actually lie outside that experience once the issue is interpreted in dancers' terms. It is the language of anthropological description, not the experience, that is unfamiliar. Take, for example, the cathartic theory, which regards dancing as a safety valve (p. 3). Every dancer, professional or amateur, has experienced such catharsis, the release of tension, in personal performance. What anthropologists do is to interpret this experience in its wider social context. Similarly, the experience of dance as stimulator and self-generator (p. 15) is part of life in any dance company as it is in many kinds of social dance, notably the emulation of disco. Through dance in such circumstances, the individual dancer can achieve qualities of performance usually beyond his everyday ability. Or again, the analysis of the masquerade dances of the Kalabari (p. 28) as ritual dramas suggests parallels with staged performances in our own society; there is a similar use of aesthetic idiom to portray an imaginary world that distorts and exaggerates our everyday reality – as indeed dance itself does – in a way that presents us with a potent image of ourselves and is capable of arousing our emotions.

It is logical to move from dance as a shared experience to dance that fortifies the sense of community to dance as a social regulator, an organ of social control, a constraint (p. 8). Dance can be an educator in traditional ways, a transmitter of cultural and social taboos, a conditioner of youthful enthusiasm. In all this it can be on the side of the political establishment. Yet the dialectic of such a functionalist theory must allow that dance and music can be also instruments of social change (p. 26). They perform such a function today in South America, reinforcing resistance to authoritarian regimes. They were and are instrumental in developing African consciousness. On the streets of London they express social protest through the Notting Hill carnivals. In many parts of the world they help to transmit and reinforce the message of Black Power movements. In this volume, Paul Spencer examines the subversive element in Samburu dancing as an integral aspect of the gerontocratic regime and one that is carefully monitored by the elders from a distance; for the duration of the dance, the normal social order is upturned and the rigidly controlled process of social development is reversed, especially with regard to the relationship between the sexes. The wonder is only that this potential

207

of dance is ignored so much by the political left or indeed by the ruling élites in most advanced industrial nations.

It is easy, then, to confirm out of the practice of professional dance the relevance of the issues quoted here and the truth of many conclusions for dance practice drawn from these anthropological studies. The notion of dance as an organ of establishment control is today one of the central problems of classical ballet. Its image is linked with class rule and élitist culture. Its future requires that this image be replaced by one which makes it accessible and attractive to audiences of a broad social mix.

Can dance itself, using the powers of imagery, directly stimulate political and social action? Certainly it cannot have the immediate impact of a politically contrived play or public speech in changing attitudes. But like other nonverbal arts, as a creature of climate, dance can generate feelings and emotions leading to the creation of ideas for action. The Notting Hill Carnival is a good example of such a dance, or again the dancing Maasai women who gathered together to take collective vengeance on a rapist (p. 26). But the latter cannot be directly compared with the Wilis – spirits of girls who have died before their wedding day because of faithless lovers – when they avenge themselves in *Giselle* by dancing to death any man who crosses their path, for this is not performed with any intention of a direct response. It is intention rather than just theme that is the keynote in this context. At most, through an exaggerated inversion, *Giselle* may arrest an audience and cultivate a greater sensitivity to the sexual inequalities and contradictions of our own society, contributing towards changing attitudes in the longer term. Again, take Kurt Jooss's *The Green Table*, produced in 1932, and still danced and relevant, illustrating the stupidity of war. It reinforced thereby the peace movement of its day. From this perhaps sprang community strength and ideas for action against war. This surely is the significance of dance in community arts. It can help create a climate leading to community action because it helps to generate feelings of strength and can disseminate a collective awareness. How this happens is illustrated in four of the studies in this volume (by John Blacking, Adrienne Kaeppler, Paul Spencer, and Andrew Strathern).

There is one area of experience, however, that most anthropologists, dancers, and dance scholars find hard to penetrate. This is the expression of inner feelings through dance. It is an intricate problem, which John Middleton seeks to clarify when considering the role of death dances in recreating order out of the disruption caused by death among the Lugbara. Often when discussing such problems a dancer will say, 'I cannot *tell* you. I can only *show* you. I must dance it.' This not only emphasises the need for a generally accepted form of dance notation, supplementing film and video as an essential tool of research in this field. (Notation could have resolved almost all the problems of dance description encountered in this volume!) It also illustrates the wide area of partnership necessary between dancers and anthropologists if what is begun in this volume is to be carried forward. Such a partnership barely exists as yet, but the rewards could be enormous.

Alfred Gell illustrates the problem using a notation he has adapted to Umeda dance. An examination of styles leads him to infer meaning that transcends the boundary between dance and nondance, so that any definition that seeks to separate the two necessarily confines itself to the form and detracts from the implicit meaning. Thus style is an aspect of dance that separates it from the nondance world, but the inherent meaning refers back to the nondance world.

It seems to me that his contribution is not only extremely perceptive in itself about the nature of dance, but also demonstrates vividly how anthropologists can throw light on some of the most difficult problems confronting dance scholars. Strathern, Kaeppler, and Blacking also contribute to the discussion about the nature and function of dance. Strathern and Kaeppler, for example, point out that in some languages there is no word for nor particular distinction of dance, so integral is it to the process of living.

Strathern illustrates the many functions of dance in the social process – commercial, political, and propagandist – through exchange ceremonies, religious rituals, and sexual display (p. 119). In other words dance derives from, and maintains, strong continuing links with surrounding circumstances of life, the cycles and creatures of nature. There is a derivation and dependence on the material world, including sexual activity as an essential part of this world. Even so he asks 'why dance?' and 'what is the expressive force of a total set of dance movements?' One Melpa big-man answered that dancing represents a unique statement of maturity or climax. Is not this another way of saying that dance is a form of communication expressing that which cannot be expressed in words? Hence the difficulty of seeking a definition in words.

Kaeppler pursues the same problem of definition in Tonga. Quite rightly, she points out the more general concepts of the creative use of human bodies in time and space. The distinction between the two is a Western distinction often signalled by the term 'dance and movement studies'. In Tongan culture the inseparability and organic unity

209

Peter Brinson

of music, words, and movement are clear, as is the importance of movement to express those areas of human experience that cannot be expressed in words. For this purpose the movement does not need to be spontaneous but can have specific choreography created by a specialist.

Blacking, too, emphasises the important link between dance and music, the connection between music and ritual and the movements of bodies in space and time. In an experience more limited than dancers', for example, all musicians know that musical performance depends on the correct performance of relevant body movements. But Blacking's exploration of the nature and function of dance leads him, more than his colleagues, to apply such anthropological lessons to problems of nonverbal behaviour, nonverbal communication, and the expression of feelings in modern industrial society.

In relation to his chapter, Blacking has noted that the education of the emotions must be a priority in modern industrial societies as it was in traditional Australian societies, in Bali, in Venda. Leisure and recreation have become crucial problems in organising the modern industrial state with important implications for the allocation of time between work and leisure (a distinction that is, or should be, artificial) and for the division of labour. Anthropological studies of work in peasant, tribal, and food-gathering economies have shown that a three-to-four-day working week had been the norm, rather than the exception in human history. It follows that we are not moving into anything new in arguing the case for a shorter working week today. Rather we are recreating on a higher plane an earlier organisation of society when time not spent in pursuit of production was spent in other ways, and such activities as ritual, dance, and music were an integral aspect of communal life.[1] The problem of leisure is really crucial for any revision of traditional approaches to dance study, whether vocational, educational, or scholastic.

Perhaps the gravest problem of dance in modern industrial society is its separation from the generality of other human activity. This, of course, also means losing from the education of children in Western societies the powerful contribution of dance to education that is demonstrated in this volume. This singularly reinforces, therefore, the arguments of many leading dance educators in our society. It recalls, for example, the work of Margaret H'Doubler, one of the most influential of dance scholars over half a century, for in the preface to her famous book she also emphasises that 'the future of dance as a democratic art activity rests with our educational system. . . . Only when

210

dance is communally conceived can it exert a cultural influence' (1940:x).

All this is an appropriate platform for asking 'why dance?' as part of the investigation of the nature of dance. Blacking shows that dance can be either a conservative or a progressive influence depending on the social context, either reinforcing existing ideas or stimulating the imagination. This leads him to suggest that while dance is a generally elusive topic, the anthropologist at least can explore each dance as an event, a minimum unit in the study of the performing arts in general, which is qualitatively different from other social events. Above all, he can follow through the implications of the conscious intentions of the participants in relation to the situational context. In this way, we can treat dance as a social fact; everything we observe in dance and intend in dancing has been processed through society.[2] As a further illustration to this point, even the cathartic element in the Temiar trance dances analysed by Jennings is portrayed as a social fact above and beyond the more obvious psychological release and the ostensible intentions of the dancers.

I hope that my references to contributors in this volume are sufficient acknowledgement to the collective value of an enterprise that demonstrates, in particular, the falsity of the romantic separation of culture from social life. Dance has suffered from this separation as much as, perhaps more than, any other art. On this account it has been thought of solely as some emanation of the spirit belonging to the area of beliefs, customs, and emotions, divorced from the conditions of existence. The alternative view is emphasised here, placing dance firmly in the context of everyday life and subject to the same forces. It is a view that emphasises the practical consciousness of dance. Dance is, therefore, as Gell, Blacking and others have shown in an anthropological context, an active creation of meanings, that is, social action dependent upon social relationships at the time. This is the reality of dance whether it takes place on the village green, in a disco, or in an opera house. To say as much is not to deny the significance of individual creation, nor the vital role of choreographers. It is merely to state the essential nature of all dance.

Twenty years ago when Peggy van Praagh and I wrote *The Choreographic Art* (1963), the anthropological study of dance was so slender we ignored its influence. Today, rewriting the book, the contributions of anthropology have not only made us reconsider our historical approach but draw a lesson for today's dance profession. If dancers wish to argue (as they do) a more secure place for themselves in our

211

Peter Brinson

society they have need of the knowledge and experience of other disciplines to present fully their case. This case is made through an increasingly wide range of models cited in this volume and elsewhere.[3]

What lessons are there here, then, of particular significance for dancers and dance studies? First, the indication that dance is an important and rewarding study in its own right, that human society cannot be properly understood without reference to the sociology of human movement within which dance is constitutive and constituting. As Raymond Williams remarks of language (1977:29–30), it is constitutive because it is biologically based there (see Blacking's chapter) and constituting because it arises and changes out of the practical consciousness of human beings, historically and socially. Anthropology demonstrates both these propositions so that the nature and entity of dance are clearly inseparable from the anthropological view of culture.

Second, the approach has a relevance for the methodology of dance study, diverting attention from some manifestation of the human spirit to the communal life of mankind rooted in his material existence. It is the articulation of experience of the real world from which comes the changing practical consciousness of human beings. Dance is not something plucked out of the air, nor dreamed from nothing by choreographers. It is a translation of practical consciousness, starting from what is, from what exists. All this teaches us to look more critically at our own dance in our own society, using similar criteria and safeguards. In this process we need to acquire inevitably a wider perspective of culture and of the nature of knowledge and its transmission. It calls in question, for instance, the line drawn for so long between verbal and nonverbal communication (p. 11). The elimination of this line is crucial as much for the future of contemporary education (where only about 11 per cent of young people are academically inclined) as it is, ipso facto, for the future of dance within that education. Rather, as Blacking shows, dance and music should be considered 'as modes of human communication on a continuum from the nonverbal to the verbal' (p. 64).

Third, such considerations have significance for the parameters of the historical study of dance. If, as the preceding chapters show, dance reflects powerful social forces, albeit still largely uncharted, then dancing has a social utility in present-day society far greater than that expressed through the theatrical performances that usually capture the headlines and the attentions of the critics. The notion, for example, of dance as an organ of social control illuminates not only our understanding of the views of Locke, Lord Chesterfield, and

212

others on the social education of children in seventeenth and eighteenth century Britain, but also the court ballet of Louis XIV, where dance was an organ of direct control over the nobility. Such interpretations are not necessarily new, but they show that the study of dance in the context of specific societies, not always primitive, can reinforce historical analyses concerning the social role and function of dance.

This leads to a fourth area of influence, the validation as it were of a sociology of dance. Sociology and anthropology, of course, are cousins, through common founding fathers – Durkheim, Marx and Weber. Durkheim especially is reflected time and again in the preceding chapters. So also are today's theories of structuralism and functionalism, common to both disciplines, although differently applied. To the extent that the pattern of dance and the array of symbols have deep down an underlying consistency, the study of dance and its ritual context is relevant to the analysis of social structure, expressed through perceptions of the body, of bodily movements, of time and space.

Anthropology thus suggests that dance can be an important tool in the analysis of society. If that is so, it is not peripheral, but central to the study of society and the education of its citizens. If *that* is so it is a challenge to the newly unfolding sociology of dance to develop the use of this tool and to demonstrate the validity of the new discipline. Indeed, it could be argued that without a coherent analysis of the relationship of dance to society provided by sociological study the argument is much diminished for funding dance out of the public exchequer of a modern industrial state. What can or does the dance artist do for modern industrial society?

Such fundamental issues indicate other questions to be explored by the partnership between anthropology and dance scholarship. How should human movement be studied? There are tentative approaches in these pages to an analysis of the nature of human movement, but no one asks whether a study of the history of human movement is possible and necessary. I believe it is necessary and that there could be developed an archive of human movement. The parameters of such an archive, indeed, are implicit in this book. Of course, human movement is *the* means of contact between human beings and their environment, the basis of human history. Therefore the *scientific* study of human movement cannot be undertaken in isolation from the scientific study of homo sapiens. Within this interdisciplinary context dance is seen, of course, as part of human movement, which is part of human biology, and therefore a manifestation of the interaction

213

Peter Brinson

between human beings and the external world. But in such interaction, as the Calouste Gulbenkian Foundation dance study (1980) pointed out, dance is more than a part of human movement. It is a part of human culture and human communication. This is the intensely rich area of new knowledge and human understanding that anthropologists and dance scholars separately may study, but that jointly they can illuminate.

NOTES

1 John Blacking's contribution here is based on a seminar paper he delivered at the School of Oriental and African Studies (London) in February 1979. In addition to citing his comments when discussing this paper, I have also drawn on an unpublished paper by him: a talk at a Physical Education course at I.M. Marsh College of Physical Education (Liverpool) in July 1978.
2 This point was made explicit in the discussion that followed Blacking's seminar paper (see Note 1 above).
3 For instance, at the Fourth Australian Musicological Symposium, which brought together musicologists, anthropologists and ethnomusicologists in a rich exchange of experience from Europe, the United States, and Oceania. The most original contributions without doubt, however, were those drawn from Oceania and particularly the research into Australian Aboriginal culture (Tunley 1982).

REFERENCES

Brinson, P., and P. van Praagh, 1963. The Choreographic Art. London: Dance Books. (Revised edition in press.)
Calouste Gulbenkian Foundation. 1980. Dance Education and Training in Britain. Report of a Committee of Inquiry into Dance Education and Training. London: Calouste Gulbenkian Foundation
H'Doubler, M. 1940. Dance: A Creative Art Experience. Madison: University of Wisconsin Press.
Tunley, D. (ed.). 1982. Music and Dance. Perth: University of Western Australia.
Williams, R. 1977. Marxism and Literature. Oxford: Clarendon Press.

Notes on contributors

JOHN BLACKING   Professor of Social Anthropology, The Queen's University of Belfast. Fieldwork among the Venda 1956–8. *How Musical is Man?* (1973).

PETER BRINSON   Principal Lecturer in the Sociology of Dance, Laban Centre for Movement and Dance, Goldsmiths' College, University of London. *Dance Education and Training in Britain* (1980, Calouste Gulbenkian Foundation, London).

ALFRED GELL   Reader in Social Anthropology, London School of Economics. Fieldwork among the Umeda 1969–70. *Metamorphosis of the Cassowaries* (1975).

SUE JENNINGS   Senior Lecturer in Dramatherapy and Social Anthropology, Hertfordshire College of Art and Design. Fieldwork among the Senoi Temiar 1974–6.

ADRIENNE L. KAEPPLER   Curator of Oceanic Ethnology, Smithsonian Institution. Fieldwork in Tonga 1964–7. 'Method and theory in analysing dance structure with an analysis of Tongan dance', *Ethnomusicology* (1972).

JOHN MIDDLETON   Professor of Anthropology, Yale University. Fieldwork among the Lugbara 1949–53. *Lugbara Religion* (1960).

PAUL SPENCER   Senior Lecturer in African Anthropology, School of Oriental and African Studies, University of London. Fieldwork among the Samburu 1957–60. *The Samburu: a Study of Gerontocracy in a Nomadic Tribe* (1965).

ANDREW STRATHERN   Professor of Anthropology. Director, Institute of Papua New Guinea Studies, Port Moresby. Fieldwork among the Melpa 1964–5 and subsequently. *The Rope of Moka* (1971).

Name index

Artaud, A., 73, 74

Backman, E.L., 4
Bailey, F.G., 22
Barlow, W., 69
Bateson, G., 39n11, 166, 192
Beidelman, T.O., 31, 39n16, 41n71
Bellman, B.L., 41n73
Benedict, R., 40n50
Benesh, R., 66
Benjamin, G., 47, 49, 55, 57, 61
Berndt, R.M., 138n6
Bernstein, B., 9
Best, D., 25, 38n2, 39n67
Birdwhistell, R.L., 12
Bishop, N., 69
Blacking, J., 1, 10, 11, 14, 38n1, 39n13,
   40n42, 41n73, 64–91, 208, 209, 210,
   211, 212
Bloch, M., 9–10, 65, 70
Boas, F., 2
Bohannan, P., 39n35
Brinson, P., 206–14
Brooks, J., 40n49
Büecher, K., 69
Bulmer, R., 137n1, 138n3
Buxton, J., 41n71

Carlsöö, S., 187
Chagnon, N., 22
Chavanne, J.M. de, 8
Chesterfield, 212
Chomsky, N., 10
Cohen, A., 23, 25
Cohen, M., 38n1
Collocott, E.E.V., 117n5
Comstock, T., 38n1
Condon, W.S., 12
Copeland, R., 38n1
Cullen, J.M., 40n52

Dentan, R., 47, 55, 59, 60
De Zoete, B., 39n27, 41n77

Dohlinow, P.J., 69
Duncan, I., 5, 7, 166
Durkheim, E., 1, 12–16, 27, 35, 82, 148,
   160, 213

Elyot, T., 8
Evans-Pritchard, E.E., 4, 38n2, 39n18,
   39n35, 40n50

Firth, R., 40n50
Forge, A., 205
Franks, A.H., 39n14
Freud, S., 4, 155

Gailey, H.A., 41n62
Geertz, C., 41n72
Gell, A., 25, 36, 39n31, 41n73, 138n8,
   183–205, 209, 211
Gillen, F.J., 39n3
Gluckman, M., 3, 5, 6, 26, 27, 31, 159,
   161
Goldman, L., 138n6
Grau, A., 70, 86
Groos, K., 69
Groves, M., 136

Hanna, J.L., 3, 6, 26, 38n1, 38n2, 40n44,
   40n62, 41n73, 73, 74, 117n1, 136
Hartwig, G.W., 5, 23
H'Doubler, M., 210
Hinde, R.A., 40n52
Hoenkamp, E., 187, 189
Holt, C., 39n11
Horton, R., 28, 30
Huxley, J., 40n52

Jennings, S., 6, 40n42, 47–63, 206, 211
Jones, K., 208

Kaeppler, A.L., 13, 37, 39n2, 39n9,
   41n73, 92–118, 203, 208, 209
Kealiinohomoku, J.W., 38n1, 40n57

217

Name index

Kubik, G., 10, 11
Kuper, H., 39n11
Kurath, G.P., 38n1

Laban, R., 2, 5, 7, 66
Lange, R., 38n1, 38n2, 39n5, 39n12, 39n18, 39n22, 40n42
Langer, S., 7, 8, 12, 15, 35, 39n5, 40n42, 40n44, 40n58, 41n64, 41n69, 72
Leach, E.R., 189
Lenneberg, E., 73
Lévi-Strauss, C., 34, 65, 155
Lewis, I.M., 3, 6, 24, 40n42, 40n47
Lex, B., 39n29
Lienhardt, P.A., 40n54, 41n71
Locke, J., 8, 212
Lomax, A., 12
Louis XIV, 213

McPhee, C., 39n27, 40n42, 41n65
Majnep, I.S., 137n1
Malinowski, B., 7, 40n50
Maquet, J.J., 40n57
Marshall, L., 5, 40n36
Martin, G., 41n73
Marx, K., 27, 213
Mauss, M., 86
Mead, M., 4, 8, 10, 39n35
Merriam, A.P., 2
Merton, R.K., 20
Metheny, E., 41n73
Metraux, A., 40n36
Middleton, J.F.M., 32, 160, 165–82, 208
Mitchell, J.C., 23
Mooney, J., 39n4, 40n49

Nadel, S.F., 39n18
Neher, A., 39n10
Norbeck, E., 3, 39n16

Ogston, W.D., 12
O'Hanlon, M., 138n6
Onwuejeogwu, M., 18
Ornstein, R., 74
Owen, C., 183

Parer, D., 128
Pemberton, E., 39n20
Pesovar, E., 41n73
Pitcairn, T.K., 66
Praagh, P. van, 211

Radcliffe-Brown, A.R., 7, 13, 14, 16, 40n36, 147
Ranger, T.C., 23, 24
Rappaport, R., 22, 138n3
Raum, O.F., 39n23, 39n35
Read, K.E., 138n6
Reay, M.O., 138n6
Rigby, P., 3, 39n16, 159, 161
Rouget, G., 39n10
Rousseau, J.J., 8
Royce, A.P., 38n1, 38n2, 39n11, 39n13, 41n73, 71, 136
Rust, F., 5, 38n1, 39n14, 39n18, 39n20, 39n22, 40n57

Sachs, C., 5, 7, 8, 15, 17, 33, 38n2, 39n22, 40n42, 68, 70
St. Johnston, R., 8
Salmond, A., 12
Sargant, W., 39n10, 39n14
Schieffelin, E.L., 16
Schleidt, M., 66
Shirokogoroff, S.M., 40n42
Singer, A., 41n73
Smith, M., 18, 39n35
Smith, M.G., 40n46
Snyder, A.F., 39n8, 40n44
Spencer, B., 39n3
Spencer, H., 4, 11, 13, 15
Spencer, P., 39n20, 140–64, 206, 207, 208
Spies, W., 39n27, 41n77
Strathern, A., 21, 119–39, 208, 209
Strathern, M., 119, 120, 132, 135
Strauss, G., 65, 71
Strobel, M., 27, 40n56

Thompson, D.A.W., 203
Tunley, D., 214
Turnbull, C., 39n35, 40n49
Turner, V.W., 27, 28, 30, 31, 34, 35, 41n68, 41n71, 41n72, 155, 156, 162

Waterman, R.A., 73
Weber, M., 17, 213
Weyer, E.M., 39n35
Williams, D., 39n29, 41n73, 41n74
Williams, R., 212
Wilson, P.J., 3, 39n16
Winter, E., 40n54, 41n71
Witkin, R.W., 65
Woodward, S., 41n73
Wundt, W.M., 73, 74

Young, J.Z., 69

218

Subject index

achievement, 7, 26, 29, 30, 133, 145; see also success
aesthetic idiom, 1, 13, 14, 30, 31, 86, 92, 96, 106, 115, 140, 165, 207
ambiguity in social relations, 22, 32, 112, 119, 132, 158, 166, 180–1, 208
Andaman Islanders, 13, 14, 16, 147
anxiety, 4, 6–8, 28, 50, 58, 60, 62, 178–81
audience, see spectators
Azande, 4, 22, 39n35

Bali, 10, 29, 37, 210
ballet, 12, 29, 35, 71, 72, 207, 208
beni-ngoma, 23–5, 32, 40n56
biological aspect of dance, 5, 10–11, 68, 73, 74, 148, 213
body decoration, 21, 36, 51–2, 119, 120, 123, 128, 140, 145, 183, 185, 186, 190
body language, see nonverbal communication
Bori, 6, 18–21, 28, 34
boundary
    display, 21–7, 38, 40n62, 124–7, 155, 170–1, 176, 192
    of sex, 26–7, 135, 143, 148, 154–5, 157
    shift, 28, 155, 202

catalyst, 18, 41n62, 61, 65
cathartic theory, 3–8, 39n18, 62–3; see also tension: release of
Chagga, 39n35
charisma, 17, 18
children (see also play)
    and dance, 5, 8–9, 41n69, 48–9, 55, 57, 70, 171
    socialisation of, 8–9, 10–11, 47, 48–9, 59, 210
Chinese dance, 71
climax, 5, 6, 16, 17, 21, 32, 54, 81–2, 84, 120, 125, 127, 129, 146, 147

collective experience, 11, 14–17, 27, 34, 55, 80, 82–4, 87, 156
communication (see also nonverbal communication)
    of emotion, 11, 13, 165
    of experience, 67
    of solidarity, 98
communion, 15, 17
communitas (fellowship of mankind), 27, 28, 30, 31, 32, 33, 34, 155, 156, 162
competition
    between sexes, 25, 150
    in context of dance, 18, 22–5, 27, 29–34, 37, 119, 167, 178, 180
    in dance, 7, 21–7, 30, 146, 148, 153–4, 157, 161, 169, 173, 175
confidence, 8, 9, 20, 150
    loss of, 9, 20, 34, 160
confrontation, 22, 24–6, 32, 119, 124–7, 145–7
confusion in social relations, 4, 21, 33, 167, 171, 178, 180
consciousness, altered state of, see transcendental state
constraint, 2, 15, 59, 147–8, 166, 199, 207, 212
context of dance
    relevance for analysis of, 2, 3, 5, 11, 14, 20, 27, 165, 182, 211
    shift of, 7, 23
Copperbelt, 23, 40n56
cosmic relations, 6, 20, 28, 31, 33, 51, 57–60, 159–61, 170, 173, 177–9, 181
courtship dances, 66, 121, 124, 168, 171–5, 177, 179, 181
creativity
    of dance, 4, 7–8, 11, 15, 33, 35, 211
    of dancers, 11, 70, 72
    of the group, 11, 24, 29
    of music, 10, 14

219

Subject index

culture
  concept of, in anthropology, ix, 2, 69, 212
  culture–nature transformation, 51, 72, 154–6, 170, 178, 183–4, 198
  diffusion of, 23, 37

dance associations, 23–4, 26–7, 29–32, 40n56
death dances, 33, 56, 131, 167–71, 176–80, 208
  and reversed behaviour, 33, 122, 133, 170–4, 178
  Dance of Death, 33
decoration, see body decoration
definition of dance, problem of, 1–2, 7, 38, 38–9n2, 70, 92–4, 114–16, 120, 165, 206, 209
discourse, 70, 140, 162; see also communication
display
  of aggression, 17, 22, 25, 173, 198
  of anger, 14, 16, 17, 26, 145, 146, 147
  bird, 22, 120, 128, 132, 135, 136, 137n1, 138n6
  boundary, 21–7, 38, 40n62, 124–7, 155, 170–1, 176, 192
  competitive, 21, 22–3, 146, 169–70, 173
  dances of, 21, 25, 77, 122–3, 146–8, 151–4
  of individualism, 33, 170, 197
  of power, 10, 21, 22, 24, 127, 157
  of protest, 3, 24–7, 32, 145, 149, 156, 157, 162–3
  sexual, 34, 120, 123–4, 134–5, 184, 197, 209
  of skill, 18, 24, 124, 148, 172
  of unity, 95, 98, 153
drumming, 13, 18, 19, 24, 29, 84, 171, 174

ecstasy, see transcendental state
education, see socialisation
effervescence, 35, 159
Ekine, see Kalabari
élite dances, 8, 23–5, 208
energy, 4, 5, 14, 16, 54, 68, 123, 159, 197, 199
Eskimo, 13, 39n35
experience of dance, 2, 11, 37, 66–9, 72, 88, 165
expression, dance as a mode of, 5, 7, 10–11, 14, 20, 24, 28, 31, 67, 71, 72, 73, 77, 88, 165–6, 181–2, 210

fertility, 28, 32, 158–61
Fiji, 101, 109, 114
flirtation, 49, 54, 142, 149–50, 153, 172
function and form of dance, 37, 70, 73, 86–7, 92–4, 132–5
functionalism and dance, 8, 11, 14, 15, 29, 207

Ghost Dance, 1, 21, 32
gift presentations, 94–6, 119, 123, 125–7, 129
Gisaro, 16
Gogo, 159

Haiti, 6
Hausa, 19–21, 28, 39n35
Hawaii, 24
healing, 3–4, 54–7
Huli, 138n6

imitation, 48, 55, 136, 153
Indian classical dance, 52, 71
individualism, 25–6, 33, 176
informal dances, 4, 8–9, 37
initiation dances
  boys', 9, 140–3, 151–3, 155, 158, 162
  girls', 8, 11, 71, 75, 76, 80–8, 155
inner response, 2, 6, 7, 10, 13–17, 38, 65–6, 165
institution, 2, 17, 21, 69
intention, 22, 50, 66, 67, 70, 208
interaction in a dance, see communication
interpretation
  in a dance, 2, 28, 64, 69
  of the dance, 5, 8, 15, 26, 31, 37, 204
Islam, 18, 20, 28

Kalabari, 28–31, 33, 207
  Ekine (men's society), 29–32
  water spirits, 29–31, 33
Kalam, 137n1, 137n2, 137n3
Kaluli, 16
Kerebe, 5, 6, 22
Kuma, 138n6
!Kung (bushmen), 5, 17, 28, 34
Kwakiutl, 21

language and dance, 9, 10, 25, 35, 36, 66–8, 71, 92, 114, 203, 212
leadership, 17, 22, 40n56, 57, 125, 146, 154, 166
legitimacy, 28, 31, 32, 160, 181
lelemama, 26, 40n56
liminality, see marginality
linguistic models, see language and

220

Subject index

poetry
  compared with dance, 36, 37, 92, 192, 203, 204
  in dance, 13, 95–6, 103–6, 109, 111, 113
possession, *see* spirit possession; trance and dance
posture, 53, 71, 77, 121, 145
power
  of community life, 2, 15, 31, 35
  of dance, 2, 13, 15, 17, 22, 35, 133, 140, 206
  political, 9, 11, 28, 31–2, 34, 87, 112, 114, 145, 161–3
  of symbols, 25, 34
presentation, *see* gift presentations
prestige, 9, 21, 23, 25, 26, 32, 37, 112, 114, 125
process in dance, 11, 15, 16, 18, 21, 27, 70
  build-up of intensity, 16–18, 21, 25, 40n41, 54, 62, 81, 83–4, 125, 145–6, 158, 174
  build-up of tension, 4, 6, 7, 8, 16–17, 142, 146, 160
  cyclical, 81–2, 120, 129, 137, 152, 161, 179, 186
  rejuvenation, 5, 63, 82, 120, 137, 152, 186
  reversion, 25, 145–6, 154–5, 171
  symbolic reduction, 132, 187, 199–202
psychological explanations, 5, 6, 15, 66, 89, 165, 166

rapport, 10–12, 16, 20, 21, 38, 150
release, 17, 27; *see also* tension: release of
religion, 6, 15, 16, 167, 169
religious experience, 2, 14, 17, 27, 32, 35, 176
reversal
  of dance, 33, 122, 131, 133, 170–4, 178
  of roles in dance, 26, 158–9, 161, 176, 180, 208
rhythm, 24, 49, 69
  in interaction, 12, 13, 14
  physiological response to, 4, 10, 29
rites of transition, 3, 11, 28, 56, 73–4, 82, 97, 167, 171, 176, 179
ritual
  action, 34, 36–8
  drama, 27–35, 38, 133, 159, 161, 181, 186, 202
  of rebellion, 3, 6, 24, 26–7, 31, 159–61
  reversal, 33, 161, 180–1
rivalry in dance, *see* competition

roles in dance, 7, 26, 28, 183
Ruanda, 24

safety valve, 3–8, 15, 161, 207; *see also* tension: release of
St John's dance, 4
St Vitus's dance, 4
Samburu, 25, 26, 33, 39n33, 40n60, 41n76, 140–64, 175, 207
  boys' dances, 149, 151–4
  boys' initiation dance, 140–3, 158
  clan dances, 148–9, 151, 153, 154
  dances of display, 145–8, 150–1, 153–4
  moran (warriors), 141, 143, 144, 148, 149, 154
  shivering/shaking, 146–51, 157
  stock theft, 145, 148–9, 160, 162, 163n4
  wedding dance, 145, 150–1, 153, 156, 158, 162, 163n3
  women's fertility dance (*ntorosi*), 157–62, 163n2, 163n3
Samoa, 5, 8–9, 10, 39n35, 111, 112
self-fulfilling prophecy, 20
Semai, 47, 59
shaman, 6, 17, 22; *see also* Temiar: shaman
social class, 8, 23, 24, 25, 27, 161, 208
socialisation, 8–11, 47, 48–9, 57, 59, 81, 85–6, 154, 210
social solidarity, 14, 15, 25, 27, 28, 32, 82, 86, 98, 110, 125, 126, 135, 151, 153, 161
songs, 9, 13, 15, 16, 26, 36, 49, 54–56, 84, 93, 95, 119, 140–3, 145, 152, 160–2, 168
space and dance, 17, 36, 38, 39n31, 75, 94, 98–9, 130, 131, 157, 180
spectacle, 1, 15, 21, 162, 171
spectators, 29, 30, 33, 54, 62, 84, 123, 125, 135, 141, 145, 153, 171, 173–4, 183, 184
  attracted by dance, 18, 19, 23, 125, 151
  interaction with dancers of, 11–12, 16–17, 20, 121–2, 196
  women as, 29, 30, 145, 153, 196, 202
speech and dance, 11, 12, 102, 103, 107, 109, 112, 115, 162, 180, 208; *see also* language and dance; poetry
spirit possession, 2, 6, 18–20, 24, 28–30, 54, 72, 79, 133, 148, 165, 167
step, *see* movement: step
structure
  ambiguity in, 36, 166, 182
  and antistructure, 27, 155, 162, 179
  and communitas, 27–8, 31, 34, 162

222